T0352683

# Judges
## and Political Reform
## in Egypt

# Judges
## and Political Reform
## in Egypt

**Edited by**
**Nathalie Bernard-Maugiron**

The American University in Cairo Press

First paperback edition 2015

Dar el Kutub No. 14010/14
ISBN 978 977 416 701 0

Dar el Kutub Cataloging-in-Publication Data

Bernard-Maugiron, Nathalie
        Judges and Political Reform in Egypt / edited by Nathalie Bernard-Maugiron.—Cairo:
    The American University in Cairo Press, 2015
            p.         cm.
            ISBN 978 977 416 701 0
            1. Judges_Egypt
            2. Egypt—politics and government
            347.014

1  2  3  4  5      19  18  17  16  15

Designed by Fatiha Bouzidi
Printed in Egypt

# Contents

# Contributors

**Ahmed Abd El-Hafeez** is a lawyer and the director of the Arab Center for Lawyers and Legal Consultants, Cairo.

**Nabil Abdel Fattah** is assistant director and chief editor of publications at the al-Ahram Center for Political and Strategic Studies.

**Mohamed Maher Abouelenen** is a vice-president of the State Council of the Arab Republic of Egypt.

**Hafez Abu Seada** is a lawyer and secretary-general of the Egyptian Organization for Human Rights.

**Hesham El-Bastawissy** is a vice-president of the Court of Cassation of the Arab Republic of Egypt.

**Nathalie Bernard-Maugiron** is a senior researcher at the French Institut de Recherche pour le Développement in Cairo. She works on the judiciary and the democratization process in Egypt and in the Arab world. Her recent publications include "Vers une plus grande indépendance du pouvoir judiciaire en Egypte?," *Revue internationale de droit comparé* (2007); "Les amendements constitutionnels de 2005 et 2007 en Egypte: vers une réforme démocratique?," *Revue française de droit constitutionnel* (2007); and "Judges as Reform Advocates: A Lost Battle?," *Cairo Papers in Social Sciences* (forthcoming).

**Negad Mohamed El-Borai** is a lawyer and the chairperson of the board of trustees of the Group for Democratic Development. He has been a project manager for dozens of projects dealing with human rights and has conducted many research projects. As part of his work on the judiciary, he has prepared two working papers, "The Servant of Justice: The

Situation of the Legal Profession in Egypt" (Lebanese Center for Policy Studies, January 2005) and "The Independence of the Judicial System in Egypt: The Fact as It Is" (Euro-Mediterranean Network for Human Rights, Project on Justice in the Arab World, 2003.

**Nathan J. Brown** is a professor of political science and international affairs at George Washington University, where he directs the Institute for Middle East Studies. He also serves as nonresident senior associate at the Carnegie Endowment for International Peace. He is the author of four books on Arab politics, including *Constitutions in a Nonconstitutional World* (2001) and *The Rule of Law in the Arab World* (1997).

**Abdallah Khalil** is a lawyer and an expert in international human rights law. He has conducted several research projects for the United Nations Development Programme, including one on public prosecutions in the Arab world.

**Mahmud al-Khudayri** is a vice-president of the Court of Cassation of the Arab Republic of Egypt and former president (until January 2008) of the Alexandria Judges' Club.

**Isabelle Lendrevie-Tournan** holds a PhD in law from University I, Panthéon-Sorbonne, in Paris. Her dissertation, "Les transferts juridiques et juridictionnels en Egypte (l'héritage des années 1875–1949)," an anthropological and historical study of legal and judicial developments in Egypt during the nineteenth century and the first half of the twenti-eth century. Her recent publications include "Le service public égyptien dans la chronique judiciaire mixte à la fin du XIXe siècle et au début du XXe siècle" (in *Histoire et Service Public*, ed. G.J. Guglielmi (2004), and "La responsabilité de l'Etat égyptien dans le droit mixte égyptien: des règles juridiques et des pratiques nouvelles en Egypte (1876–1922)" (in *La coutume, la tradition, la pratique et le droit écrit*, special issue, *Revue Méditerranée*, L'Harmattan, no. 37, 2004).

**Tamir Moustafa** is an associate professor of international studies and the Jarislowsky chair in religious and cultural exchange at Simon Fraser University in Vancouver, Canada. His teaching and research deals with comparative law and courts, religion and politics, and state–society relations, all with a regional focus on the Middle East. He is the author of *The Struggle for Constitutional Power: Law, Politics, and Economic Development in Egypt* (2007).

**Atef Shahat Said** is an Egyptian human rights lawyer and researcher. He is a sociology PhD candidate at the University of Michigan. Since 1995, he has been working with non-governmental human rights organizations in Egypt, where he has directed research projects and written a number of reports and studies (in Arabic) about human rights and the judiciary in Egypt and the Arab world. His research interests are the sociology of law, the judiciary, and human rights and colonialism. His proposed dissertation involves an exploration of human rights and humanitarianism in settings of authoritarianism and imperialism.

**Mohamed Sayed Said** is deputy director of the al-Ahram Center for Political and Strategic Studies, and editor in chief of the independent newspaper, *al-Badil.*

**Mustapha Kamel al-Sayyed** is a professor of political science at Cairo University and at the American University in Cairo. He is the director of Partners in Development, a think tank devoted to issues of development. He works mostly on questions of political economy, human rights, and civil society. His writings have been published by *World Policy, Middle East Journal, Arab Studies Quarterly, Maghreb-Machrek,* and *Cairo Papers in Social Science.*

**Sherif Younes** is a historian of ideologies and political thought in the modern Middle East. He is a lecturer of modern and contemporary history at Helwan University in Egypt.

# Acknowledgments

I wish to thank the Cairo Institute for Human Rights Studies, without which the 2006 conference, "The Role of Judges in the Process of Political Reform in Egypt and the Arab World" could never have been convened. I also thank the Institut de Recherche pour le Développement and the European Commission for their financial support.

The work of bringing this volume together was a massive undertaking, and I could not have done it without the substantial help and support of Nabil Abdel-Fattah, who was a member of the conference's scientific preparatory committee and edited the Arabic version of this volume; Hesham El-Bastawissy, a member of the conference's scientific preparatory committee; and Enid Hill, who carefully read the papers one by one and whose thoughtful comments were invaluable to the revision process. I also enjoyed able assistance from Hebatallah Ghali, who helped me check the translated chapters in this volume as well as carry out the initial editing work, and the editors and staff of the AUC Press whose diligence and meticulous revision and final editing added more clarity and precision to the final content.

# Preface

The years 2005 and 2006 were marked by growing tensions between the judicial and the executive branches of government in Egypt. In order to get concessions from the executive, judges went so far as to threaten to boycott the supervision of the presidential and legislative elections slated for autumn 2005. The struggle between the two branches was in full swing when the conference that gave rise to this book, "The Role of Judges in the Process of Political Reform in Egypt and in the Arab World," was held in Cairo from 1 to 3 April 2006.

The conference was organized by the Cairo Institute for Human Rights Studies (CIHRS), in cooperation with the Institut de Recherche pour le Développement (IRD), the International Federation for Human Rights (FIDH), and the Euro-Mediterranean Network for Human Rights (EMNHR), and with the support of the European Commission and the Institut de Recherche pour le Développement. The conference's Scientific Preparatory Committee was made up of Nabil Abdel Fattah (assistant-director of the al-Ahram Center for Political and Strategic Studies), Hesham El-Bastawissy (a vice-president of the Egyptian Court of Cassation), Nathalie Bernard-Maugiron (IRD), Mo'taz al-Fegiery, and Bahey al-Din Hassan (CIHRS).

The aim of the conference was to discuss the role judges play in the political reform process in the Arab world, with a special focus on Egypt. The demands of Egyptian judges and the reactions of political actors and civil society were studied and compared with the current legal and political contexts of judges in other countries in the Arab world. A particular emphasis was placed on the events that took place in Egypt in 2005 and on the conflict between Egypt's judicial and executive branches.

This book contains most of the conference papers that dealt with Egypt.[1] Despite the high quality of the papers on other Arab countries, the Scientific Preparatory Committee decided the book would be more coherent and balanced if it focused on Egypt alone.

# Introduction

## Nathalie Bernard-Maugiron

If justice in the Arab world is often marked by the judiciary's lack of autonomy in relation to the executive branch, one of the characteristic features of the Egyptian judiciary is its strength and activism in defense of democratic values. Judges have been struggling for years to enhance their independence from the executive power and to exercise full supervision of the electoral process. In order to introduce the reader to the issues that will be discussed in the book, I first will present a short chronology of the main events of the judges' struggle in 2005–2007. Next, I will present the organization of the judiciary and judges in Egypt. Finally, I will introduce the main demands of Egypt's reformist judges.

## Events Involving Egypt's Judiciary (2005–2007)

The institutional crisis between the judiciary and the executive branch started with an incident in Alexandria in April 2005. A judge was physically attacked by a group of lawyers who wanted him to acquit their client. The Alexandria Judges' Club held an emergency general assembly during which judges criticized the absence of a reaction from the president of the court where the incident took place and, more generally, criticized the failure of the government to protect their independence. They called for judicial reform. The general assembly linked the independence of the judiciary to election transparency and threatened to boycott the upcoming elections.

On 13 May 2005, the Cairo Judges' Club also held an emergency general assembly, during which it authorized its members to monitor a referendum on a constitutional amendment slated to occur on 25 May.[1] The club threatened not to supervise the upcoming presidential and parliamentary elections if the members found a lack of transparency during the 25 May referendum. In July, the Judges' Club published a fairly critical report entitled *Egypt's Conscience*,[2] in which the authors questioned the soundness of official figures related to electoral participation and vote counting. They stressed the fact that members of judicial bodies were allowed to supervise only 5 percent of the polling stations during the referendum. That same month, the 1956 Law on the Exercise of Political Rights, which regulates the voting procedure for parliamentary elections, was amended, and an electoral commission was established to supervise the entire election process.

The Judges' Club held a second extraordinary general assembly on 2 September 2005, during which it decided to allow judges to supervise the elections out of concern that a boycott would open the door to wholesale fraud. The presidential elections took place on 7 September, and President Hosni Mubarak won with an overwhelming 88.5 percent of the vote. The Judges' Club published a report on these elections in November, denouncing several types of abuse the judges had witnessed. It also strongly criticized the attitude of the Presidential Elections Commission. Starting in October, the ministry of justice suspended the annual financial subsidy it gave to all judges' clubs throughout Egypt, which was the clubs' main source of funding.[3]

The parliamentary elections took place in November and December 2005. On 24 November, Noha al-Zini, a female member of the Office of Administrative Prosecution,[4] publicly denounced the fraud she had witnessed in the electoral constituency where she was supervising an auxiliary station.[5] The Judges' Club decided to lead an inquiry into the allegation and to interrogate the judges who had supervised other polling stations in the same constituency. According to the club, 151 judges out of 160 agreed to testify, and they confirmed al-Zini's testimony that the Muslim Brotherhood candidate received three times as many votes as the ruling National Democratic Party's (NDP) candidate.[6] A complaint was filed at the general prosecutor's office, but it received no response.

The Judges' Club held its regular general assembly on 16 December. The club president was reelected and his list won all the seats on the board of directors. On 17 February 2006, the Alexandria Judges' Club organized a sit-in for judicial independence in front of its premises. On 17 March, shortly before another extraordinary general assembly of the Cairo Judges' Club, judges demonstrated silently for half an hour in the street in front of their premises, wearing their official red and green sashes.

Toward the end of March, the board of the Cairo Judges' Club agreed to meet representatives of Human Rights Watch (HRW), an American non-governmental organization (NGO) anxious to discuss the club's concerns over judicial independence. The club then withdrew its agreement to the meeting, however, after the presidents of the eight courts of appeal met on 29 March and adopted a joint statement accusing HRW of being a biased American and Zionist organization.[7] These judges claimed that meeting with HRW would permit foreign interference in internal matters.

In the early hours of 24 April 2006, the Egyptian police attacked a peaceful pro-reform camp set up in front of the Judges' Club in Cairo and a judge was beaten and his arm broken. That May, Counselors Hesham El-Bastawissy and Mahmud Mekki, both vice-presidents of the Court of Cassation, were summoned to appear before the disciplinary council to answer charges of defamation of a fellow judge. They were suspected of accusing that judge of vote rigging in *Sawt al-umma*, an independent newspaper. The newspaper had published a "blacklist" with the initials of all judges suspected of participating in the fraud. Demonstrations of popular support took place and some participants were arrested. All charges were dropped against Counselor Mekki, while Counselor El-Bastawissy received a reprimand.

On 25 May, judges participated in another sit-in in front of the High Court in Cairo, on the anniversary of the 2005 constitutional referendum. In June, the 1972 Law on Judicial Authority was amended, but the amendment did not meet reformist judges' expectations.[8] The following month, Mamduh Mar'i, former chief justice of the Supreme Constitutional Court and president of the Presidential Elections Commission, was appointed the new minister of justice. This promotion was considered by some judges a way for the government to thank Mar'i for the Presidential Elections Commission's support during the presidential elections.[9] After becoming minister, Mar'i refused to talk to the Cairo Judges' Club,[10] to visit its premises,[11] and to accept any invitation from the club's representatives.

In September, the Court of Cassation issued a finding that fraud had been committed in the constituency supervised by the judge who had brought charges against Counselors Mekki and El-Bastawissy and issued a decision that the elections in that constituency should be considered void.[12] In early December, the judge dropped the complaint he had filed against *Sawt al-umma* for having published the "blacklist." The People's

Assembly did not follow up on the report of the Court of Cassation and refused to void the elections in the constituency.

In October, the Judges' Club decided to raise its monthly membership fee to LE20 from LE5 in order to ensure financial independence.[13] The minister of justice began to establish organizations parallel to the judges' clubs that offered similar services to judges. This was perceived by some as an attempt to undermine the role of the original clubs. In November, the president of the Cairo Judges' Club stated that Egyptian society was not yet ready for the appointment of women judges.[14] This statement drew criticism from civil society organizations that had so far stood by the clubs.[15]

In December, the Central Auditing Agency requested an audit of the annual budgets of all judges' clubs since 2001. In January 2007, the minister of social affairs publicly declared that the Judges' Club should register as an association in conformity with the 2002 Law on Associations and stated that he was ready to proceed upon the club's request.[16] This statement was perceived as a threat to dissolve the club.

On 26 March 2007, a new referendum on the amendment to the constitution took place.[17] Among the thirty-four provisions that were revised, amended Article 88 took away judges' responsibility to supervise the balloting process during elections. In the same month, thirty women were appointed judges for the first time. They were chosen from members of the Office of Administrative Prosecution and placed in courts of first instance in Cairo and Alexandria.[18]

In April, the 1972 Law on Judicial Authority was amended again, this time to delay the age of mandatory retirement of judges from sixty-eight to seventy—a measure the Judges' Club had opposed several times before. On 29 April, an extraordinary general assembly of the Cairo Judges' Club was organized in protest of the extension of the retirement age. Fewer than a hundred members attended and the suggestion to hold a sit-in or even a protest march was dropped.

At the end of November 2007, the ministry of justice drafted a bill that established a new Council of Judicial Bodies. That draft law was rejected by judges as an attempt to tighten the grip of the executive on judicial affairs. President Mubarak finally announced on the day of the general assembly of the Judges' Club, 30 November, that the draft law had been withdrawn. On the same day, the reformist list won the five seats open for renewal of the club's board of directors. This development showed that reformist judges still enjoyed strong support within the judiciary.

## The Judicial Hierarchy in Egypt
### Judiciary Laws

Reformist judges refer with nostalgia to Law 66/1943 on the Independence of the Judiciary, which, according to them, was the best judiciary law Egypt ever had. Several judiciary laws were adopted under Gamal ʻAbd al-Nasser that deprived judges little by little of their independence until Decree Law No. 82 was adopted in August 1969. This law abrogated the Supreme Judicial Council and replaced it with an appointed Supreme Council of Judicial Bodies (al-Majlis al-Aʻla li-l-Hay'at al-Qada'iya) headed by the president of the republic. It dealt a severe blow to the independence of the judiciary by making the judges subordinate to the executive branch, represented by the president of the republic and the ministry of justice.

In 1971, a new constitution was adopted that included Articles 165 and 166, which provided for the independence of judges and of the judiciary. In 1972, Law 46/1972 on the Judicial Authority was adopted by decree of President Anwar al-Sadat. Many judges criticized this law and have been striving since the 1970s to amend it and reinforce their independence. In 1984, these judges succeeded in having some amendments introduced: the Supreme Judicial Council was reinstated by Law 35/1984, and members of the Office of Public Prosecution were protected from removal. The minister of justice retained most powers of appointment, transfer, and promotion of judges but after the amendment had to seek the agreement or at least the opinion of the Supreme Judicial Council.

Judges were not fully satisfied with the amendments introduced in 1984 and called for more judicial independence. They complained that the minister of justice retained important powers and decided to continue their struggle. Full judicial independence was one of the main recommendations of the 1986 National Conference on Justice organized by the Judges' Club.[19] In January 1991, the general assembly of the Cairo Judges' Club approved a proposal for amending the 1972 Law on Judicial Authority. The draft law was sent to the minister of justice and was shelved in his office. The Judges' Club attempted to persuade him to submit the draft to the People's Assembly for consideration but to no avail. The draft law was amended in 2004 by the general assembly of the Judges' Club.

In 2005, the ministry of justice formed a committee to draft amendments to the 1972 law. The president and the secretary-general of the Cairo Judges' Club participated in these discussions. In May of that year, the ministry of justice's draft law was sent to the Supreme Judicial Council for its opinion in conformity with Article 77 bis (2) of the 1972 Law on Judicial Authority. The council decided to consult the general assemblies of all the courts before giving its consent. The council finally submitted its opinion to the minister of justice in January 2006, but that opinion was not made public.

In June 2006, Law 46/1972 was finally amended on the basis of a new draft proposed by the political committee of the NDP. The committee did not incorporate many of the judges' recommendations. The Judges' Club issued a press release in which it called some points of the new law positive but noted that key demands had been rejected and that the law failed to meet the judges' expectations.

## Ordinary Courts

The Egyptian judicial system is divided into three branches: the 'ordinary' judiciary *(al-qada' al-'adi)*, which is competent in civil and criminal matters; an administrative justice system that rules on administrative matters;[20] and a constitutional justice system, which is specified in the 1971 constitution as the competence of the Supreme Constitutional Court.

The ordinary judiciary is competent in civil, commercial, and criminal matters, as well as in questions regarding personal status. It is organized in a pyramidal form. At the lowest level are more than two hundred summary courts *(mahkama juz'iya)* established by the minister of justice within the jurisdiction of the courts of first instance, according to the burden of work. They have one judge and are competent in minor criminal and civil matters. Appeals from decisions of ordinary courts are made before courts of first instance.

Courts of first instance *(mahkama ibtida'iya)* consist of chambers with three judges. There are twenty-four such courts in Egypt—one in each governorate, except Cairo, which has two, and Matruh, Damietta, and the Red Sea, which have none. They sit as courts of first instance for civil matters in cases that are not within the competence of the summary courts. They also hear urgent or temporary cases. Their decisions can be appealed at a court of appeal.

Courts of appeal *(mahkamat al-isti'naf)* are composed of civil and criminal chambers each with three senior judges (counselors, or *mustasharun)*. There are eight courts of appeal in Egypt. Their criminal chambers, called criminal courts *(mahkamat al-jinayat)*, judge felonies, that is, acts liable to more than three years imprisonment or the death penalty. With the exception of the death penalty, which must be confirmed by the Court of Cassation before being carried out, the rulings of courts of appeal are not subject to appeal except before the Court of Cassation on points of law. Courts of appeal can hear complete retrials of the facts of the case as well as review application of the law, in recognition of the principle in code-based legal systems that everyone is entitled to two hearings of his or her case.

The Court of Cassation (Mahkamat al-Naqd) is at the apex of the ordinary justice hierarchy. It is composed of a president, vice-presidents, and counselors. It is divided into two chambers, one for civil and commercial cases, including personal status cases, and another for criminal cases, sitting in groups of five judges. Its main function is to control the judgments of courts of appeal on the basis of a motion founded on an error of law. The control of the Court of Cassation bears only on these questions and not on the facts of the case.

## The Office of Public Prosecution

The Office of Public Prosecution (al-Niyaba al-'Amma) is in charge of protecting the general public interest and of investigating and prosecuting crimes. It has wide-ranging powers of investigation and interrogation, as well as authority over the judicial police. The record it compiles is the basis for the trial of the accused. The Office of Public Prosecution, therefore, is charged with seeking the truth of a case rather than simply collecting incriminating evidence. In the beginning of the 1950s, Egypt eliminated the investigation judge *(juge d'instruction)* and incorporated his functions into the Office of Public Prosecution, which confusingly melded the investigatory function with the responsibility to prosecute (see Chapter 4 in this volume, by Abdallah Khalil).

The Office of Public Prosecution is presided over by the general prosecutor *(al-na'ib al-'amm)* and is hierarchically organized. Its members are found at all levels of the court structure. According to Article 119 of the Law on Judicial Authority, the president of the republic appoints, by his sole decision, the general prosecutor from among the vice-presidents of the courts of appeal, counselors of the Court of Cassation, and chief public attorneys *(muhami 'amm awwil)* or higher ranks within the Office of Public Prosecution. Judges criticize the fact that the appointment of the general prosecutor is a political decision.

The Office of Public Prosecution is organized by Law 46 on the Judicial Authority. As in the French legal system (*parquet*, or *ministère public*), the Office of Public Prosecution belongs to the judiciary and not, as in common law systems, to the executive branch. Members of the Office of Public Prosecution are supposed to be independent from the state and thus from the ministry of justice. Until 2006, however, its members were subordinate to their immediate superiors, to the general prosecutor, and to the minister of justice (Article 125 of Law 46/1972). The amendments of 2006 eliminated their subordination to the minister of justice. Members of the Office of Public Prosecution have the same rights and immunities as judges. With the 1984 amendments of the 1972 judiciary law, the principle of irrevocability was extended to the members of the Office of Public Prosecution (Article 67). They now are allowed to serve until they reach the age of retirement.

## Ordinary Judges

Article 38 of the 1972 judiciary law puts conditions on candidates who seek appointment to the judiciary. They must have Egyptian nationality and be law graduates. The candidates also must present all required guarantees of morality and reputation (*mahmud al-sira husn al-sum'a*) and enjoy their civil rights. The minimum age for working for the Office of Public Prosecution is twenty-one. The minimum age for a judge is thirty. Newly recruited magistrates work for the Office of Public Prosecution until they reach the age of thirty and then may request to be appointed a judge. Once they reach the age of thirty-eight, they can be appointed to a court of appeal. When they reach age forty-one, they can be appointed to the Court of Cassation (a measure adopted in 2006 through amended Article 38.2). The Supreme Judicial Council makes hiring decisions. A widespread complaint is that sons of counselors or well-known personalities close to the government manage to get hired even though their exam results at the law faculty are inferior to those of other candidates.[21]

Eligibility for promotion in the judicial hierarchy is governed by certain requirements, such as holding a certain rank for a certain period of time. As mentioned above, since April 2007, judges retire at seventy years of age instead of at sixty-eight. Reformist judges accuse the government of having tailored this amendment to reward pro-government judges who are approaching retirement age.[22] They also argue that the amendment prevents young reformist judges from being promoted to high-ranking posts in the near future.[23] The amendment was justified by the government as allowing the judiciary to benefit from the experience of veteran judges,[24] which helps speed up the flow of court cases. Judges reply that the older one is, the less acute one's mental capacities.[25] Besides, they argue, most senior judges have administrative and leadership responsibilities and do not sit on the bench anymore.[26]

Until 2007, no women judges sat on the ordinary judiciary even though no provision of the 1972 law prohibited women from becoming judges.[27] After a lengthy debate, thirty women were appointed judges in courts of first instance in March 2007, as mentioned above.

The career course of judges is the same as that of members of the Office of Public Prosecution, and movement between the two spheres is open. In fact, trainees in the Office of Public Prosecution assist in provincial courts as part of their training.

The hierarchy of judges from highest to lowest is as follows:

President of the Court of Cassation *(ra'is mahkamat al-naqd)*
Vice-presidents of the Court of Cassation/presidents of courts of
    appeal *(na'ib ra'is mahkmat al-naqd/ra'is mahkmat al-isti'naf)*
Vice-presidents of courts of appeal *(na'ib ra'is mahkamat al-isti'naf)*
Counselors of the Court of Cassation/counselors of courts of appeal
    *(mustasharun)*
Presidents of courts of first instance *(ra'is mahkama ibtida'iya)*
Judges *(qudah;* singular, *qadi)*

Law 46/1972 grants extensive powers to the executive, represented by the president of the republic and the minister of justice. The executive appoints individuals to the most important positions in the judiciary. The general prosecutor and the president of the Court of Cassation are appointed by the president of the republic.[28] Vice-presidents of the Court of Cassation are appointed by the president of the republic with the agreement of the Supreme Judicial Council on the proposal of the general assembly of the court (Article 44, paragraph 3). Counselors of the Court of Cassation are appointed by the president of the republic with the agreement of the Supreme Judicial Council. There are two candidates for each vacant position—one is recommended by the general assembly of the court and the other by the minister of justice (Article 44, paragraph 4). Presidents of courts of appeal are appointed according to their seniority.

Presidents of courts of first instance are appointed by the minister of justice for one year renewable. They are chosen from among the counselors of the court of appeal within whose jurisdiction the first instance court falls, subject to the agreement of the Supreme Judicial Council (Article 9). Reformist judges argue that the executive enjoys considerable influence over the judiciary through the appointment of presidents of courts of first instance because these presidents have significant powers, including, in practice, the referral of particular cases to particular judges. The 1991 draft amendment of the judiciary law prepared by the Judges' Club was transferring these powers to the general assemblies of the courts of first instance and restricting the role of these presidents to administrative duties.

A Judicial Inspection Department (Idarat al-Taftish al-Qada'i) is in charge of the technical evaluation of judges and presidents of courts of first instance. The department prepares the annual judicial "movement" project, which is a rotation of judges, and holds judges accountable for their acts and rulings (Article 78). Senior judges *(mustasharun)* are not assessed by this department.[29] The Judicial Inspection Department consists of judges seconded to the ministry of justice. In their draft law, the Judges' Club sought to place this department under the control of the Supreme Judicial Council, instead of the ministry of justice.

Judges enjoy immunities, including irrevocability *('adam qabiliya li-l-'azl)*, which protects them from dismissal without serious cause (Article 67). Reformist judges would like to change the conditions of temporary secondment *(nadb)*, transfer *(naql)*, secondment abroad *(i'ara)*, and disciplinary complaints. They consider the current conditions detrimental to their independence, as they give the executive a powerful means by which to reward and punish judges without reference to clear criteria. The Judges' Club's draft law decreased the powers of the executive in this field.

The judiciary law of 1972 includes rules of professional conduct (Article 72) and stipulates that courts should not express political opinions and that judges should not be involved in political activities (Article 73). Since the 2006 amendment of Law 46/1972, the judiciary enjoys an independent budget.

## Judicial Bodies
### The Supreme Judicial Council and the Supreme Council of Judicial Bodies

The Supreme Council of Judicial Bodies (al-Majlis al-A'la li-l-Hay'a al-Qada'iya) was first constituted by Decree Law 82/1969 to replace the Supreme Judicial Council (Majlis al-Qada' al-A'la). Article 173 of the

1971 constitution confirmed its existence and Law 46/1972 invested it with significant powers. It was presided over by the president of the republic and composed of the minister of justice, the president of the Court of Cassation, the presidents of the State Council, the Supreme Constitutional Court, the Cairo Court of Appeal, the general prosecutor, the presidents of the Office of Administrative Prosecution and the State Litigation Authority, and the most senior vice-presidents of the State Council and the Cairo first instance court (Article 3 of the 1969 Decree Law). According to Article 173, the Supreme Council of Judicial Bodies supervised the affairs of all judicial bodies, which placed their affairs under the control of a common council instead of several special councils.

The Supreme Council of Judicial Bodies lost most of its powers when separate councils for the main judicial bodies were reestablished in 1984. For instance, the regular judiciary recovered its Supreme Judicial Council and, through new legislation, the State Council was given its own Council of Administrative Affairs (al-Majlis al-Khass li-l-Shu'un al-Idariya). These judicial organs were granted autonomy in the administration of their internal affairs. Since the 2006 amendments, the Supreme Council of Judicial Bodies has played only a minor role, such as giving its opinion on the appointment of judges to the Supreme Constitutional Court.

Unlike the Supreme Council of Judicial Bodies, the Supreme Judicial Council is composed entirely of judges. It is presided over by the president of the Court of Cassation and includes the president of the Cairo Court of Appeal, the general prosecutor, the two most senior vice-presidents of the Court of Cassation, and the two most senior presidents of the courts of appeal (Article 77 bis of the 1972 law as amended in 1984). Reformist judges criticize the fact that the council's members sit *ex officio* on the basis of the position they occupy in the judicial hierarchy. In their 1991 draft amendment, the judges proposed that four of the council's members be elected by the general assemblies of the Court of Cassation and the Cairo Court of Appeal. Having been entrusted with most powers so far held by the Supreme Council of Judicial Bodies, the Supreme Judicial Council supervises the entire judicial system with respect to judges and with respect to members of the Office of Public Prosecution. It makes decisions or is consulted in matters concerning the careers of members of the judiciary. It oversees hiring, appointment, promotion, transfers, salaries, and disciplinary actions.

The constitutional amendments of March 2007 amended Article 173 of the constitution. The Supreme Council of Judicial Bodies is to be replaced with a council presided over by the president of the republic, or by the minister of justice as the president's representative, and composed of the presidents of judicial bodies. This council will be in charge of overseeing the joint interests of all judicial bodies. In November 2007, the minister of justice presented a draft law to implement the new Article 173 of the Constitution and establish this new council. The draft law gave important powers to the council, which may have led to interference with the internal affairs of the judiciary. All concerned judicial bodies strongly protested the draft law. After the minister of justice agreed to amend some provisions of the draft, the president of the republic finally decided to withdraw it.

**The Judges' Club**
The Judges' Club was founded in Cairo in 1939 to solidify relations among judges. It has evolved into an unofficial professional association and a forum for public issues relating to the judiciary. Any member of the ordinary judiciary or the Office of Public Prosecution can join it. Still based in Cairo, it has more than nine thousand members.

In addition to the Cairo Judges' Club, Egypt has more than twenty regional judges' clubs. The most important is the Alexandria Judges' Club, which was established in 1941 to provide services to the large number of judges in that city. The other clubs were created by the minister of justice in 1980, during Sadat's regime, in order to decrease the influence of the Cairo Judges' Club, which had strongly criticized new laws of that era.[30]

The legal status of the Judges' Club is controversial. The club refuses to register as an association in order to avoid falling under the supervision of the ministry of social affairs. Judges argue that, as a gathering of members of the judiciary, their club should be organized under the judicial authority law and responsible only to its own general assembly.

## Reformist Judges' Main Claims
The June 2006 amendments to the 1972 judiciary law diminished the powers of the minister of justice regarding court supervision and the right to address warnings to judges and discipline them. The 2006 law also provided that the judiciary have an independent budget. The other

main claims of reformist judges were not satisfied, however. According to them, the executive branch retains the means to influence judicial affairs through the president of the republic, who nominates the general prosecutor and the president of the Court of Cassation, signs the decisions of judges' nomination and promotion, and selects judges to be commissioned abroad or assigned to the ministry of justice. In addition, executive influence is exercised through the minister of justice, who appoints the presidents of courts of first instance, selects the members of the Judicial Inspection Department, and introduces requests for retirement or transfer to non-judicial functions. Judges also complain that the executive has the means to exert pressure on them not to issue decisions that would displease the government.

Judges maintain that there is a link between judicial independence and election transparency, and they emphasize that free and fair elections cannot take place without independent judges. Since 1990, they have been calling for full supervision of the electoral process. This was one of the main recommendations of a symposium on the transparency of the electoral process organized by the Judges' Club in June 1990.[31] Until 2000, judges monitored only general polling stations, where vote counting takes place, while state employees oversaw the auxiliary stations where voting itself occurred. By a decision handed down in 2000,[32] the Supreme Constitutional Court ruled that according to Article 88 of the constitution,[33] members of judicial bodies should supervise both general and auxiliary polling stations.

Thus, judges supervised both types of polling stations for the first time in the elections of 2000. They witnessed widespread fraud and irregularities and complained that they were asked to certify rigged elections. They threatened to refrain from monitoring future elections if their main demands were not met. They wanted full supervision rights over the entire election process, from the preparation of voter lists to the announcement results.

In 2005, judges began resorting to new tools in their struggle for judicial independence, such as the media, boycott threats, and even a sit-in. The reaction of the executive branch was proportional to the threat that such a revolt of the judiciary represented to the state's institutions. Several reformist judges were referred to the general prosecutor for investigation, and their immunity was lifted by the Supreme Judicial Council. The judges failed to get substantive concessions from the executive and were subjected to a variety of countermeasures.

On 26 March 2007, Article 88 of the constitution was amended. The election process was limited to a single day to prevent it from occurring in several rounds as had been the case in the 2000 and 2005 elections, to compensate for the insufficient number of judges. In addition, the amendment put the electoral process under the supervision of a higher commission composed of current or retired judges. The amended Article 88 also states that general committees in charge of vote counting should be composed of members of judicial bodies. That provision is silent, however, regarding the composition of supervising committees at auxiliary polling stations, with the implication that these stations could be staffed by state employees, as they were until 2000.

The government justified this amendment by pointing to the growth of the voting population and the need to establish an ever-increasing number of polling stations. It also argued that the involvement of judges in the supervision of elections occurred at the expense of their main responsibility, which is settling judicial disputes in the courts.[34] Another justification given by the government is that it aims to preserve the dignity of judges because some of them were insulted during the 2005 elections and even physically assaulted while attempting to perform their duties at polling stations.[35] It also pointed out that judicial supervision of both general and auxiliary polling stations had not prevented vote rigging in the 2000 and 2005 elections.[36]

Ahmad Mekki, a vice-president of the Court of Cassation, denies that the dignity of judges was harmed by their monitoring of the 2005 elections, saying, "Quite the opposite. We won the support of the public due to our stand during the poll."[37] Judges suggest that the number of auxiliary polling stations could be reduced. They also insist that parliamentary elections take place only every five years, which means that judicial supervision would not have such negative consequences on the speed of the judicial process. Some judges suggest that the elections take place on public holidays or during the summer judicial break.[38]

On 26 March 2007, the day of the constitutional referendum, the Judges' Club of Alexandria flew its flag at half-mast. Its president called on the Egyptian people to wear black to mourn democracy.[39] He himself was wearing a black tie.

This book is dedicated to exploring the relationship between judges and political reform in Egypt. It begins with a general introduction to the judiciary in Egypt by Nathalie Bernard-Maugiron, followed by a political analysis of the judges' crisis by Mohamed Sayed Said. These two papers should help the reader understand the legal and political contexts of the crisis. The book is then divided into four parts.

The first part, "The Independence of the Judiciary: Past and Present," deals with the historical shifts in the independence of the Egyptian judiciary. In "The Development of Relations between the Mixed Courts and the Executive Authority in Egypt (1875–1904)," Isabelle Lendrevie-Tournan shows that judges and the executive branch were already in conflict in the nineteenth century. The khedive and the British authorities attempted several times to paralyze the regular operation of the mixed courts and to hinder the execution of the courts' judgments. The courts initially resisted such pressure, but had surrendered to it by the beginning of the twentieth century.

In "The Law on Judicial Authority and Judicial Independence," one of the most prominent reformist judges in Egypt, Counselor Mahmud al-Khudayri, analyzes different forms of interference by the executive branch in the affairs of the judiciary. Counselor al-Khudayri discusses the main amendments to the judiciary law made in June 2006. This paper is particularly important because amendment of the 1972 judiciary law was one of the two main demands of the reformist judges.

Abdallah Khalil, in "The General Prosecutor between the Judicial and Executive Authorities," discusses the specific relationship between the general prosecutor and the executive authority, and its consequences for the protection of human rights.

Part two of the book, "Pushing the Judiciary into Politics," tackles the question of how judges have been drawn into politics. In "The Political Role of the Egyptian Judiciary," Nabil Abdel Fattah explains how this phenomenon is characteristic of the Egyptian judiciary. Through concrete examples, he identifies the factors and results of the judiciary's political role, drawing a distinction between direct and indirect political roles.

Tamir Moustafa, in "The Political Role of the Supreme Constitutional Court: Between Principles and Practice," focuses on the political role of the Supreme Constitutional Court, which is constitutionally charged with judicial review of the constitutionality of laws. Through an analysis of cases dealing with political rights, he shows how the court has provided opposition and human rights groups, as well as individuals, with the institutional possibility of challenging the state. He also identifies the limits of the activism of the court and shows how the government has tried to challenge its power. Let us not forget that it was the Supreme Constitutional Court's 2000 decision that required parliamentary elections to be organized under the full supervision of the judiciary. That decision is indirectly at the origin of the revolt of the judges, who considered full supervision to mean that they should supervise the election process from the preparation of the voters' list to the announcement results.

In "The Role of the Judges' Club in Enhancing the Independence of the Judiciary and Spurring Political Reform," Atef Shahat Said discusses the most important past and current contributions of the main actor in the struggle against the regime—the Judges' Club—and how that actor has contributed to the defense of the independence of the judiciary and of democracy.

Nathan J. Brown, in "Reining in the Executive: What Can the Judiciary Do?," also focuses on the role played by the Judges' Club and discusses how judges can resist executive domination and whether they represent a genuine prospect for change.

Finally, Sherif Younes, in "Judges and Elections: The Politicization of the Judges' Discourse," analyzes the judges' discourse from the 2005 elections and how the reformist judges' two main claims, namely full judicial supervision of elections and increased judicial independence, became politicized.

Part three, "The Crisis of the Efficiency of the Judiciary," aims to explain how the judiciary crisis came about. The papers presented here deal with three different means used by the executive to deprive citizens of their right to a legal remedy before their "natural judge" (al-qadi al-tabi'i). The first means is presented by Hafez Abu Seada in "Exceptional Courts and the Natural Judge." The author describes the different exceptional courts, including state security courts, military courts, courts of values, and the court of party affairs, established by the political regime to withdraw sensitive cases (not necessarily dealing with state security) from ordinary courts. The purpose is, of course, to avoid presenting these cases before judges from the regular judiciary, which violates citizens' rights.

Mohamed Maher Abouelenen, in "Judges and Acts of Sovereignty," presents another government tool for avoiding judicial accountability. He presents situations in which the State Council and the Supreme Constitutional Court found themselves required to declare their lack of competence to rule in cases involving an act of sovereignty or a political act.

Finally, Negad Mohamed El-Borai, in "The Government's Non-execution of Judicial Decisions," describes the increasing phenomenon of non-execution of judicial rulings by the executive branch. The author classifies the different forms of non-execution, provides the reasons given, and includes some concrete examples of this third means that the government uses to avoid accountability to the judiciary.

In part four of the book, "Civil Society and the Judiciary," the authors discuss relations between judges and Egyptian civil society. These three papers demonstrate that the courts represent a last and sometimes sole resort for civil society groups unable to find a remedy through normal political means. Because they lack venues through which to address conflicts and voice demands, political actors have found in courts a place to express opinions that the closure of the political field has otherwise made virtually impossible to express. Judges often accept the responsibility of deciding on such cases, and many of their decisions have had important consequences on the political level.

In "Egyptian Parties and Syndicates vis-à-vis Judicial Decisions," Ahmed Abd El-Hafeez analyzes several decisions by Egyptian courts involving political parties and syndicates. Mustapha Kamel al-Sayyed, in "The Judicial Authority and Civil Society," analyzes several court rulings dealing with NGOs and their rights. In "The Relationship between Judges and Human Rights Organizations during the 2005 Elections and the Referendum," Nathalie Bernard-Maugiron focuses on the relationship between NGOs and the judiciary in the specific framework of the 2005 elections. She shows how an informal coalition between judges and NGOs emerged during that time and how they supported each other in their struggle for transparent elections.

In conclusion, Counselor Hesham El-Bastawissy, in "The Independence of the Judiciary as a Democratic Construct," argues that the establishment of an Arab Union of Judges would help increase the independence of the judiciary in Arab countries generally and in Egypt in particular. Counselor El-Bastawissy is in many respects the most prominent of the Egyptian reformist judges. His thoughts are thus a fitting conclusion to this volume. This section includes the document, "The Draft Constituent Declaration of the Union of Arab Judges."

# 1

# A Political Analysis of the Egyptian Judges' Revolt

*Mohamed Sayed Said*

Egypt stands alone in witnessing a strong judges' revolt. Nowhere else have judges engaged in such a prolonged protest for their independence, whether in another Arab or Islamic country or in Europe or the west. Because of its uniqueness, the Egyptian judges' movement captures the imagination of all who dream of democracy and the rule of law. It is well known that Egypt exercised legal and judicial regional influence, in particular due to its school of law, which has distinguished itself internationally by combining the Islamic tradition and modern standards for an extended period, beginning in the 1860s.

The judges' revolt itself is a testament to longstanding injustice: the loss of the guarantees of justice, the marginalization of the law, and the use of the judiciary to punish the political opposition. These phenomena occur in nearly all Arab countries, but without judges' refusal to allow the judicial apparatus to use them against public freedoms and the law. In most Arab and Islamic countries, judges, instead of taking on the burden of a lengthy struggle, have been partners in the executive's authoritarianism in exchange for individual and group privileges.

The Egyptian judges' revolt "gladdens the heart," as we say in Egypt, because it absolves the judges of responsibility for the oppression of average Egyptians in the name of the judiciary, but by persons and entities who are outside it. Through their protest, the judges have strengthened their reputation in the eyes of Egyptians and the world.

However, a broad alliance of interests and social forces wants the judiciary to remain under the tutelage of the authoritarian system.

The most important point in this long struggle is the alternative law for the judicial authority presented by the Judges' Club in 1991. This draft continues to be the main point of reference for the club's demands more than fifteen years after it was elaborated and submitted to the minister of justice. The Judges' Club's legal struggle for the independence of the judiciary has become a political and social battle.

## When Did the Revolt Really Start?

Attempts to determine when the judges' revolt began reveal several possible moments. It can be said to have begun in April 2006, when two leading judges from the Judges' Club were referred to a disciplinary council composed of figures known for their enmity toward the club and its stances. These disciplinary procedures were widely seen as an attempt to punish the club for its boldness, especially in issuing reports on the violations its members observed during the May 2005 referendum on the amendment of Article 76 of the constitution and during the presidential and legislative elections of autumn 2005. The revolt was emboldened by the fierce dispute that emerged over the sense and meaning of "full judicial supervision of the elections," as stipulated by the constitution.

The judges' protest also can be said to have started when the Judges' Club formed a committee to investigate the widespread falsification of the results of the legislative elections. Several of the most revered judges went public with these violations after Noha al-Zini, a young female member of the Office of Administrative Prosecution, emerged as an inspiring hero for people of all ages by giving her account of what happened in the constituency of Kafr al-Zayat. The club then became intent on collecting the testimony of its members who participated in supervising the elections, particularly in that constituency.

Another starting point could be the discussions about full judicial supervision of the referendum on amending the constitution that began immediately after the amendment was proposed on 26 February 2005. These discussions heated up in May of the same year with the start of that bewildering referendum, which few in Egypt considered credible, and with subsequent political and constitutional processes, including the presidential election. Its beginning also could have been in the political dynamism of spring 2005, which highlighted Egyptians' discontent over longstanding political stagnation, the continuous violation of the spirit and letter of the law, and the growing possibility that the president would be succeeded by his son, an idea intensively promoted by the NDP since that time.

The judges' revolt may have started much earlier, in 1991, when the Judges' Club drafted a law for the judicial authority to amend Law 46/1972. The draft was the root of exhaustive negotiations between the club and the ministry of justice that failed to achieve anything. It also may go back to the first Justice Conference in 1986, which gave rise to outstanding resolutions of the sort necessary to liberate Egypt from the government's massive arsenal of exceptional laws and authoritarian legislation and to foster democratization.

The revolt's beginning also could be placed at the founding event of the judges' struggle: their refusal to join the Arab Socialist Union (ASU). Established in 1962 by President Gamal 'Abd al-Nasser, the ASU replaced Egypt's political parties. Membership in it was meant to be a requirement for holding a judicial post. The judges' refusal to join the ASU resulted in dozens losing their jobs in what is known as the Massacre of the Judiciary of 1969.

## The Judiciary and the Repression of Political Opposition

Law No. 46 of 1972 is the means the state uses to employ the judiciary for political ends and to frighten, punish, and thus control political opposition figures, particularly in cases of a political nature and those related to political corruption.

Giving the appearance of supporting the independence of the judiciary, the law forbids the arbitrary dismissal of judges and pressure being placed on them to provide certain rulings. Thus, the only way for the government to influence rulings is either to intimidate judges (using transfer and forbidding them from profitable secondment or temporary assignment) or to entice them with privileges (once again, through secondment or temporary assignment to non-judicial appointments that bring them financial or non-financial privileges). The regime has repeatedly resorted to these methods, mainly enticement, giving some judges political posts, particularly governorships. Real independence of the judiciary would mean an end to such intimidation and enticement. It requires that judicial institutions decide all matters relating to judges' performance, including appointments, promotions, transfers, and disciplinary measures. Decisions in these matters also must be based on clear and objective criteria.

Doubtless, one of the most important aspects of executive domination of the judicial system is the executive's control over the Office of Public Prosecution, specifically the position of the general prosecutor. This is the executive's key to the entire judicial process. It is able to put opposition figures on trial and extricate others from trial, particularly by monopolizing the process of launching criminal complaints. Another tool that has been used to wide effect by the executive is the provision for "precautionary custody," which allows opposition figures to be jailed for six months or more without trial and without evidence that they have committed any offense.

Unless the judiciary resumes control of the Office of Public Prosecution, freedom is impossible. Unless the judiciary takes control of its financial, administrative, and disciplinary affairs, some judges will be given positions for making rulings favorable to the government, whether out of fear or ambition.

## A Political Battle?

The judges' revolt implies condemnation of the regime and its apparatuses for violating human rights night and day for decades. For this reason, it was predictable that a massive campaign would be waged in the state media against the judges. The aim of that sweeping campaign was to create a smokescreen to obscure the truth of the judges' cause. An army of journalists working for the state press participated in the campaign because of their longtime ties and service to the security apparatus. They partially succeeded in clouding the view of many average readers about the cause of the judges' revolt.

The aim of the media strategy was to sidetrack discussion of the Judges' Club's demands. Instead of presenting positions for or against particular views on the matter, the press stepped up its battle against opposition political forces or figures to the extent that the issue itself—its basis and meaning—was almost absent from the public field. The most important accusation made by newspapers and the security apparatus was that the judges were engaging in political activity. Yet, the value of the judges' draft law lies precisely in its insistence on guarantees of the political neutrality of the judiciary and on an end to the exploitation of the judiciary for political ends.

The judges and their club were accused of overstepping the bounds of their judicial authority into an area that is the purview of the legislative assemblies. This begs the question of whether the judges have the right to make suggestions for profound legislative reforms to guarantee the independence of the judiciary or if that is the role of parliament, in accordance with the principle of separation of powers.

Among international legal scholars, no one questions the right of the judges, whether in their capacity as judges or as a professional grouping, to call for everything that guarantees their independence and protects them from subordination to the executive branch, whether by order, coercion, or enticement. Accordingly, the response to the accusation that the judges have been departing from judicial traditions is that, in fact, the judges who tailored the interpretation of laws to the specifications of the executive are the ones who violated judicial traditions hallowed by democratic societies. What politicizes the judiciary and judges is forcing a judge to obey the executive's orders by blocking a law that includes guarantees for judicial independence.

## A Social Battle for Independence

The conflict over the judicial authority law was the most important and uninterrupted political phenomenon in Egypt in the first half of 2006. The conflict intensified in early summer, when the two judges leading the revolt were referred to a disciplinary council. At that time, people gradually came to recognize the nature of the matter and began to hope for a peaceful resolution that would enable Egypt to rebuild its judicial system. The desired system would not be characterized by orders from the executive or by politically motivated rulings. It would reject bribes and all manner of corruption. It also would stand firm against intimidation campaigns.

In mid-May 2006, the police began making shows of force harsher than any before. Concurrent with the start of the disciplinary hearings for the two judges, massive, well-equipped security forces appeared in the vicinity of the Judges' Club, the Court of Cassation, and the journalists' and lawyers' syndicates in downtown Cairo. This was an attempt by the government to reestablish a culture of fear among professional organizations that for centuries have formed the heart of political and social movements in Egypt. The goal was not only to prevent demonstrations in support of the judges and their club but also to prevent citizens from exercising their constitutional and human right to hold a political demonstration—an indivisible part of freedom of expression that has become the demarcation line between democratic and authoritarian states.

The judges and their club received extensive support from the political reform movement in Egypt and from all professional syndicates and political parties, with the exception of the ruling party. In return, it seems that supporters of the authoritarian system began to shake off their laziness and reliance on the security apparatus and to plunge into the battle on the media and political fronts, alongside the actual use of force. Debates on the judges' revolt intensified during the spring and summer of 2006.

On the social front, the regime's camp rallied an ever-increasing number of supporters, who accused the judges of every possible shortcoming. These supporters adopted the guise of struggle by targeting the Muslim Brotherhood in their attacks and attributing the judges' revolt to it. The overwhelming majority of the supporters come from pro-regime camps in the state apparatus, the media, universities, research centers, and the judicial corps. On the other side, reformist forces in the professional syndicates, political parties, and intellectual circles, as well as reformist writers, university professors, students, recent graduates, journalists, and others, rallied around the Judges' Club and expressed a startling readiness to risk everything, including jail, in support of the judges.

The matter seems paradoxical because a relatively small number of supporters confronted the mechanisms of the state security forces and brutish administrative authorities in every institution controlled by the state. From a social standpoint, however, the matter is entirely logical, as the conflict centers on the principle of the independence of society—all of its institutions, not only the judiciary—from the state. Authoritarianism does not spare any social institutions but works to control them all through monitoring and stringent subordination to security.

In every profession in Egypt that is linked to the production of knowledge and opinion making, there is a minority (albeit an important one) of university professors, journalists, and engineers struggling for the independence of their institutions and guarantees that the rule of law will prevail in the institutions and in Egypt as a whole. In response, security forces intervene on behalf of particular social interests (also a minority, but a powerful one). The majority remains silent, apprehensively awaiting the outcome of each conflict. This has happened in most, if not all, social and state institutions in Egypt, with the exception of the judiciary, where a clear majority, particularly from younger generations, was behind the judges and formed the body of the revolt.

In truth, the judges' revolt and the social conflict it occasioned revolved around loyalty versus merit in the holding of public office and, thus, the principle of the rule of law versus arbitrary and police rule. Egypt experienced a unique cultural conflict that was parallel to its ongoing social and political conflict.

## Conclusion

The issues I am discussing were decisive in the transition of western societies to modernity—a transition that Egypt has not yet succeeded in making. Put simply, western societies progressed because the majority of their structures adopted the idea of law in the most fundamental sense of the word. Both Arab and European cultures understand law to mean respect for logic and a system of scientific explanation, but Arab societies have declined into a strange state of submission to contradictory chaos in the intellectual field. Independence of the judiciary is the principle that underpins a form of thought and behavior that respects the truth and the law and, accordingly, aims to uncover their precise form with respect to justice. The police state's cause is the opposite: to defend the purported achievements of an arbitrary authority that does not even want to abide by its own laws.

The battle for the independence of the judiciary is thus one of reason against powerless submission to the authorities, particularly old forms of authority. The battle for the independence of the judiciary is one of knowledge against ignorance, of proficiency against failure, and of the desire to be upstanding against greedy self-hatred.

The matter, then, is not about the Muslim Brotherhood or other political forces encouraging the judges to confront the state. Rather, it is about individual patriots endowed with a moral legacy unique among Arab and Islamic countries, and perhaps in the world, who have engaged in a protracted struggle to reclaim fundamental guarantees for their independence as an institution. Their struggle represents an important element in the vision of a democratic and free future for Egypt. Indeed, it is the noblest battle that Egypt has entered in its contemporary history.

# 2

# The Development of Relations between the Mixed Courts and the Executive Authority in Egypt (1875–1904)

*Isabelle Lendrevie-Tournan*

With the construction of the Suez Canal (1859–1869), the Nile Delta region became an international crossroads. During the reigns of Viceroy Sa'id Pasha (1854–1863) and Khedive Isma'il (1863–1879), Egypt experienced an economic boom as a result of an increased volume of commercial transactions between Egypt and Europe,[1] an extensive influx of European capital (mainly French),[2] and the settlement of numerous Levantines and Europeans in Egypt. On the legal level, commercial and civil disputes involving these foreigners (especially regarding real estate) were settled through diplomatic channels, which was the traditional mode of conflict resolution between the Egyptian state and European and Ottoman individuals.

During that period, Egyptian reformers, after the pattern of Ottoman viceroys,[3] considered that one of the ways to settle such disputes within a context of modernizing the country was to modify the administration of justice and the legislation according to a European model.[4] The khedive, for his part, had endeavored to modify the capitulation system,[5] restore Egypt's sovereignty, reaffirm its political authority vis-à-vis the European powers, and gain additional attributes of sovereignty vis-à-vis the Sublime Porte. To organize a reformed judicial system in favor of the political authority, Nubar Pasha, Isma'il's minister of foreign affairs, introduced two new features to Egypt: European and Christian magistrates and control of the administrative and legislative activity of the government by courts.[6]

After eight long years of diplomatic negotiations, Nubar's "courts of the reform," which became known as mixed courts *(al-mahakim al-mukhtalata)*, were finally approved in July 1875 at the Palace of Ras al-Tin in Alexandria. In the same year, the Egyptian government published the six "Mixed" Codes, new civil and commercial legislation inspired by and closely copied from European continental legislation (notably the Napoleonic Code and other code legislation), which the mixed courts were to apply. In February 1876, the various mixed courts (summary courts, courts of first instance, and the Mixed Court of Appeal in Alexandria) held their first sessions.

I will focus on the beginning of the mixed courts (1875–1904). During this period, these new "Egyptian" mixed jurisdictions went through multiple crises, notably the debt of the Egyptian state in 1876 and the 'Orabi Revolution in 1881, which provoked the 1882 British Occupation.

The relationship between the mixed judicial authority and the government was complicated and conflicted. The khedive and the "Anglo-Egyptian" (colonial) authorities attempted several times to paralyze the regular operation of the mixed jurisdictions and hinder the execution of their judgments. Many political trials jeopardized the "courts of the reform." Nevertheless, the courts "succeeded," at least in their beginning phase, in surviving these ordeals. Their firmness in dealing with the government even reinforced their independence. For that reason, in 1926, the general prosecutor of the mixed courts, Léon Pangalo, called that period a "heroic age."[7]

I will show how until 1904 the mixed courts resisted executive authority, at first from the khedive and then from the occupying British power. I will next discuss the consequences of this judicial independence and then consider the conflicting relations between the executive authority and these mixed jurisdictions by examining lawsuits with political overtones that occurred starting in 1876, virtually from the beginning of these courts. These lawsuits raised a number of issues, including the viability of control by civil judges over administrative and legislative acts taken by the khedival government.

## The Resistance of the Mixed Courts toward the Executive Authority

In order to show how the mixed courts resisted interference by the executive authority, I will briefly review the historical context within which the birth of the judicial reform of 1875 took place. Then I will look at the founding texts of this reform, which encompassed the Regulations for the Organization of the Mixed Judiciary and the mixed civil code. I also will discuss the influence of liberal-minded Egyptian political figures and Ottoman and European legal scholars.[8]

## Origins of the Mixed Courts' Independence
The last quarter of the nineteenth century was an important era for legal development, when judicial authorities and legal sciences were totally reformulated in Egypt. New actors in law, like European and Ottoman judges and lawyers of the mixed courts, appeared on the scene. Such judicial and legal changes would not have occurred without the "persistent endeavors exerted by the great Egyptian statesman,"[9] Nubar Pasha.

## Defenders of the Independence of the Mixed Jurisdictions
Alongside Nubar Pasha, the main figure of the 1875 judicial reform, numerous European and Ottoman legal scholars and magistrates defended the concept of the independence of the new mixed jurisdiction vis-à-vis the executive authority.

### Nubar Pasha's Reformist Project
With the new mixed jurisdiction, Nubar Pasha, the foreign minister of Khedive Isma'il, aspired to unify legislation in Egypt, especially in the civil and commercial fields. He also hoped to introduce the system of separation of powers. Finally, the ultimate goal of his reform was to adjust legal relations between Egypt and foreigners. Assurance needed to be given to foreigners that in exchange for the partial suspension of their jurisdictional immunity attached to the system of capitulation, they would be tried before new courts that would have all the required guarantees of neutrality, especially independence from the khedival authority.

Nubar Pasha faced relentless objections and opposition. From 1867 to 1875, he had to defend his project not only before the Sublime Porte and Khedive Isma'il but also before the foreign powers, primarily the European countries whose nationals had commercial relations with Egypt. The Sublime Porte viewed such judicial reform as an infringement on the territorial rights and sovereignty of the sultan.[10] Nubar Pasha responded that the 1867 decree[11] had granted Egypt full autonomy at the political level. In order to put in place the new mixed courts, which he argued were necessary for the "moral redress of the country" and for its judicial and legal unification, Nubar Pasha assumed that "there was a lack in material and men and that they had to be searched for in Europe."[12] He suggested to the sultan that he grant Egypt full autonomy in order not to be "held accountable for the actions of the Egyptian viceroy before the public opinion of Muslims."[13]

In fact, Nubar Pasha aspired to make Egypt the first enlightened monarchy based on justice in the Ottoman Empire. Nevertheless, he had to convince his "prince," Khedive Isma'il, of this concept, as Isma'il had followed in the footsteps of his predecessors in regard to exercising absolute power over the country. Khedive Isma'il at first did not like the concept of independent justice and liked even less the idea of new courts exercising control over his actions or those of his family or the government. The Egyptian minister explained to his sovereign that establishing impartial justice was the only way to put an end to the "secular arbitrariness of Egyptian governments" and to enable Egypt to become "independent and powerful."[14]

Nubar Pasha also could not neglect the opinions of the foreign powers. He addressed particularly the United States and Italy,[15] once more using his personal connections. During the 1870s, he was close to certain Italian legal scholars and politicians, such as Pasquale Mancini,[16] whereas his relations with the French were not as good. France had considered the Mediterranean its geographical axis of expansion since the Ancien Régime and viewed such judicial reform as the end of the capitulation system, of which it was the primary beneficiary.[17] Finally, the fact that many nations agreed to the reform can be attributed to their intention to use the new courts to enhance their power in Egypt. This applies to Belgium, Italy, the Netherlands, Spain, Sweden, Denmark, Portugal, Russia, the United States, Germany, and Austria-Hungary.

### Shadow Men

By ratifying the project at the last minute, France did not have sufficient time to appoint a large number of French magistrates to the mixed courts, which eventually set the stage for the presence of Belgian and Italian judges. The Belgian and Italian influence was not restricted to the new judicial system. The liberal legal concepts of the two nations also inspired European and Ottoman legal scholars during the preparatory work for the reform.[18] The concept of separation of powers, the corollary of which is the independence of the judicial authority, had penetrated most European countries by the second half of the nineteenth century. In Egypt, Italian legal scholars laid the cornerstone for including a provision requiring the adoption of the Belgian system of judicial defense of citizens' rights in the 1875 Regulations for the Organization of the Mixed Judiciary.[19]

In 1876, the birth year of the mixed judiciary, fifteen countries finally agreed to the reform that led to the establishment of a court of appeal in Alexandria, three courts of first instance, in Cairo, Alexandria, and Mansura, and a number of summary courts. These courts, in the exercise of their jurisdiction in civil and commercial matters and within their limited competence in penal law, were to apply the six codes known as the Mixed Codes,[20] submitted by Egypt to the foreign powers. Pursuant to Article 9 of the Regulations for the Organization of the Mixed Judiciary, the mixed courts were competent to settle all disputes in civil and commercial fields between Ottomans and foreigners and between foreigners of various nationalities, except in matters of personal status. The jurisdiction of the courts extended to all real estate controversies between all peoples, including those with the same nationality.[21]

In fact, correspondence between the new magistrates and members of their European hierarchies is a good source of information on the personnel of the mixed courts residing in Egypt starting from February 1876. Such correspondence includes, for instance, a letter of thirty-five pages, dated May 1876, sent by Alfred Vacher, a French public attorney at the Mixed Court of Appeal in Alexandria, to Emile Valot, the personnel manager at the ministry of justice in Versailles. The letter shows that the mixed court personnel in Alexandria included:

> An ex-public prosecutor of the king in Bruges, who was appointed as general prosecutor, and five public attorneys, among whom two were Ottomans between twenty-eight and thirty years old, and three foreigners of the same age, one of them a German from Wilmonski (alternative judge at Berlin), another an Italian, Mr. Bernardi (the special secretary of the minister of justice in Rome), and the third is French (author of the present letter).[22]

The mixed court in Alexandria included the Court of Appeal, the two circuits of the Mixed Court of First Instance, and the Summary Court of Justice. It is important to underline the significant role played by the magistrates of the Mixed Court of Appeal in Alexandria, Ottoman lawyers (Egyptian or not), and European attorneys of the mixed bar. The

Belgian legal scholar, Maurice de Wée, states that "since the start of its activity, the Mixed Court of Appeal decided that the rules relative to its competence belonged to the public order." He highlights that "it was a good means to prevent the parties from concluding conventions attributing competence to one jurisdiction or another in the country."[23]

The Mixed Court of Appeal took measures that normally belong to the legislative domain, since it established on its own initiative rules relating to the public order. In May 1876, there were "sixty-six lawyers enrolled, without taking into account a lot of businessmen who sought to work in trade or summary justice in the capacity of agents."[24]

## The Mixed Courts: An International Institution that Protected European Interests

From 1876 to 1904, the mixed courts could have been considered an international institution. Through the European judges in the courts (of more than ten nationalities), the European countries exercised legislative influence in Egypt.

### The Regulations for the Organization of the Mixed Judiciary

The Regulations for the Organization of the Mixed Judiciary were signed by the foreign powers that were party to the establishment of the mixed courts; hence, they acquired the form of an international treaty. According to Article 5 of the regulations, the khedival government was not totally free to select the judges. The khedive was vested with the authority to appoint them but had to "officially address the minister of justice abroad, and to appoint only those who obtain their government's permission and agreement." At the same time, discipline, promotion, and transfer of magistrates from one mixed jurisdiction to another "were matters where the local authorities are not permitted to interfere."[25] According to Article 24 of the regulations, discipline of a judge was within the jurisdiction of the Mixed Court of Appeal. Article 20 gave the Mixed Court of Appeal jurisdiction over promotion and transfer.

### The Mixed Civil Code

In accordance with Article 7 of the mixed civil code, the mixed court defined the competence of the government when a foreign interest was at stake. They promptly exercised control, particularly over the decisive administrative actions of the government.[26] The judges of the Mixed Court of Appeal, inspired by the French theory of acts of government, made a distinction between the administration and the government, separating acts of government (assimilated to the acts of sovereignty) from acts of administration. This distinction between acts of sovereignty and traditional administrative acts was made at the outset of the mixed courts.[27]

Mixed jurisprudence did not develop objective litigation, however, as had happened in French administrative jurisprudence. The mixed courts were not competent to repeal illegal administrative acts but were able only to provide redress to foreign individuals (and later, the Ottomans) in pursuance of Article 7, in case a vested right was damaged by virtue of an administrative act. On the basis of Article 7, the mixed jurisdictions considered themselves competent to rule on the validity of a government seizure action that prejudiced one of the foreigners (a decision by the Mixed Court of Appeal on 20 April 1883) or about requests for compensation presented by foreigners against the Anglo-Egyptian government for losses caused as a result of administrative acts (a decision by the Mixed Court of Appeal on 4 February 1885).[28]

In accordance with Article 7 of the mixed civil code, "The Mixed Courts can decide in cases provided by the Civil Code on damages occasioned to a vested right of a foreigner that is caused by an administrative act, while they do not have the right to decide upon the property of public space or on the interpretation or suspension of the implementation of an administrative decision." With reference to Article 12 of the mixed civil code, the Mixed Court of Appeal exercised legislative powers by virtue of delegation from the capitulatory powers. The Court of Appeal had the right to approve legislative decisions issued by the Egyptian authorities that were applicable to foreigners.

Article 12, before its amendment in 1911, read as follows: "Additions and amendments to the current laws will be enacted in accordance with the binding opinion of the magistrates and, if necessary, following their suggestion." According to some specialists of the mixed courts at the time,[29] Article 12 was never applied and the khedival authority persistently pursued diplomatic means to amend the mixed legislation. In an article on "les sources du droit mixte" featured in the periodical, *Egypte contemporaine*, Salvatore Messina adopted Abdel Salam Zohny's hypothesis that Article 12 was to be considered a dead letter. According to the Egyptian lawyer, "the Egyptian government hesitated to cling to a provision that had not been inserted into the Regulations for the

Organization of the Mixed Judiciary and thus did not have the power of the international agreements consecrated by this regulation, or it did not wish to grant the Mixed Courts judges too substantial powers because the government feared they might interfere in its own powers if it were to have associated legislative powers."[30] According to Messina, the Egyptian government wanted to keep for itself "the authority to enact laws applicable to foreigners, through the establishment of a legislative entity that would make sure that the government ensured a maximum of autonomy, especially through the reform project of the Regulations for the Organization of the Mixed Judiciary, presented by Riaz Pasha to an international commission in 1880."[31] This project was subsequently abandoned.

## Consequences of the Mixed Courts' Independence: Extension of Their Judicial Competences

In this international context, the mixed courts easily extended their competence to almost all important administrative, civil, and commercial litigation in the country.

### Extensive Competences in the Field of Administrative Litigation

Upon reviewing the judgments of the Court of Appeal in Alexandria over the last twenty-five years of the nineteenth century,[32] I noted that most cases submitted to the mixed courts in their early years were related to real estate and administrative litigation. The mixed courts settled a considerable number of cases that opposed the khedival state—the private administration (al-da'ira) of the khedive, the members of the royal family, and other branches of the public administration, such as the ministry of awqaf —to European and Ottoman individuals. The mixed jurisdictions were equally involved in cases between nationals (Ottomans and Egyptians) and foreigners. In the field of real estate, the 1875 judicial and legal reform occurred at a time of diminished competence of traditional Islamic justice. In fact, Nubar Pasha was pressured by the European powers to transfer to the mixed jurisdictions jurisdiction over real estate.

According to Article 10 of the Regulations for the Organization of the Mixed Judiciary, relations between foreigners and the government, the administration, the private administration of the khedive, and the khedive's family fell within competence of the mixed courts, "within a purely civil frame, and in accordance with the rules of civil responsibility."[33] On the basis of Article 11 of the regulations, the mixed jurisdiction allowed foreigners, and later Ottomans, to file indemnity actions against the local government, although they were not allowed, theoretically, to intervene in the administrative workflow.

One of the goals of the judicial reform was to reduce the number of actions filed against the Egyptian state.[34] Such actions, which were settled through diplomatic means, were characterized by high costs and impeded the regular administrative workflow in the state. In addition, they did not prompt the state to undertake new public works, which generally were contracted out to European companies.[35]

After the 1875 judicial reform, foreigners continued to enjoy a kind of jurisdictional and legal immunity. The question was whether they could enjoy equal "administrative immunity," or, more precisely, if they could escape being subjected to administrative regulations. According to Pélissié du Rausas, director of the Cairo French Law School,[36] and Henri Lamba, professor at the Cairo Khedival Law School,[37] the legal immunity granted to foreigners through the capitulations and renewed by the 1875 reform prohibited the Egyptian government from enacting any administrative rule or taking any police measures against foreigners.

The practice in the mixed courts undermined this hitherto dominant doctrine. From 1876, the Mixed Court of Appeal, which dealt with all rulings and decisions issued by the 'commissions' (also called special chambers)[38] established to judge old cases filed against the Egyptian government and not decided before 1875, adopted a different approach. Decisions of the mixed courts given after the decisions issued in 1876–1877 by the special chambers of the Alexandria Mixed Court of Appeal confirm this shift. In *Soliman Elias al-Charkaoui v. State Railway Administration 1892* (considered a mixed administration),[39] a decision of the Mixed Court of Appeal on 13 April 1892, the plaintiff was a national subject who had been fired by the Railway Administration. The administration referred to Article 11 of the regulations, contending that administrative measures taken against Egyptian employees, which were criticized by employees as prejudicing their vested rights and breaching laws and decrees, were not within the field of competence of the mixed courts. The administration also attacked the competence of the mixed courts by claiming that the litigation was between an Egyptian administration and a national subject.

The Mixed Court of Appeal rejected the arguments of the administration. It first gave a definition of "mixed interest":

> Unlike the government as such and a number of other state administrations, the Railway Administration was subject to adjudication in the mixed courts not only in litigation with foreigners, but even in litigation with national subjects. The Railway Administration is, in accordance with the conditions of appointment and nomination of its senior officials and the powers and competences delegated to such officials and with its numerous existing interests and finally with the special allocation of its incomes, an entity of a mixed interest and mixed nature, and therefore it is subject to the provisions of international conventions.

The court also defined an administrative act, or "administrative measure," stating that "the debate did not concern an administrative act in the sense related to Article 11 of the Regulations for the Organization of the Mixed Judiciary, that had been consecrated by jurisprudence, that is, a general measure or a particular measure taken in the general and public interest. On the contrary, the debate dealt with a personal measure related to an employee, a simple act of discipline and dismissal."

Article 5 of the mixed civil code enabled the mixed court to deal comprehensively with real estate litigation: "The new courts will decide all litigation in both civil and commercial fields between nationals and foreigners, and between foreigners of different nationalities. Except for personal status cases, these courts are also competent to decide all real estate actions between all persons, even belonging to the same nationality."

## Competence in Islamic Law

Articles 8, 22, and 37 gave to the courts the possibility of settling a significant portion of litigation related to *waqf*s in Egypt.[40] In accordance with Article 8, "Actions filed by foreigners against a religious establishment for the purpose of claiming *waqf*s as part of their real estate are not submitted to these courts. They will be competent, however, to decide upon actions filed on the question of legal possession, regardless of the identity of the plaintiff or the defendant."

Long before the attempts to codify Islamic law of the so-called liberal years (1922–1949),[41] part of the traditional Islamic doctrine of the Hanafi rite had been set in 1875 with the drafting of the Code of Personal Status (Hanafite rite) under the mandate of the Egyptian minister of justice, Qadri Pasha. With the rise of the mixed doctrine and jurisprudence and the application of new sources of law related to *waqf*s, this Islamic doctrine lost its influence. On the judicial level, the competence of the mixed courts (like that of the 1883 national courts) regarding *waqf*s stripped Islamic religious courts *(mahakim shar'iya)* of part of their jurisdictional competence.

### Expanded Competences in the Civil and Commercial Fields

On the basis of the provisions of the regulations and of the mixed civil code, the mixed courts' competences expanded to include the civil and commercial fields. Their rulings, for instance, helped in the development of the credit system based on real estate mortgages linked to cotton production. They also succeeded in gaining the trust of rich European and Ottoman traders.

Because the mixed legislation was incomplete, the mixed courts, having relied in their work on numerous local and foreign references,[42] showed real legal creativity. They had to adopt legal rules and "decide on legal issues totally absent from the Mixed Codes."[43] Article 11 of the mixed civil code allowed judges of the mixed courts, "in case of the absence of a legal provision or its insufficiency," to take a decision "in conformity with the principles of natural law and the rules of equity." Thus, the mixed courts extended their competence to litigation between Ottomans, relying on the concept of mixed interest that they had developed in administrative litigation.

On the basis of this theory of mixed interest, the mixed courts considered themselves competent, for instance, to examine major cases related to commercial law. When a "foreign interest" was involved, the "courts of the reform" declared their competence in litigation implicating major companies, whether anonymous or established by public concession,[44] and became the "locomotive of commercial development."[45]

## The "Legal-political" Conflicts between the Mixed Courts and the Executive Authority (1876–1904)

This last section is about the attempts of the executive authority to limit the mixed courts' influence and the two-fold nature of the courts: judicial and political. By presenting some major trials, I will illustrate the role the courts played in the political life of Egypt between 1876 and 1904.

## Restrictions Imposed on the Independence of the Mixed Courts under the Khedival Authority
### Political Control through Symbols

The sovereignty of the political authority usually involves a degree of control over justice. The government under Khedive Isma'il was no exception. Until the British Occupation in 1882, the khedive sought to exercise his authority through the new mixed courts. This authority was at times symbolic. Isma'il imposed on the judges of the mixed courts the wearing of the national costume, characterized at the time by the *stambouline* and the *tarbouche*.[46] Through such symbols, among which the judicial robe was the strongest, Khedive Isma'il meant to remind mixed court judges of his power. The symbols were, for him, a means to "remind them, at the same time, that he was the sovereign and the first judge."[47]

### Establishment of the State Litigation Committee in 1875

With the 1875 reform, the mixed courts (and later the national courts) started examining the acts and decisions of the state in the same way they were examining those of individuals. The executive authority decided in 1875 to be represented in these administrative cases by counselors of the State Litigation Committee, often (wrongly) called the State Council at that time.

## Restrictions Imposed under the British Occupation
### Attempts to Suppress the Mixed Courts (1896–1897)

In 1879, Nubar Pasha wished to complete the reorganization of the Egyptian judicial system by creating, along with the mixed courts, competent local courts to settle controversies between Ottomans in civil and commercial matters. The project was stopped by the 1882 'Orabi Revolution and resumed only under the British Occupation, during which the national courts were created in 1883. These courts were competent to examine civil and commercial cases between Ottomans, except those pertaining to personal status. In criminal cases, the courts had jurisdiction to examine all petty offenses, misdemeanors, and felonies that had not been reserved to the mixed courts by the international treaties. The national courts exercised an authority parallel to that of the mixed courts: they could order the government to pay compensation if an administrative act violated a law or decree.

Judges of the national jurisdiction also established a distinction between acts of sovereignty and administrative acts on the basis of Article 15 of the Regulations for the Organization of the Judiciary in National Courts,[48] as well as on the basis of some decisions of the mixed courts.

After the *Da'ira Saniya Case* in 1876 and the *Dongola Expedition Case* in 1896, the British decided to add three European magistrates to the bench of the national court of appeal. The court of appeal, which was composed of twenty counselors (thirteen "Egyptians" and seven Europeans), was enlarged on 30 December 1896, to include ten European counselors. According to a member of the British Cabinet, as quoted by the French Consul at the time, "the intrusion of foreign members in the Egyptian judiciary will certainly furnish, in the future, a pretext to abolish the Mixed Courts."[49]

Many articles published in the pro-British local press or the English press (*The Times* in 1897) at the end of the nineteenth century condemned the control exercised by the mixed courts over acts of sovereignty of the Anglo-Egyptian government.[50] These articles also highlighted the open conflict between the two sovereignties. After the British occupation of Egypt, the mixed courts were in an uncomfortable position. Thus, when the question of the renewal of their competence was raised in 1899, the British parliament considered limiting their authority or even abolishing them.[51]

## The Anglo-Egyptian Statutory Authority

The Anglo-Egyptian executive authority could not legislate alone in areas pertaining to foreigners or in cases of violation of foreigners' vested rights. The authority had to obtain the agreement of all the delegates of the capitulatory powers in the framework of an international conference. The issue of legislative autonomy was raised many times, particularly in 1889 and 1891, regarding the executive's authority in police matters.

Police regulations approved by the Mixed Court of Appeal in conformity with the decree of 31 January 1889, became binding on all foreign subjects under the competence of the mixed courts, however they had been promulgated (whether in the form of laws, decrees, or decree laws). The first of these regulations to come into force was the regulation of 17 December 1890, regarding the obligatory vaccination of infants and newborns. The second, dated 9 June 1891, established the registry of the civil state in Egypt. The third regulation was the min-isterial decision of 13 June 1891, on the practice of medicine, equally applicable to dentists. The last regulation, also adopted in June 1891, imposed the necessity of applying for a license from the public author-ity prior to opening any public establishment, such as coffee shops, pubs, theaters, circuses, and clubs.

## Two Examples of "Legal-political" Cases

The first example of such a case was the 1876 case, commonly known as the *Da'ira Saniya Case*, which opposed the *Da'ira Saniya* (or private administration of the khedive) to European holders of treasury bills. The second case was the *1896 Dongola Expedition Case*, also known as *The Sudan Expedition Case*. In both cases, the mixed courts condemned the khedive's government and later the Anglo-Egyptian (colonial) government by referring to Article 11 of the 1875 Regulations for the Organization of the Mixed Judiciary. The concept of "vested rights of foreigners" stipulated in Article 11 allowed the mixed courts to extend their control over many government acts, whether financial or military.

### Cases in 1876 between European Holders of Treasury Bills and the Da'ira Saniya

The actions filed before the mixed courts starting in May 1876 occurred in the context of the 1873 world economic crisis, which resulted in the cessation of European capital exportation to Egypt and caused the khedive and his country to fall into unprecedented indebtedness.[52] I will not examine here the political aspect of the French-English financial custodianship or the financial control system that was established in May 1876 (based on the Debt Fund, a mixed entity first established by four European members). I will focus on the effect of this debt on the judiciary.

Many European owners of Egyptian treasury notes, issued in the form of bills of exchange, ventured to summon the *Da'ira Saniya* before the mixed court of commerce. The principle of separation of pow-ers that had been proclaimed in the 1875 reform did not actually apply in Egypt during the last quarter of the nineteenth century. Before the issues that emerged through the creation of the Debt Fund, there was no real separation of powers or separation between public funds and khedival private funds.

The *Da'ira Saniya* defended itself by claiming that the court lacked competence. First, it considered that "the Mixed Courts were not allowed to rule in the presence of a decree passed by the sovereign power of the Khedive and having the force of law." Second, the case, according to the French attorney, Alfred Vacher, pertained to civil justice and not to commercial justice. The court declared itself incompetent as a commercial court but laid down the following principle: "In accordance with Article 11 of the Regulations for the Organization of the Mixed Judiciary, the Mixed Courts were competent to decide on administrative measures infringing on vested rights of foreigners. The present case was about an administrative measure, and the Mixed jurisdiction could therefore examine it." The Mixed Court of Appeal in Alexandria decided upon the appeal case on 3 May 1876, and confirmed and broadened this principle. The court decision stated, "After the reform of the Mixed judiciary, khedival laws and decrees, whatever they are, shall be considered as administrative measures the court may be ruling on regarding damages caused to foreigners. For such laws and decrees to be binding on them, they should have been passed with the support of the magistrature in accordance with Article 12 of the Mixed Civil Code."[53] According to Vacher:

> This theory, substantiated in length, was formulated by the judgment in the most absolute terms. . . . the court had rightly decided that the commercial court was competent to examine the substance of the case, since the treasury bills had been issued in conformity with the Ottoman code, according to which a bill of exchange is a commercial act. . . . It also decided, on the merits of the case, that the Da'ira shall pay the value of the bills in question.[54]

On 7 May 1876, the decree of consolidation of debt was issued, unifying all the debts of the government and of the *Da'ira*. Key French bankers and financial institutions undertook the task. Another decree created the Debt Fund, managed by foreign commissioners appointed by the international powers. This step was the result of the efforts of European and Egyptian diplomats over several months. The legal settlement was expected to avert, inter alia, judicial actions. Nonetheless, a group of treasury bill holders brought new cases against the *Da'ira* alone, or both the *Da'ira* and the Egyptian government. These actions were examined by the mixed court (first chamber) in a session held on

17 May 1876. The question of lack of competence was raised again and argued at length by both parties. The European members of the State Litigation Committee came to the court and submitted their conclusions on 18 May 1876.

The French attorney explained that:

> He preferred to bow before the decisions of the Mixed Court of Appeal, although he deemed the consequences drawn from the decision exaggerated, and that the theory raised could have been avoided while reaching the same results. . . . It was incumbent in such a grave situation, and at the outset of the judicial organization, to give an example of due respect to the decisions passed by the magistrature in its most sovereign expression, since there was no Court of Cassation in Egypt.[55]

## The Dongola Expedition Case

Referring once again to Article 11 of the Regulations for the Organization of the Mixed Judiciary, the Mixed Court of Appeal, on 2 December 1896,[56] condemned the Anglo-Egyptian government for having used the funds of the mixed administration (the Debt Committee) to finance a military expedition to Sudan instead of to pay off the debt.

The court first decided on the competence of the mixed courts, referring to Article 11 of the regulations: "The decision, taken by the government in agreement with the Debt Committee to deduct an amount of the reserves to be used for a particular purpose, shall be considered as an act of government; or, in other words, an act of sovereignty that is not subject, by its nature and by virtue of the general principles of public law, to examination or evaluation by the judicial authority." However, the court also stated, "By the publication, with the agreement of the Powers, of the liquidation law passed on 17 July 1880, which aimed at settling old issues and fixing the future financial situation in the country, the Egyptian government gave to the various decrees which created and organized the Debt Fund a real contractual character."

The court then decided that the government had "transgressed the limits of the mandate delegated to it by the Powers" and had "acted beyond the cases defined in the contract." Lastly, it deemed the agreement of the Debt Commission to be vitiated by an excess of power, which made the decision taken by the government an illegal administrative act and not an act of sovereignty. Therefore, this decision fell within the competence of the mixed courts.[57]

The Mixed Court of Appeal also decided on the matter of the ability of simple treasury bill holders to file lawsuits, administrators of state property, and commissioners of the Debt Commission. It considered the actions of simple bill holders and administrators of state property inadmissible, whereas it accepted those of the commissioners. The court said that "they are in a different position"[58] because Article 38 of the 1876 liquidation law had "invested the Debt commissioners with the mandate to defend the collective and international rights of the creditors in their interests and . . . each one of them has also been invested with the personal right to act individually."[59]

Regarding the merits of the case, the court upheld the arguments of the debt commissioners, who argued that "the Anglo-Egyptian government can not make a request for funds, and the commissioners are not entitled to grant from the reserve fund the necessary amounts for financing the military expedition to Sudan. Such expenses are not incorporated in the anticipated extracurricular expenses, set forth in Article 3 para. 3 of the decree issued on 12 July 1888."[60]

As the mixed courts played a substantial role both at the level of "the mechanisms of European monitoring over the economy" and on the political scene, one can easily understand why the executive authority,[61] both khedival and Anglo-Egyptian, wanted to control at all cost this new judicial authority.

## The Fate of the Mixed Courts

Over the years of their existence, the mixed courts took on an institutional persona of their own. From 1904 to 1949, the year of their abolition, matters became complicated. The French/British Entente Cordiale in 1904 marked the end of the internationalization of Egypt and the beginning of real British "legal colonization."[62] Following it was a period of the demise of the influence of the mixed courts and the establishment of British hegemony over them, although this does not mean that their economic influence declined.

As previously discussed, the competence to legislate vis-à-vis foreigners did not make for an easy reform process because every amendment had to be approved by the foreign powers. However, the amendment of Article 12 of the mixed civil code enabled the Anglo-Egyptian government to remedy the legislative paralysis that prevented it from carrying out some of its colonial schemes in Egypt. By officially and legally associating the legislative power with the Mixed Court of Appeal, the British succeeded in reducing the autonomy of the mixed judges. In one case, *Bencini and Quistas v. Egyptian and Sudanese Governments* (11 April 1910), the Mixed Court of Appeal ruled in favor of the Anglo-Egyptian government and officially recognized that "Great Britain could invoke not only the title of the occupying power in Egypt, but also and especially, according to the *droit des gens*, the acquired right to conquest."[63] The British power was free to govern in this region, as its acts would no longer be controlled by the authority of the mixed judiciary.

With the rise of Egyptian constitutional government during the 1920s and increasing nationalist hostility toward the mixed courts, mixed courts were denounced as having taken the place of the consular courts, which caused them to be viewed as "exceptional" courts. The colonial and Egyptian governments wanted to control the mixed judiciary. The mixed courts had no choice—in order to preserve their judicial authority, they became subservient to the power of the British protectorate. Their mantle passed to the national courts and to the new State Council (1946), which took on the protection of judicial independence from the executive authority.

The year 1949 saw the end of an institution that for three-quarters of a century was one of the privileged witnesses of the progressive conquest of Egypt's autonomy.

# 3

# The Law on Judicial Authority and Judicial Independence

*Mahmud al-Khudayri*

Democratic states should be governed by the principle of the separation and independence of their three powers—executive, legislative, and judicial—in terms of their respective roles and missions and the tools used in the performance of their specified tasks. This separation of albeit necessarily interdependent powers contributes to mutual cooperation in realizing a greater benefit for the state and its people. While the executive authority is the oldest one as a result of the historical development of societies, the separation of powers was the outcome of peoples' desire not to have all power controlled by one authority, as this had caused governments to be autocratic. Countries that do not have a real separation of powers still suffer from an excess of executive power.

Since its formation, the Egyptian judicial authority has been suffering from the intervention of the executive authority. Before the inception of the progressive and advanced form of state, the ruler decided disputes among his people. The executive authority sometimes still intervenes in the affairs of the judiciary, as it seems often to consider that any form of autonomy enjoyed by the judiciary may diminish its own authority. Hence, the judiciary finds obstacles placed in the way of its legitimate work.

The judicial authority has assiduously endeavored and bitterly struggled for years to gain guarantees of its autonomy. For instance, the judiciary in Egypt acquired irrevocable appointments ("irrevocability") in three phases. First, it was confined to judges, provided they had spent three years in their positions, to ensure their competence and efficiency before they enjoyed irrevocability.[1] In the second phase, starting from 1972, judges acquired irrevocability upon appointment, but members of the Office of Public Prosecution, including the general prosecutor, were deprived of it. In the last phase, the Office of Public Prosecution, in accordance with Law 35/1984, amending Article 67 of the Law on Judicial Authority, became irrevocable, with the exception of auxiliary prosecutors. Each phase was preceded by strife and bargains that ended in the fulfillment of some demands, leaving the unfulfilled demands for another round of strife. Judges found themselves unable to achieve all their demands and eventually accepted the fulfillment of only some.

Since the beginning of the 1990s, judges have been endeavoring to see some of their unmet demands fulfilled. To this end, they have held private meetings and convened in the general assembly of the Judges' Club. They have even entered into bargains with the government, which has attempted to foment dissension among them by turning some judges against the majority that has been calling for more guarantees in the law. The Judges' Club prepared a draft amendment to the 1972 Law on Judicial Authority in 1991 and amended it in 2004. Judges struggled desperately to have this draft adopted by the People's Assembly, but it remained in the office of the minister of justice' office. The government even urged other entities to submit conflicting bills in an attempt to overwhelm judges and block their effort to achieve financial and administrative autonomy from the executive authority. The government's stance was strongly resisted by the judges. The ministry of justice formed a committee that included two members from the Judges' Club's board of directors—its president and its secretary-general—to draft amendments to the law. The draft was sent to the Supreme Judicial Council in May 2005 for its opinion, pursuant to Article 77 bis (2) of the judicial authority law. The council declined to examine the bill for a long while, on the pretext that it should consult the general assemblies of courts, as well as the members of the Office of Public Prosecution. When the council finally submitted its opinion on the draft law, no one was allowed to see it.

Law No. 46 of 1972 was finally amended in June 2006 by Law No. 142, based on a draft prepared by the Political Affairs Committee of the NDP. Only a few of the proposals in the Judges' Club's draft were in the new law, and the executive authority retained most of its forms of intervention in the judiciary.[2]

## The Main Forms of Executive Authority Intervention in the Affairs of the Judicial Authority

The executive authority intervenes in the judiciary through several legal means allowed by Law 46/1972. Among its main tools are the affiliation of the judicial inspection department with the ministry of justice, the composition of the Supreme Judicial Council, the rules of transfer, secondment, and secondment abroad, and the role played by the ministry of justice in the supervision of the courts. Until 2006, the tools included the judiciary's lack of an independent budget.

### Judicial Inspection Affiliation

According to Article 78 of the judicial authority law, "A department of judicial inspection shall be formed in the ministry of justice to inspect the work of judges and presidents of courts of first instance." This judicial inspection department deals with all aspects of the work of members of the Office of Public Prosecution and of judges up to the grade of president of court of first instance. These judicial personnel attach great importance to the matter of evaluation because it affects promotion. The judicial inspection department investigates complaints against judges and suggests penalties. It also is responsible for preparing the project of the annual judicial "movement" (rotation of judges), which includes promotions, transfers, and secondments.

Judges should have a say in these matters to prevent their use by the executive authority to control the fates and futures of members of the judiciary. Besides, it is strange that this law has the judicial inspection department directly reporting to the minister of justice, who represents the executive authority. The law contains no binding provision for the government to choose the minister from the members of the judiciary, and the government often appoints persons who are far from the judiciary, such as lawyers and academics. Even if the government selects the minister from among counselors in the ordinary courts or from the State Council, he thereupon becomes a member of the executive power and thus should have no authority over the judiciary, in conformity with the principle of separation of powers.

The draft amendment prepared by the Judges' Club in 1991 and adopted by its general assembly aimed to put the judicial inspection department under the supervision of the Supreme Judicial Council. The department would be in charge of inspecting the work of the presidents and judges in courts of first instance, as well as of chief prosecutors, public prosecutors, and assistant prosecutors, except for the members of the technical office of the Court of Cassation and its Office of Public Prosecution. The council would prepare a regulation that would specify the competences of the department, the rules and procedures to be applied in its work, and ways to evaluate efficiency. Judicial independence would be supported by the transfer of the affiliation of the department, influential for the life and future of judges, to an entity belonging to the judicial authority and free from the influence of the executive authority.

Why, indeed, should the department of inspection of courts be affiliated with the minister of justice when the department that inspects the work of members of the State Council is affiliated with the president of the State Council, not the minister of justice? This paradox also occurs with the departments of technical inspection, which inspect the work of the Office of Administrative Prosecution and the State Litigation Authority, as these departments are affiliated with the presidents of these two entities. Hence, members of the State Council, the Office of Administrative Prosecution, and the State Litigation Authority are more independent in this regard than judges of the ordinary courts and members of the Office of Public Prosecution.

The project prepared by the committee established by the ministry of justice did not provide for affiliation of the inspection department with the Supreme Judicial Council. After the general assembly of the Judges' Club refused the exclusion of this provision from the project, the minister of justice sent a letter to the club declaring that the ministry did not object to the affiliation of the judicial inspection department with the Supreme Judicial Council. Law 142/2006, amending Law 46/1972, did not amend this provision, however, meaning that the judicial inspection department is still affiliated with the ministry of justice.

## Composition of the Supreme Judicial Council

Free and fair elections are the best means to select individuals to a post who are capable of selfless service to the people and who expect no benefit other than the people's confidence and respect. Such individuals would not expect any gains from the executive authority, as they would be selected by the will of the people who trust them and not by the executive. As for those appointed by the government, they rarely take the people's will into account because the people neither reward nor punish them. They know that the resentment or satisfaction of the public is of no consequence so long as the power that appointed them is satisfied with their work.

It has become common in Egypt to avoid elections for leadership positions. Such attitudes are evident in universities, where elections for deans have been abolished on the pretext that they lead to divisions in faculties that should be dedicated to knowledge and education. This is a flimsy pretext because elections generate strength capable of resisting power when it attempts to interfere in the affairs of the university. The executive authority should have sought to deepen the sense of democracy in Egypt by extending elections to all university presidents and deans, instead of expanding the practice of appointment to include deans. This new policy was criticized in some newspapers, the audio and visual media, and in the street. Despite criticism, officials did not revise the policy. Elections should occur for all leadership positions, including that of governor, in order to deepen an experience of democracy that would push the country toward more progressive institutions.

The project prepared by the Judges' Club wished to incorporate elected members into the Supreme Judicial Council. The council currently is composed of the following members: the president of the Court of Cassation, the president of the Cairo Court of Appeal, the general prosecutor, the two most senior vice-presidents of the Court of Cassation, and the two most senior presidents of the courts of appeal.[3] This composition denies judges representation on the council, as all members are appointed. This is why the Judges' Club proposed that the council be formed of the president of the Court of Cassation, the president of Cairo Court of Appeal, and the general prosecutor, as well as two members of the Court of Cassation and two members of the Cairo Court of Appeal, elected by the general assembly of their relevant courts for a one-year term of office.

According to the project prepared by the ministry of justice, the council would include the president of the Court of Cassation, the president of the Cairo Court of Appeal, the general prosecutor, the two most senior vice-presidents of the Court of Cassation, the four most senior acting presidents of the courts of appeal, two members of the Court of Cassation, and two members of the Cairo Court of Appeal, elected by their relevant general assemblies for a one-year term of office. Chairmanship of the council would be granted to its most senior member, except for the general prosecutor. This proposal differed slightly from the one proposed by the Judges' Club, particularly regarding the chairmanship. This is a sensitive point for counselors of the Court of Cassation and the courts of appeal, although it is of little consequence to the bill. Both texts ratified the judges' request to have an elected element in the council.

Law 142/2006, amending Law 46/1972, did not amend the composition of the Supreme Judicial Council. Members of the council resisted the addition of elected members, especially as the council's powers would increase if the judiciary budget and the judicial inspection department were added to its jurisdiction. The absence of elected members on the council after the addition of these competencies may turn the council into a tyrannical entity that manipulates helpless judges.

## Codifying Rules of Transfer, Secondment, and Secondment Abroad

Among the elements that influence the lives of judges on the material and moral levels are transfer *(naql)*, secondment *(nadb)*, and secondment abroad *(i'ara)*. Because of aging, the difficulty of transportation, problems with children, and working wives, judges are greatly concerned with the location of their workplace, and equally with the place they will be in the future. Their location may affect the stability of their family and their job performance. Secondment means judges get financial and other benefits but are far from judicial work. This worries judges and makes them wonder whether they really need the position or whether it is appropriate for them. Secondment abroad enables judges to settle their financial affairs and those of their family.

General and abstract rules should therefore be established in these fields to enable judges to define their positions without having to resort to any powerful official to insure equitable treatment.

### Transfer

While the rules concerning transfer of counselors are settled, those dealing with judges and presidents of tribunals and with members of the Office of Public Prosecution in similar grades change every now and then. They change by virtue of determining equivalencies between the term of office spent in the Office of Public Prosecution and that of judicial work. Transfer depends on the decision of the Supreme Judicial Council, which opens the door wide for fraud in the application of transfer rules. General and abstract rules need to be set up in relation to transfer.

The draft project of the Judges' Club stipulated in Article 77 bis (4) that the Supreme Judicial Council would set regulations to govern the exercise of its competencies and the preparation of the project of judicial movement by the judicial inspection department after having consulted the general assemblies of the courts. The regulation would compare the term of office spent in courts to that spent in the Office of Public Prosecution and take into consideration the wishes of judges according to their seniority and place of residence. This would put judges' minds at rest as to the fairness and openness of the process. It would be even better if this regulation were adopted by a presidential or ministerial decree and thus could not be easily amended depending on the mood of the council. Another positive outcome would be that the regulation would be conditioned on the approval of the general assemblies of the courts.

Law 142/2006, which revised Law 46/1972, amended Article 77 bis (4) to specify that the Supreme Judicial Council would be in charge of drafting the rules to be followed by the judicial inspection department in the preparation of the annual judicial movement. The law added that the wishes of judges should be taken into consideration. The law did not mention, however, that the general assemblies of the courts should be consulted.

**Secondment**

According to Article 62 of Law 46/1972, the minister of justice can request that a judge or a president of a court undertake legal or judicial tasks outside of his or her tribunal instead of or in addition to ordinary work, on a temporary basis, after having consulted the general assembly of the court to which the judge belongs and with the approval of the Supreme Judicial Council. The latter determines the indemnity the individual should receive. According to Article 64 of the law, secondment should not exceed three consecutive years.

Legally speaking, only the Supreme Judicial Council can specify the financial compensation that a judge deserves for his or her additional work. This is a significant power as it is aimed at preventing any pressure on judges that might influence their legal decisions. In practice, however, the council does not exercise this competence properly. This was obvious during the elections of 2005, when the executive authority generously rewarded judges supervising elections in order to influence them. The Commission on Presidential Elections also controlled the judges' remuneration, stoked dissension among them, and excluded some judges from supervision of the elections on the pretext that they had political tendencies. Hence, the judicial authority was forced to resort to courts to complain against such unjust decisions. If the Supreme Judicial Council had properly exercised its power in seconding judges and specifying their rewards, such injustices would not have taken place and judges would have maintained their dignity and prestige.

The draft law prepared by the Judges' Club aimed at amending Article 62 of the law to stipulate that a judge could not be seconded to another position or given additional assignments, except for judicial assignments specified by this law or any other law. The decision should be taken by a decree from the minister of justice, with the approval of the general assembly of the court with which the judge belongs (or the general prosecutor, as appropriate) and the approval of the Supreme Judicial Council. Only the council would be competent to determine a judge's financial compensation.

This proposal differed from that of the law of 1972 because it did not allow secondment except for judicial assignments and required the approval of the general assembly of the court with which the judge is affiliated or of the general prosecutor, not only their opinion. Law 142/2006, amending Law 46/1972, only changed the length of secondment. According to Article 66, secondment should not exceed six years during all of an individual's career, instead of three consecutive years as was previously the case. Article 66 was amended again by Law No. 17 of 2007 and no longer provides for a maximum length of secondment, meaning the three-year limit stated in Article 64 should apply again.

### Secondment Abroad

According to Article 65 of the judicial authority law, judges can be sent to a foreign government or an international organization by a decree of the president of the republic after having taken the opinion of the general assembly of the court to which the judge belongs or of the general prosecutor, as appropriate, and the approval of the Supreme Judicial Council. This provision specifies that the maximum duration of secondment abroad is four continuous years. It can be extended in case of national necessity, to be determined by the president of the republic. Practically speaking, this provision has opened the door for unlimited extension of secondment abroad, as some judges resort to influential connections in the executive authority to have their secondment extended. This exposes judges to shame and violates the rights of others by not granting them opportunity. Since secondment abroad affects the financial status of judges, general and abstract rules should be set to ensure that every judge receives his rights without intervention from the administration in terms of granting or preventing secondment.

The text prepared by the Judges' Club limited the period of secondment abroad to four years, and only those seconded in the field of judicial inspection and in the technical office of the Court of Cassation and its Office of Public Prosecution were to be excluded from the application of that rule. Long absence from the courts reduces a judge's efficiency. The bodies excluded from the rule were viewed as undertaking judicial work that does not keep judges away from the courts. Moreover, the draft law proposed that judges could only be seconded abroad after having spent four years in office and received a good evaluation in their latest performance reports in order to ensure that they had adequate professional experience and would act as good ambassadors in the countries where they would be working.

The draft law prepared by the ministry of justice limited the length of secondment abroad to six years. Law 142/2006 of June 2006 amended Articles 65 and 66 to state that secondment abroad could not exceed six years during the career of a judge. The procedure and conditions for secondment have not been amended. These provisions were amended again in 2007 by Law No. 17 to reestablish a maximum of four continuous years, as was the case before 2006.

## Sanctions and Supervision of the Minister of Justice over Courts

Article 93 of the 1972 Law on Judicial Authority stipulated that the minister of justice had the right to supervise all courts and judges. Article 94 added that he could issue a warning *(tanbih)* to presidents of courts of first instance and judges from violations of their duties or job obligations. The right to address warnings also belonged to the president of the court, on his own initiative or upon a decision of the general assembly, after hearing the judge's testimony. Warnings could be given orally or in writing. If a warning was written, individuals were entitled to object before the council. A copy of the written warning was also given to the minister of justice.

It is quite clear from these provisions that the power granted to the minister of justice under the judicial authority law to impose warnings was important and entailed grave consequences for the judge. Among these consequences was that the judge's promotion may be postponed or that he may be deprived of secondment or secondment abroad. This represents a grave intervention by the executive authority in the affairs of the judiciary.

The draft law presented by the Judges' Club attempted to avoid such intervention by amending Articles 93 and 94. According to Article 93, the minister of justice would exercise administrative supervision over courts, and the president of the court and the general assembly would exercise administrative supervision over the judges affiliated with them. Thus, the supervision of the minister of justice and of the president of the court would be restricted to the court's employees and not extend to judges whose work does not require any form of supervision, except by their conscience and the law.

Law 142/2006, amending Law 46/1972, amended Article 93 to state that the minister of justice has the right to supervise courts (and not judges), and adds that this is administrative supervision. The president and the general assembly of each court are now in charge of supervising the judges affiliated with them. This provision, though, does not limit this supervision to administrative supervision, contrary to the drafts laws of both the Judges' Club and the minister of justice.

Article 94 in the club's draft law stateed that the general assembly could, on its own initiative or upon a request of the president of the court, address warnings to judges on violations of their duties or job obligations, after hearing their testimony. This could be done orally or in writing. The minister of justice would have no power to impose such a significant penalty as a warning to judges. The president of the court also would be deprived of the power to impose this significant penalty. Only the general assembly of the court to which the judge belongs would be entitled to do it, on its own initiative or upon a request from the president of the court. Therefore, the affairs of the judge in question would be decided by his fellow judges, who are the most capable of evaluating his performance.

Law 142/2006, amending Law 46/1972, changed Article 94 to transfer from the minister of justice to the director of the judicial inspection department the right to address warnings to judges and presidents of courts of first instance.

The draft law submitted by the committee of the ministry of justice would have given such a right to the president of the court, with the approval of a committee to be established by amended Article 35, and to the general assembly of the court. The draft prepared by the Judges' Club, therefore, gave more security to judges, as it placed this important penalty only in the hands of the community of judges represented by their general assemblies.

As for the Office of Public Prosecution, Article 125 of the 1972 law stated that its members are responsible first to their superiors, then to the general prosecutor, and then to the minister of justice. This provision was amended by Law 142/2006 to delete the reference to the minister of justice. Article 126 of the 1972 Law on Judicial Authority stipulated that the minister of justice and the general prosecutor are entitled to address warnings to members of the Office of Public Prosecution who make slight mistakes concerning their duties, after hearing their testimony. The warning could be oral or written. The draft laws prepared by the Judges' Club and by the minister of justice gave that right to the general prosecutor only. Law 142/2006 revising Law 72/1972 amended Article 126 in that manner. Only the general prosecutor now can address warnings to members of the Office of Public Prosecution.

Article 129 of the 1972 law allowed the general prosecutor to file a disciplinary case, on a request from the minister of justice. The general prosecutor can decide to suspend the work of the member of the judiciary during the investigation process. The draft amendment prepared by the Judges' Club confined this right to the general prosecutor, on his own initiative. Article 129 of Law 142/2006, amending Law 72/1972, states that the general prosecutor can file a disciplinary case on his own initiative or on a proposal (no longer a request) by the minister of justice.

## Toward Budgetary Independence from the Ministry of Justice

The most prominent drawback of Law 46/1972 was the domination of the executive authority, through the ministry of justice, over the budget of the judiciary. The ministry could control the destinies of judges by assuming full control over their financial affairs. This type of domination greatly affects judicial independence, as the executive authority uses the control as a means to intervene in the affairs of the judiciary and to attempt to control judges. Nor is this in the interest of the people. Among those in the civilized world who respect courts and fully believe in the necessity of the autonomy of the judicial authority, it is acknowledged that the judiciary should enjoy financial independence based on the independence of its budget. The judicial authority should control its own budget without any intervention from the executive. The draft bill by the Judges' Club added Article 77 bis (5) to the law. This proposal provided for the judicial authority to have an independent budget to be set out in the same manner as the state public budget, starting at the beginning of the fiscal year and ending at its end. The resources of the judiciary would comprise the judicial fees paid before the courts and fines in criminal and civil cases, goods and surety confiscated by the courts, and adequate resources allocated by the state in its public budget. The president of the Supreme Judicial Council would prepare the draft budget and allocate it. He also would be in charge of defining its conditions and areas of expenses to be submitted, after examination and adoption by the council, to the competent entity. This draft further stated that:

> The Supreme Judicial Council shall exercise the responsibilities assigned by the relevant laws and regulations to the minister of finance regarding the implementation of the budget of the judiciary. The President of the Council shall also exercise the powers assigned to the minister of administrative development and to the Chief of the Central Agency for Organization and Management. The provisions regarding the state public budget shall apply to the budget of the judicial authority and to the balance sheet, if the law does not stipulate other provisions.

The draft bill prepared by the ministry of justice did not include an independent budget. After the general assembly of the Judges' Club refused the exclusion of this provision from the project, the minister of justice sent a letter to the club in which he declared that the ministry did not object to the inclusion of such a provision.

The amendments finally adopted by the People's Assembly in June 2006 included an Article 77 bis (5) providing for an independent budget for judges and the Office of Public Prosecution. This provision will only enter into force, however, starting with the budget of 2008 (Article 7 of the law). The amendment gives an important role to the minister of finance in the preparation of the budget and the allocation of funds.

## Other Important Issues

According to the current law (Article 44), the president of the Court of Cassation is appointed by presidential decree from among the vice-presidents of that court after the Supreme Judicial Council has given its opinion. The draft law submitted by the Judges' Club provided that he would be chosen by the general assembly of that court from among the five most senior vice-presidents who had chaired one of the court's chambers during the previous three years. The draft law of the ministry of justice stipulated that the most senior vice-president of the Court of Cassation should be appointed president, with the approval of the Supreme Judicial Council. This provision was not amended by Law 142/2006.

The approval, and not only the opinion, of the Supreme Judicial Council (with some elected members in its composition) should be requested in matters such as appointments, transfers, secondment, secondment abroad, and imposition of penalties. Article 1 of Law 142/2006, amending Law 72/1972, required the approval and not only the opinion of the Supreme Judicial Council in all matters, except three, which include the nomination of the president of the Court of Cassation.

## Conclusion

In a statement published in June 2006, the Judges' Club expressed its disappointment with the amendments adopted by Law 142/2006. The members admitted that some points in the law were positive, such as the announcement of the annual judicial movement before it is adopted, the granting of an independent budget, and the possibility of challenging decisions adopted by the disciplinary council. Among negative developments, they underlined that the conditions of secondment had not been changed, which may lead to corruption; the judicial inspection department is still affiliated with the ministry of justice; the presidents of courts still could require the general assembly of the court to delegate to them part of its powers, which may allow them to assign a specific judge to decide a particular case; the composition of the Supreme Judicial Council remains the same and the period of secondment and secondment abroad has been raised; the conditions of the choice of the president of the Court of Cassation remain the same and, in particular, the general assembly is not required to give its approval of the choice; and no provision in the law guarantees the independence of the Judges' Club. In July 2006, the club announced that it had decided to draft a whole new law on the judiciary to replace the current one.

The optimum guarantee for judges would be to have all their affairs decided by their fellow judges, and not by the executive authority represented by the minister of justice. All important decisions regarding their careers, therefore, should be in the hands of either the general assemblies of the courts or the Supreme Judicial Council, on the condition that it contain elected elements. The legal system thus would be liberated from the influence of the executive power, whose current influence conflicts with the principle of separation of powers on which a democratic system is based.[4]

# 4

# The General Prosecutor between
# the Judicial and Executive Authorities

## *Abdallah Khalil*

With the establishment of the mixed courts in 1875, Egypt became the
first Arab country to incorporate the office of the general prosecutor
into its legal system. Since then, that office has been trapped between
the executive and the judicial authority and has lacked real independence from the ministry of justice.

In this study, I will trace the historical evolution of the role of the
general prosecutor in Egypt and the office's relation to the executive
power since its introduction. I will clarify the relevant laws and related
developments of the office in an effort to reveal how the relationship
has evolved, giving concrete examples of lack of independence.[1]

## The Historical Evolution of the Role of the Office of Public Prosecution and its Relationship to the Executive Power

### 1875 to 1952

In 1875, the first statute for the organization of the mixed courts
established the office of the public prosecutor (*al-na'ib al-'umumi*) to
defend public rights. The public prosecutor was appointed by order
of the khedive and could be removed or transferred. In the beginning,
foreigners dominated the Office of Public Prosecution, with lawyers
coming from Europe to fill the post.[2] Later, Egyptian prosecutors were
appointed and performed satisfactorily, many of them having been
educated in law in France. They were often treated with arrogance by
foreigners, however.

When the national courts were established in 1883, their statute affiliated the public prosecutor *(al-na'ib al-'umumi)* with the minister of justice. The British Occupation power chose a British subject to be the first public prosecutor before these courts. An Egyptian was appointed to the post in 1895.

Under British Occupation, the public prosecutor had to offer help to the minister on the one hand and be responsive to the prosecution-based inspection department dominated by foreigners on the other. Therefore, this appointment became a political affair. With the establishment of the Court of Cassation in 1931, the public prosecutor started to be chosen from among that court's counselors (senior judges).

The Office of Public Prosecution had numerous prerogatives and combined investigative and prosecutorial functions. The executive authority tried to bring it under its control by allowing the minister of justice to supervise, admonish, and dismiss prosecution personnel. Because of the desire of the political authority to control the powers of the Office of Public Prosecution, the British deliberately abolished the criminal investigation judge *(juge d'instruction)* and handed his powers to the Office of Public Prosecution with an 1895 decree.[3]

In reference to the office, the 1923 constitution only stated that "the appointment and dismissal of members of the Office of Public Prosecution shall be subject to the conditions established by the law."[4] The Office of Public Prosecution suffered in terms of appointments and promotions, which were given based on political considerations rather than efficiency or qualifications. Events showed how the prosecution could be manipulated in favor of the ruling party against its opponents. Prosecution staff without political connections failed to be promoted, to the extent that they filed complaints before the High Commissioner, the official representative of the British government in Egypt.

After ratification of the agreement that abolished the capitulations in Egypt,[5] signed in Montreux in 1937, the new Judicial Organization Regulations, issued by Law 49/1937, stated that the public prosecutor of the mixed courts had to be of foreign nationality and assisted by an Egyptian first (senior) public prosecutor *(afukatu 'umumi awwil)* and a foreign second public prosecutor *(afukatu 'umumi thani)*. Britain managed to sideline the rest of the countries and seized these positions (Articles 16 and 17).

The subordination of the Office of Public Prosecution to the executive power remained under Law No. 66/1943 on the Independence of the Judiciary and continued after the abolition of the mixed courts, but the job titles of public prosecutor *(na'ib 'umumi)* and public advocate *(afukatu 'umumi)* were changed to general prosecutor *(na'ib 'amm)* and public attorney *(muhami 'amm)*. The general prosecutor was appointed by royal decree and took the official oath before the king in the presence of the minister of justice.[6] Auxiliary prosecutors were appointed on a probationary basis pursuant to a decree of the minister of justice for a minimum of one year and a maximum of two years.[7] The assistant prosecutor was required to pass an exam, the terms and conditions of which were to be decreed by the minister of justice.[8]

Prosecution members were responsible to their superiors and the general prosecutor, and all of them were responsible to the minister of justice, who had the right to control and supervise the Office of Public Prosecution and its personnel.[9] He also had the right to direct warnings to members of the prosecution who failed to fulfill their responsibilities.[10] Matters did not change significantly in Law 147/1949, and prosecution officials remained subordinate to their superiors, as well as to the minister of justice.

## Since July 1952

After the 1952 Revolution in Egypt, the government maintained the system of prosecution-based investigations. It did not get rid of the occupational heritage that had infiltrated the Egyptian judicial system, only of the material presence of the occupation.

Elaborating on developments after 23 July 1952, and the promulgation of Decree Law 188/1952 on the Independence of the Judiciary, no change transpired. Matters actually worsened when the minister of justice was vested with the power to suspend members of the prosecution under investigation pending the settlement of a disciplinary case.[11] The new government was given the right to dismiss any prosecution personnel. The only requirement was to have the opinion of the newly established Higher Consultative Council of the Office of Public Prosecution (Majlis Istishari A'la li-l-Niyaba al-'Amma) for low-ranking Office of Public Prosecution staff and the opinion of the Supreme Judicial Council (Majlis al-Qada' al-A'la) concerning senior prosecution officers up to the general prosecutor.[12] The minister of justice, upon a proposal by the general prosecutor, also had the right to transfer members of the prosecution and to second them to positions other than within the prosecution office to which they were affiliated,[13] besides the right to direct warnings to them.[14]

Under subsequent judicial authority laws such as Law 56/1959 and Law 43/1965, the office of the general prosecutor continued to be subject to the executive authority, and the government perpetuated its domination of members of the Office of Public Prosecution. Prosecution staff continued to be subordinate both to their superiors and to the minister of justice.[15] The government retained the right to dismiss prosecution staff or to transfer them to non-judicial offices without applying disciplinary rules.[16] Auxiliary prosecutors were recruited on a probationary basis for at least one year.[17] Moreover, Law 353/1952 abolished the criminal investigation judge (juge d'instruction) system that had been reinstated into the revised 1951 Code of Criminal Procedure.

The 1952 Revolution government also established a State Security Investigation Department to tighten its grip over investigation of political crimes and to ban the Office of Public Prosecution from conducting investigations of crimes allegedly perpetrated by public officials and security forces.

## The Office of Public Prosecution and the Executive Authority under Law No. 46 of 1972[18]

Under Law 46/1972, currently in force, the subordination of the Office of Public Prosecution to the executive authority remained, though it has been lessened by amendments introduced in 1984 and 2006. Concrete examples will help the reader understand this lack of independence.

### Hierarchy of the Office of Public Prosecution

The Office of Public Prosecution is hierarchically organized under the ultimate supervision of the general prosecutor. The hierarchy of its members from the highest to the lowest grade is the following:

General prosecutor (al-na'ib al-'amm) (1)
Assistant general prosecutor (al-na'ib al-'amm al-musa'id) (1)
Chief public attorney (muhami 'amm awwil) (22)
Public attorney (muhami 'amm) (69)
Chief prosecutor (ra'is niyaba) (297)
Public prosecutor (wakil niyaba) (1688)
Assistant prosecutor (musa'id niyaba) (817)
Auxiliary prosecutor (mu'awin niyaba) (194)[19]

Prosecution members are found at all levels of the court structure. Assistant general prosecutors perform the tasks assigned or delegated to them by the general prosecutor. They are chosen from among the vice-presidents of courts of appeal or counselors of the Court of Cassation. The most senior of them replaces the general prosecutor and assumes all his functions in the event of the general prosecutor's absence or impairment, bearing in mind that at present there is only one assistant general prosecutor.

A chief public attorney is attached to each court of appeal. He represents the Office of Public Prosecution before that court and exercises all the duties and enjoys all the rights of the general prosecutor within the district of this court. He also has the right to supervise the staff of the court of appeal.

Public attorneys are appointed in courts of first instance to exercise all functions relevant to the general prosecutor with regard to initiating a criminal action and following it up. They have the right to control and supervise the prosecution staff attached to their courts (chief prosecutors and public prosecutors).

The function of the Office of Public Prosecution at the Court of Cassation are carried out by an independent public prosecution office composed of a director chosen by the minister of justice from among Court of Cassation or court of appeal counselors or public attorneys. The director is assisted by an adequate number of members ranked no lower than public prosecutors.

The project of judicial movement is prepared annually by the office of the general prosecutor after consultation with the inspection department. It is then submitted to the Supreme Judicial Council for approval, then to the president of the republic to issue decrees of nomination.

A basic principle proper to the Office of Public Prosecution is indivisibility, which means that each member represents the general prosecutor and can be substituted for any other member.

## Appointment of the General Prosecutor

Under the 1972 Law on Judicial Authority, the general prosecutor is appointed by presidential decree from among vice-presidents of courts of appeal, counselors of the Court of Cassation, or chief public attorneys (Article 119). The general prosecutor's appointment, therefore, is not conditional upon the consent or even opinion of the Supreme Judicial Council, and no specific qualifications or conditions are required of the new appointee.

The appointment of the general prosecutor has remained a political decision made solely by the political authority, which is the president of the republic. The office has suffered from appointments and promotions often made for political reasons, irrespective of efficiency or qualifications. For instance, the appointment of Counselor Raja' al-'Arabi in 1991 gave rise to much criticism, as he was appointed on the basis of his previous job in the Office of State Security Prosecution. In 2000, Counselor Mahir 'Abd al-Wahid was appointed general prosecutor, although he was not at the time a counselor (senior judge) at the Court of Cassation or a court of appeal, or even a chief public attorney *(muhami 'amm awwil)* working for the Office of Public Prosecution. Rather, he was seconded from his position as assistant to the minister of justice.

Voices resound at the Judges' Club, in human rights organizations, and among some opposition parties, calling for full independence of the Office of Public Prosecution from the executive authority, the end of its subordination to the minister of justice, and withdrawal of the political leadership from the task of appointing the general prosecutor.

## Appointment of Other Members of the Office of Public Prosecution

Law 46/1972 requires that candidates to the post of assistant prosecutor *(musa'id al-niyaba)* satisfy conditions related only to nationality, age, and education, that they do not have a criminal record, and that they present all the required guarantees of morality and reputation.[20] Candidates must undergo a test whose conditions and criteria are specified in a decision by the minister of justice, with the consent of the Supreme Judicial Council.[21] The law is devoid of any provision requiring specific tests regarding legal knowledge or professional integrity and enthusiasm for hard work, and it does not require training in a judicial academy.

Appointment in the Office of Public Prosecution is subject to special criteria related to security investigations. The candidate is not informed of these standards, nor is he permitted to respond to them. Because of the absence of objective selection methods and standards and the domination of the supreme leadership of the judicial authority, the appointment process in the prosecution has been said to breach the nondiscrimination principle.[22]

## Powers of the Minister of Justice over Prosecution Members

Until the amendment of Law 46/1972 by Law 142/2006, all prosecution members were responsible to the minister of justice.[23] This is no longer the case. However, the law still stipulates continued subordination of prosecution members to their superiors and to the general prosecutor.[24]

The minister of justice can now exercise only administrative supervision over members of the Office of Public Prosecution, while before he was vested with the right to supervise them with no limitations.[25] Until 2006, the minister of justice could address warnings to members of the Office of Public Prosecution in the event of their failure to perform their responsibilities well. Now, only the general prosecutor can exercise this power.[26] Disciplinary action against prosecution members used to be filed by the general prosecutor upon the request of the minister of justice, who at the same time had the right to suspend the prosecution member subject to investigation pending settlement of the action.[27] Since the 2006 amendments, the general prosecutor can file a request on his own initiative and not only following a proposal (no longer a request) by the minister of justice. Now only the general prosecutor can decide now to suspend the prosecution member subject to investigation.[28]

The Office of Public Prosecution Judicial Inspection Department is competent to evaluate the performance of members of the Office of Public Prosecution, make reports on their efficiency, and suggest their promotion. The minister of justice decides who is transferred and seconded to work in premises other than the Office of Public Prosecution headquarters with which they are affiliated.[29] Delegation of prosecution officers to other assignments or the addition of other tasks to their functions affects their independence and neutrality. Seconding or assignment to the State Security Affairs Office,[30] in addition to their original job, is a prominent example of actions that threaten the independence of members of the judiciary. Such actions politicize the Office of Public Prosecution and the judiciary as a whole. Such an assignment entails financial remuneration in addition to the salary of the assigned prosecution member, and thus is a tool of temptation. Until 1984, Prosecution personnel were vulnerable to dismissal. Law 35/1984 amended Article 67 of Law 46/1972, establishing the principle that the general prosecutor and members of the Office of Public Prosecution are not removable.

## Functions and Competence of the General Prosecutor

The general prosecutor is charged with representing the public interest in a lawsuit and following up on its proceedings pending final judgment. His competence involves investigation and conviction powers and applies to all of Egypt and all types of crimes. The general prosecutor also supervises the affairs of the Office of Public Prosecution, enjoys administrative powers in relation to its staff members (for example, transfer, seconding, warnings, and lodging of disciplinary action), and is entrusted to initiate disciplinary actions against judges. The general prosecutor functions on a personal basis and may ask prosecution staff to act on his behalf. The two most important functions of the Office of Public Prosecution are investigation and accusation. The Office of Public Prosecution is also in charge of prisons inspection.

### Power of Preliminary Investigation

The general prosecutor is in charge of conducting investigations. He will search for all case evidence, assess it neutrally and without prejudice against the accused, and search for all evidence of guilt or innocence. After a record is compiled, a decision is taken regarding the sufficiency of evidence for referring the accused to court. This means that the investigation authority should not adopt an antagonistic stance vis-à-vis the accused but, rather, should seek to learn the truth, even if it is against the authority and its interest. Thus, whoever carries out the investigation must be a neutral judge who stands between the accusation and the accused.

The general prosecutor can use several procedures in that regard. The office has the power to issue warrants for arrest and for search of property. However, the general prosecutor has long drawn criticism for failing to conduct fair investigations into torture incidents and the cases of political opponents. The office has been characterized by lack of credibility and bias toward the governing party, settling some political accounts by following the orders of the executive authority and the minister of justice, as illustrated by the following examples.

### Investigation of Torture Cases by Police Officers

The relationship between the Office of Public Prosecution and the police has deep roots and goes back to British Occupation. Because of the nature of police work, policemen are entitled by the law to become judicial officers who assist the prosecution authority in conducting criminal investigations by pooling information on crimes and referring it to the Office of Public Prosecution for assessment. The Office of Public Prosecution also needs the police for all kinds of coercive measures (for example, to arrest suspects, carry out property seizures, search homes, or bring witnesses).

In practice, the Office of Public Prosecution stands by policemen who misuse their power. A high number of detainees die from torture and maltreatment in custody, prisons, detention centers, and police stations at the hands of policemen. Although the law holds the Office of Public Prosecution liable for investigating claims of torture and for immediately producing evidence of such abuses, the prosecution often abdicates this responsibility, providing proof of traces of torture in a few cases only, without indicating the reasons for injuries often proven by medical reports.

The Office of Public Prosecution is reluctant to refer people who claim to have been tortured to forensic medicine before the traces of torture heal. For instance, the High State Security Court (created pursuant to the Emergency Law) decided in July 1991 to send a court member to investigate allegations of torture by those accused in the case of the assassination of the head of the People's Assembly, Rif'at al-Mahjub. This decision was issued after torture was substantiated by reports of forensic medicine officials, even though the prisoners had been taken for a forensic medical inspection many weeks after the alleged torture.

The prosecution also has displayed great reluctance to pursue criminal cases against officials involved in any of these acts. Only in a very few cases has the prosecution worked to bring such cases to court. The courts, in turn, have ruled to acquit those accused of torture because, although the torture suffered by the victim was not denied by the court, the litigant failed to identify those who tortured him because they blindfolded him during the torture.

In cases of citizens detained on political grounds or because of conversion from one religion to another, no officer has ever been prosecuted, even though torture has been substantiated by forensic medical reports and those claiming torture have managed to recognize their attackers.

### Sexual Abuse of Demonstrators

Tension has increased recently because of the Office of Public Prosecution's stance in some cases, such as investigations into the violations committed on 25 May 2005, against opponents of the referendum on the amendment of Article 76 of the constitution, which deals with the election of the president of the republic. Many Egyptian and foreign journalists suffered sexual abuse and attacks with legs and sticks at the hands of NDP supporters, yet security forces turned a blind eye to these violations. The Office of Public Prosecution concluded that there was no reason for filing a lawsuit for the time being, as the perpetrators were unknown. The 2005 report of the National Council for Human Rights stated:[31]

> The fact that the investigation was filed and put away gave rise to much criticism from political powers and those concerned with the public welfare, as well as human rights organizations, since the assaults had taken place in thee presence of heavy security, who did not move to prevent the occurrence of the assaults or to arrest the criminals on the spot or even pursue them afterwards and hand them over to investigation bodies. This generates the ideas of complicity, and undercover protection, as means of intimidating demonstrators, with the assistance of supporters of the National Democratic Party.[32]

### Security Forces Violations Inflicted on Judges in the 2005 Parliamentary Elections

On the occasion of the 2005 parliamentary elections, human rights organizations and the Judges' Club reported a number of electoral crimes against judges supervising the electoral process, such as their being assaulted by security forces.

More than 129 complaints have been lodged by judges and judicial bodies about the violations inflicted on supervisory judges. Only two cases have been referred to criminal courts, and all the other complaints went unanswered.

### Power of Accusation

The power of accusation means filing a criminal case, gathering evidence supporting the accusation, and presenting it before a court. The core of the role of accusation is to formulate the charges and present the supporting evidence in fact and in law. The filing of a criminal case by an accusation authority means that the authority is fully convinced by the accusation and that the accused should be charged. This power lasts while the case is deliberated and referred to the court, through the representation of the plaintiff before the court, the appeal, and the judgment's execution.

The 1883 Penal Investigation Law separated the powers of investigation and accusation, but the 1895 decree regrouped them, allegedly because of the insufficient availability of investigation judges.[33] The

1950 Code of Criminal Procedure separated the two authorities again, but Decree Law 353/1952 reverted to the combined authority of charging and investigation.

The 1950 code also established an accusation chamber to decide whether a felony should be brought before the competent court. Law 107/1962 replaced the accusation chamber *(ghurfat al-ittiham)* with a referral counselor *(qada' al-ihala)*, whose office was then abolished by Law 170/1981, which transferred competence to prosecutors.

The explanatory note of Decree Law 353/1952 referred to two main reasons for the Office of Public Prosecution having the authority of both investigation and accusation: 1) comparative legislation tends to gather both authorities, and 2) combining both jobs within the jurisdiction of the prosecution eventually would facilitate procedures, especially since the relationship between judges and judicial officers is limited.

In fact, the investigation judge system was abolished because of the wish of the political authority to have full control over political cases and over the authorities of accusation and investigation in political crimes.[34] Combining the authorities means that the overall interest of the investigating authority is to gather evidence against the accused, and that its interest in scrutinizing such evidence in favor of the accused ranks second. When the accusation authority combines the jurisdictions of investigating and prosecuting the case, it inevitably is suspected of prejudice because of the opinion it has already formed supporting the validity of the accusation against the accused. Even if this is not necessarily the case, it is perceived to be so by the public, the accused, and the judiciary. This contradicts the condition of neutrality that should characterize the investigator and enable him to reach the truth, be it against or in favor of the accused.

## Protection of Detainees

The Office of Public Prosecution is the body responsible for inspection of prisons and detention centers and for ensuring that no detainee is wrongfully held, pursuant to Article 42 of the Code of Criminal Procedure and within the scope of the provision of Article 85 of the Prisons Regulation Law. The Office of Public Prosecution is directed by this law to check prisons at least once per month, and the inspection is to be carried out abruptly, without previous notice to the prison directors, in order to enable the prosecution to detect the true status of the internal administration of the prisons.

No doubt, such legal provisions are essential for the protection of prisoners and detainees against any potential transgressions against them in prisons. In practice, however, the protection is ineffective. A number of detainees who have served long sentences in prison state that they have never met with any officers from the Office of Public Prosecution, despite the mistreatment they suffered while in jail. Some detainees have disappeared, and the Office of Public Prosecution has yet to announce the whereabouts of these 'disappeared' persons. The presence of State Security Investigation officers inside prisons, who have permission to transfer detainees from prisons to the premises of State Security Investigations to torture them, raises questions as to the role of the prosecution in putting an end to such infringements.[35]

## Conclusion

The 2006 amendment of Law 46/1972 only partially improved the independence of the Office of Public Prosecution from the executive authority. The general prosecutor is no longer under the authority of the minister of justice, but he remains discretionarily appointed by the president of the republic. The minister of justice can no longer address warnings to members of the Office of Public Prosecution, this right now being limited to the general prosecutor, but the general prosecutor is still chosen by the executive authority. The general prosecutor also continues to have the authorities of both issuing charges and investigation. While the Office of Public Prosecution is considered part of the judiciary, it maintains close links with the executive power legally, as well as, and more importantly, politically.

# 5

# The Political Role of
# the Egyptian Judiciary

*Nabil Abdel Fattah*

The debate around the role of the Egyptian judiciary was a main axis of the political, constitutional, and legal discourses of the government, the opposition, and the new protest movements, such as Kifaya, from 2004 until the 2005 presidential and parliamentary elections. This interest, although not new, has intensified and become more prominent in public debate.

The political role of judges in political and constitutional discourses is one of the characteristics of Egyptian politics. It also is recurrent in the history of the authoritarian political system that was established after the 1952 Revolution. This can be attributed to several factors.

Since July 1952, Egyptian constitutions have concentrated constitutional powers and competencies in the position of the president of the republic, leading to a continuous violation of the principle of separation of powers and creating a state of imbalance among the authorities. Thus, the question of judicial independence and its role in maintaining the constitutional balance of powers, protecting the rule of law, and enforcing individual rights and freedoms has become part of the political discourse.

The professional traditions and ethics of the judiciary played a fundamental role in the diffusion of its values and strengthened its authority in the face of the imbalance of powers. The judiciary has adapted western, man-made laws to Egyptian social, political, and economic realities.[1] The discourse of the judiciary, as diverse as it may be, has acquired an overall respect at various levels. There is general respect for the judiciary among several social categories, especially in terms of the judiciary maintaining public and individual rights and settling disputes. It is considered a neutral and impartial body. The judiciary is valued by civil society organizations.

The demands of the judiciary and of its elected representatives in the Judges' Club and regional judges' clubs for the independence of the judiciary are a main issue for most opposition groups, such as the Wafd Party, the Progressive National Unionist Party, and the Muslim Brotherhood, which is legally banned. Linking political reforms to the independence of the judiciary is part of the relative political opening that occurred in Egypt during 2004 and 2005. It also demonstrates that constitutional and legal issues are back on the list of interests of the majority of the political elite, writers, intellectuals, artists, and of some journalists.

The ruling elite itself respects judges in its official political discourse, considering them a part of the structure of the Egyptian state. This group avoids the ordinary judiciary, however, and has established special and extraordinary judicial entities, including State Security courts, military courts, the socialist public prosecutor, and the courts of values (see Chapter 10 in this volume, by Hafez Abu Seada).

The increased interest of most political actors in the judiciary emerged as a result of the relative political opening in Egypt, the emergence of new protest movements, and the issuance of important judicial decisions regarding monitoring by civil society organizations and their activists during the presidential and parliamentary elections following the 2005 amendment of Article 76 of the constitution (see Chapter 15, by Nathalie Bernard-Maugiron, in this volume). This interest among activists also emerged as a result of the Judges' Club's reports on low turnout at the referendum and the elections, the violations that damaged the integrity of the electoral process, and rigging in some constituencies in favor of candidates of the NDP. The judges' reports and their neutral stance during the elections highlighted their importance to the political reform process that the political opposition and the new protest movements promote, as well as to the critical discourse of some Egyptian intellectuals and writers, beginning with those of the 1970s generation.

The statements of the general assemblies of the Cairo and Alexandria Judges' Clubs on the draft amendment of the 1972 judicial authority law and the discourse of senior judges highlighted the link between the independence of the judiciary,[2] the rule of law, and constitutional and political reform. The judges used the support of political parties and protest movements for the independence of the judiciary to reinforce the legitimacy of the proposed amendment of the 1972 law drafted by senior judges and approved by the general assembly of the club on 18 January 1991.[3]

The judges demanded an end to the state of emergency and an abrogation of exceptional laws. Their struggle for full supervision over all elections and rulings of the Court of Cassation and State Council has enhanced their position despite pressure by the executive authority and the ruling elite.

I will start the discussion of the political role of the Egyptian judiciary by presenting the different meanings of a political role for judges. I will then discuss the effectiveness of, reasons for, and actors in such a role.

## The Political Role of the Egyptian Judiciary: Meanings

I will start with a study of the meaning of politics and then make a distinction between the direct and indirect political roles of the judiciary.

### The Meanings of Politics

The executive authority in Egypt always calls for the judiciary to keep away from politics. The official discourse in some of the state-owned media labels any criticism of the state of emergency and the exceptional laws a political act. Calls for judicial supervision over the electoral process also were given the same label until a ruling of the Supreme Constitutional Court mandated full supervision of elections by judges, pursuant to Article 88 of the constitution.

Critics of the judges' supervision of elections aim to prevent judges from performing one of their main roles. When judges discuss the separation and balance of powers, they discuss matters that pertain to the organization of power within the constitutional and political system— matters that lie at the heart of the role of the judiciary. When judges discuss the independence of the judiciary and call for an end to exceptional laws and exceptional courts, they are fulfilling their judicial role.

The concept of politics in the discourse of the executive authority and of the government is that of conflict, competition, partisan rivalry over public policies, and the negative aspects of politics, such as political deviance, fabrications, evasive language, and deception. The politics condemned by the official political discourse is that of judges participating in partisan work and favoring or joining a political party or a legally banned religious political group, such as the Muslim Brotherhood or radical political Islamic groups. In this context, the government's calls for keeping judges away from politics aim, on the surface, to place judges on a pedestal that keeps them from indulging in the inferior world of politics, as it is defined. Of course, stating the problem in this way invites the approval of many people.

However, politics also means establishing a balance and separation among powers. It means protecting individual rights, and eliminating vagueness, conflict, and accumulation of legislation. All these issues are political, but at the same time they are constitutional and legal issues that fall under the mandate and functions of all powers. Addressing these issues is, therefore, acceptable in constitutional and political terms. Judges are entitled to adopt political and ideological stances as they choose, as long as their choice remains in the field of convictions and intellectual pursuit and does not interfere with the judicial process and their enforcement of constitutional and legal rights. If judges show a bias, it becomes the role of the Court of Cassation or the Supreme Administrative Court to investigate and rule on appeal.

At the same time, when judges call for the end of exceptional laws and exceptional courts, their demands are perceived by the government as dealing with politics, even though the role of this exceptional judiciary is to implement political provisions and regulate political issues, as defined by the executive, which violates the right to resort to one's natural judge. There is also a judicial role in the supervision of presidential or parliamentary elections, in what has come to be known as the judicial management and oversight of elections,[4] which is an openly political role of the judiciary.

Rulings also play an important role in the Egyptian social system and in political relations. The principles embedded in judicial decisions that touch upon rights and legal positions have in themselves social and political values. They may affect the philosophy and other aspects of legislative policies. Some rulings may call for amendments to laws if two laws are in conflict, more than one law organizes the same legal positions and relations, a law is not fair or violates human rights, or a law does not fit with the new realities of society. Rulings have criticized the executive authority or the police for using torture, for failing to implement the law or otherwise favoring some people over others, and for implementing social policies or issuing decisions that affect the lives of the majority and that may lead to disturbances, violence, transgression, or violation of the law.

A well-known example is the case of the January 1977 demonstrations during the Sadat era. The High State Security Court ruled that the only and direct reason for the events that took place on 18 and 19 January 1977 was the government's decision to raise the prices of certain basic commodities so as to change the country's economy.[5] The court was convinced that the demonstrations were causally linked to this decision and that they could not be logically linked to any other cause. The decision had been issued unexpectedly and had surprised everyone, including the security forces, which implies that no one could have planned to use that measure to incite people. The court added that no time had elapsed between the issuance of the decision and the people's taking to the streets. In a general introduction to its decision, the court referred to some general principles pertaining to public rights and freedoms, including the Universal Declaration of Human Rights and Egyptian constitutions from 1923 to 1971.[6]

Rulings in cases of torture or corruption in the economic system, banking, or the export-import sector, which led to the conviction of some politicians in Nasser's era, could be regarded today as a source for studying that era. These cases reflect the political influences on the executive and legislative decision-making processes in Egypt.

I will now explore the extent to which the judicial process currently plays a direct and indirect political role in Egypt.

## Direct Political Role of the Judiciary

The judiciary can play a direct and unequivocal political role through the Judges' Club and through the Supreme Constitutional Court's decisions on the economic system and those that uphold fundamental freedoms.

### The Judges' Club

The Judges' Club plays a direct political role when it is the general will of the group, as represented in its general assemblies, that all exceptional laws and exceptional courts that diminish the authority and competence of the judiciary be abolished. This also applies when the group calls for complete supervision of the electoral process to guarantee its transparency so that any falsification of the will of the voters cannot be said to have occurred under the judges' supervision. They do not want their supervision to be used as a cover for the illegal practices of the executive authority and the police, as was the case prior to the Constitutional Court's ruling. The same applies to the statements and reports adopted by the committees established by the club to monitor the 2005 electoral processes.

The Judges' Club can promote the social interests of judges in terms of salaries, housing, and health or social care. All these are matters connected to defending the social status of judges as a professional group, which can be regarded as part of their rights or as a measure for ensuring that they are not subject to pressures or promises made by any of the state's powers or litigants. Declaring or demanding these social rights is a political expression, no matter what form it takes.

The executive authority has attempted repeatedly to control the club so as to avoid such a direct political role for the judiciary. Historical facts show that the executive authority and the ruling political elite in Egypt have recognized the importance of the role of the Judges' Club as a forum for judges, an expression of their interests, a means for defending judges' positions on general matters as Egyptian citizens, a way for judges to struggle for the independence of the judiciary, and a living collective conscience for the nation. They also are cognizant of its influence.

The general assemblies of the Judges' Club and the elections for the club's board of directors, therefore, usually are subject to certain forms of indirect interference by the executive authority through the secondment of certain judges, rewards for others, and various kinds of pressure aimed at shifting judges' support to a specific list of candidates. The results of several elections show that these attempts usually do not succeed.

The fact is that the political role of the club is in accordance with the conventions and declarations of the United Nations, according to which judges' unions or union-like institutions are entitled to express and defend the rights of judges in the face of all other government authorities. This is a legally acceptable practice.

## The Supreme Constitutional Court

The direct political role of the judges is also based on the competence that the Supreme Constitutional Court assumes in its rulings. Some of the court's rulings have had an effect on the legal provisions regulating the economic system. When the 1971 constitution was written, the economic system was based on a socialist ideology of central planning, a strong public sector, and public ownership of the most significant means of production. Since the Egyptian regime and its ruling elite adopted the policies of privatization and structural adjustment in the early 1990s, or economic reform as it was called, the Supreme Constitutional Court has tried to reconcile constitutional provisions with the economic and political reality in Egypt in order to avoid major contradictions that would affect the constitutional legal order.

In this context, the court has questioned the legality of laws related to the sale of public sector units, especially as the 1971 constitution emphasized socialism in Articles 1 and 4. The original Article 1 stated in 1971 that "the Arab Republic of Egypt is a *democratic socialist state* based on the alliance of the working forces of the people. The Egyptian people are part of the Arab nation and work for the realization of its comprehensive unity" (author's emphasis). After the amendments of 22 May 1980, Article 1 read, "The Arab Republic of Egypt is a *socialist democratic state* based on the alliance of the working forces of the people. The Egyptian people are part of the Arab nation and work for the realization of its comprehensive unity" (author's emphasis).[7] Legal experts deemed this amendment "a slight amendment limited only to the wording and not affecting the content of the text."[8]

Article 4 of the constitution addresses the economic system. Before the 1980 amendment, it read, "The economic foundation of the Arab Republic of Egypt is a *democratic socialist system* based on sufficiency and justice, in a manner preventing exploitation, *aiming to suppress class distinctions in society*" (author's emphasis). After the 1980 amendments, it read, "The economic foundation of the Arab Republic of Egypt is a *socialist democratic system* based on sufficiency and justice, in a manner preventing exploitation, *narrowing the gap between incomes, protecting legitimate earnings and guaranteeing the equity of the distribution of public duties and responsibilities*" (author's emphasis).[9]

Despite the 1980 amendments, the socialist system existed in the constitution until the amendments of March 2007.[10] The aim of the system was to prevent people from exploiting each other.

Constitutional Article 23 states that "the national economy shall be organized in accordance with a comprehensive development plan which ensures raising the national income, fair distribution, raising the standard of living, eliminating unemployment, increasing work opportunities, connecting wages with production, and fixing a minimum and maximum limit for wages in a manner that guarantees lessening the disparities between incomes."[11] The fact that the constitution includes a comprehensive plan is ideologically quite different from what was common when the constitution was drafted. The prevailing concepts used to be the control of the people over the means of production (Article 24);[12] public ownership as the ownership of the people, confirmed by the continuous consolidation of the public sector (Article 30);[13] and the public sector as the vanguard of progress in all spheres and the main responsible actor in the development plan (Article 30, paragraph 2). One of the issues that legal experts regard as clear is that "public property is the general rule for ownership of the means of production. The ownership of the state is represented in the public sector that leads the development project and on which the state primarily depends for the success of the programs and aims of the plans."[14]

The selling of public sector units within the privatization policy raised questions about the constitutional legality of such actions. The Supreme Constitutional Court resolved the dispute by ruling on 1 February 1997, that Public Business Sector Law No. 203 of 1991 was constitutional. The court stated that constitutional provisions should not be interpreted as a final and permanent solution for economic situations that differed from those that existed when the constitutional provisions were adopted. Adopting, insisting on, and blindly applying these provisions would be pointless. They should be understood in the light of values that are aimed at liberating the homeland and the citizen politically and economically. The court added that subjugating constitutional provisions to a specific philosophy does not allow for their usage to reach new horizons. In this instance, the constitution would become an obstacle to achieving positive change, not a sponsor of it.[15]

The rulings of the Supreme Constitutional Court are one of the components of the political role played by the judiciary. The court validates the constitutionality of laws that affect economic and political systems, as well as public freedoms.

**Protection of Freedoms: Freedom of the Press and Freedom of Belief**
Ordinary courts and the State Council have played an important role in the protection of fundamental rights and freedoms, such as the rights to security and freedom of expression.[16] Various judicial rulings and principles have addressed constitutional and legal cases and positions of a political nature. One of the main political roles of the judiciary is its defense of freedom of the press and freedom of belief.

Rulings issued by different courts, whether ordinary, administrative, or constitutional, aimed at protecting the freedom of the press have not only implemented the provisions of the law but have also established legal and political principles. For instance, the Court of Cassation stated that constitutional rulings and legislation have granted the press its freedom, thus protecting it from interference or imposition of restraints by the state. In its ruling, the court stated:

> The press is the voice of the nation and a window allowing citizens to see the facts that should not be withheld from them, especially the right of the group to defend its interests, and the rights of citizens that should not be violated or breached. However, legislators, guided by the beacon of perpetual rules and public morals, have regulated the practice of this freedom by imposing restrictions. Such restrictions aim at protecting the freedoms and dignity of honest people from the domination of pens that might use newspapers as an abusive tool, through insults, defamation, or other acts that legislators should not approve of, under the guise of the freedom, sanctity, or protection of the press. The doctrine of freedom does not accept the removal of all boundaries, the violation of the rights of others, or domination over people. Nothing can be free from all restrictions.[17]

In many of its rulings, the Court of Cassation has stated that a person can change his or her religion, school, or sect and have free will, provided that the said person has legal capacity.

The State Council also has played a prominent role in protecting citizens' basic rights of religious freedom or freedom of performance of religious rites and recognizing the principle of equality before the law and the judiciary in public offices. For instance, the Supreme Administrative Court, headed by Dr. 'Abd al-Raziq al-Sanhuri, ruled on the freedom to build temples and churches, stating, "The provisions stated in the document presented by the ministry of the interior dated 9 December 1933, on the condition of granting permission for the establishment of new churches, will apply only if they do not contradict the principle of freedom of performing religious rites, in accordance with the observed tradition represented by the [Ottoman firman of 1856]."[18] The court added that the stipulations for granting permission for the establishment of places of worship stated in the firman should be limited, stating that they:

should not be used as a pretext to pose unjustified obstacles that hinder the establishment of such places, since such a practice would violate the freedom of performing religious rites. The permission mandated by the [firman] was not intended to be used to hinder the performance of religious rites, but to ensure that the places of worship are established in a respectable environment that fits the dignity and purity of the religious practices and does not cause any friction with other religious communities. Within these reasonable parameters, the permission should be granted. Furthermore, legislation should be promulgated to stipulate and simplify the requirements for establishing a place of worship. Once the requirements are met, the permission should be granted within a timeframe to be specified by the legislator. Since the permission was not granted within the specified timeframe, the applicant was free to establish the place of worship applied for."[19]

## Indirect Political Role of the Judiciary

The judicial process and judicial rulings may result in the judiciary having a political role in society and an influence on the decision-making process of the legislature and the executive authority. For instance, rulings of the Supreme Constitutional Court have led to changes in legislation and the policies of the government in several fields, such as taxes and education. Court rulings have also had other indirect effects, such as assisting in the development of social and political trends and the management of crises.

### Assisting in the Development of Social and Political Trends

Court rulings may assist in developing social and political trends that contribute to the formation of civil society. They do this through litigation and cases of a political nature that deal with the violation of individual or collective rights. Court decisions have condemned the use of violence and physical or psychological torture. The most prominent example is the litigation for compensation for torture filed by Marxists and Muslim Brothers arrested in state security cases and subjected to humiliation, degradation, and torture. In one significant example, the defendants in a case against the Islamic Jihad group were found innocent. In its famous ruling on this case, the State Security Court condemned all types of physical and morally degrading treatment and torture practiced by the police. The court found innocent many of the defendants, who had been subjected to physical duress and had confessed under its influence, which made their confessions and the evidence ensuing from the confessions null and void.

Some court rulings have considered as one category the basic rights and freedoms of citizens as individuals and as groups organized in associations, unions, or clubs. A number of cases and legal disputes have dealt with the legitimacy of the actions of boards of directors of sporting clubs, associations, and unions. Court rulings in these cases undoubtedly have established legal frameworks and work ethics for these different entities, which allow professional and other members to monitor and supervise their activities. This highlights the role of such groups and institutions in mobilizing and defending the social, professional, and even promotional interests of their members. Such litigation promotes the individual as a producer and as a social actor, despite the structural obstacles that hinder individuality and the productivity of individuals in Egyptian society.

The judiciary has ruled on the basic rights and freedoms of professional and social sectors that the political system and the ruling authority do not recognize or promote. This role of the judiciary has increased in recent years, especially in cases that favor the social power of persons prosecuted for political reasons. These can be called the "silent social powers," as their social and political movements do not attract as much attention from the ruling political elite as do the activities of some professional and middle class groups, such as lawyers, engineers, and doctors. Workers constitute one of these politically prosecuted groups. Despite the importance of workers, a group that has been growing over the past two decades and has been active lately, organizing strikes, sit-ins, and demonstrations, with the rise of privatization programs and the selling off of the public sector, all types of political and union movements are faced with opposing security measures.

The Egyptian judiciary has recognized some of the basic rights of workers, such as the right to hold strikes. This right was recognized in the ruling of the High State Security Court of Cairo (established under the emergency law) in 1987.[20] In that decision, the court ruled that Article 124 of the penal code, which considered strikes a crime, had been implicitly repealed by Article 8 of the International Covenant on Economic, Social, and Cultural Rights, which Egypt had ratified. According to Article 151 of the constitution, international conventions ratified by Egypt have the force of law. The court called upon the legislature to hasten to put the necessary regulations in place to guarantee this right, adding that it should be done in a way that ensured the best interests of the state and of the workers at the same time. In this way, it argued, chaos would not occur, the best interests of society would be served, the main public utilities would not be compromised, the means of production would not be destroyed, and non-strikers would not be harmed. This decision underlines the importance of the judiciary in the establishment of basic rights and freedoms for a range of social and economic sectors. It shows how judges can legally reinforce human rights in political as well as social relations despite the non-democratic features of the political and legal systems.

The judiciary has allowed some social sectors to adopt political ideologies that were illegal, such as Marxism. The law penalized those adhering to or joining an organization that advocated Marxist ideas. The reason the government gave for this penalization was that such ideas and organizations are corrosive to the political system. The High State Security Court put restrictions on the implementation of this provision, stating that mere convictions and adherence to a philosophy or political system could not be penalized.[21] Only joining an entity that engaged in violence to achieve its goals was forbidden. The use of force, terrorism, or any other unlawful means had to be part of the goals of the group for its members to be penalized. It would not be sufficient if these means were an expression of the opinions of some group members but not of the group itself. The assumption that the accused were Marxists was not in itself evidence of their intention to use force and violence to reach their goals. It only indicated their political and economic tendencies in addressing the problems facing the country.

This ruling highlights the role played by the judiciary in the defense of freedom of thought and of political, social, and cultural convictions. Criteria identified through judicial interpretation, when they are applied in specific cases, are safeguards of rights and basic freedoms. I consider this an indirect political role, and a creative role, for the Egyptian judiciary.

### The Judiciary as an Indirect Mechanism for Political Determination

The judiciary has played an important role during periods of political and social transition, especially during the last few decades. When political and social crises arise, the judiciary is sought as an indirect tool to manage them.

For instance, prominent elements in the ruling elite—ministers, the inner circle of former President Sadat, leaders in the ruling party, and members of the People's Assembly—were charged with structural political and social corruption in the early 1980s. The crisis was managed at two levels. First, a cabinet shuffle was organized to give the impression of a change in individuals and policies. This action conveyed the message that the president and the ruling elite were not defending political corruption. Second, files of political corruption were opened, referred to the judiciary, and exposed to intensified media coverage, although the president was shielded from criticism.

The dangerous aspect of this strategy is that such matters are left to be resolved within the judicial process instead of being dealt with politically or socially by the executive authority. The strategy is still being used in the work of the ruling political elite and the regime, and the negative effects of this approach during past crises are still being felt in the country.

## Efficiency, Reasons, and Actors
The political role of the judiciary raises questions concerning its efficiency, the reasons for its political role, and its main actors.

### Efficiency
The problem is that the scope of the judicial process and its mechanisms and nature are not equipped to deal with the complex aspects of social, economic, and political phenomena. These are matters that should be the concern of those working within the executive and legislative authorities. They should be left to the policymakers at the top of the political pyramid, who are supposed to be well informed of changes in the political and economic arena and better equipped to identify and analyze the situation and come up with solutions.

For example, the organization of elections for the People's Assembly and the Consultative Council and the laws regulating some professional unions, such as the syndicate of engineers, are issues that can be considered political. The ruling power needs to identify a vision for political and legal planning of such political actions. These important matters have been left to the judiciary, however, when politics has involved planning, organizing, dealing with variables and pressures, balancing, maneuvering, prioritizing, and deciding between opposing political and social interests.

For instance, Law 125/1981 on the Lawyers' Union and Law 38/1972 on the People's Assembly, as amended by Law 114/1983, which established elections by list, were found to be unconstitutional by the judiciary. In these cases, the judiciary played an indirect political role by pointing out the need for political and legislative changes through executive decisions or laws.

Examples of this trend in rulings issued in social or political cases abound.[22] The most significant such ruling is that of 4 May 1985, which declared the unconstitutionality of Law 44/1979, which amended some provisions of the personal status law. The most important aspect of this ruling is that it shows the role rulings can play in sorting out the chaos of legislative politics. The parliament, which is dominated by the executive, particularly by the presidency, relinquishes its role and function, even in fields that normally are within its competence. It grants the president of the republic exceptional legislative powers to issue decrees with the force of law in contradiction to constitutional and legal restrictions, and it does not even carry out its subsequent supervisory role in regard to these decrees. The Supreme Constitutional Court ruled that it was competent to rule on the constitutionality of presidential decree laws adopted under Article 147 of the 1971 constitution. This right, granted to the president, is supposed to organize relations in urgent and exceptional circumstances. The decree laws should be submitted to the People's Assembly to ensure that they are in accordance with constitutional provisions.[23] In practice, the president has used this article extensively and the People's Assembly has neglected its supervisory role.

The Supreme Constitutional Court also has checked the constitutionality of laws and presidential decrees to ensure the principle of equality and equal opportunity for all citizens. It has emphasized that education is a right guaranteed to everyone in accordance with this principle. Some students were accepted into institutions of higher education without having the required grades on the general certificate of secondary education. Some were granted this privilege based on being family members of individuals who hold certain offices, who shoulder certain burdens or responsibilities, who were martyred or lost their lives, or who were lost or injured performing certain tasks, and so on. Other students were granted this privilege on the basis of their own circumstances, such as being injured in military action or being honored for their services. The Supreme Constitutional Court recognized that students who had scored higher grades would lose their places in favor of those granted exceptional rights. The court ruled that this was in contradiction to the nature, objectives, and requirements of higher education, and that it constituted an infringement on the rights of those with higher grades. It decided that this provision violated the principle of equal opportunity and equality before the law.[24] In such ways, the judiciary has played a major political role in identifying the basic rights and principles upon which constitutional system of government is based, and which the Egyptian legislative and executive authorities have violated.

The High State Security Court of Alexandria ruled that a state of emergency should not be declared except with the approval of a properly formed People's Assembly, meaning an assembly whose members were validly elected. The court declared that the approval of the People's Assembly on 20 March 1988, of the renewal of the state of emergency until 31 May 1991, was constitutionally flawed, as some members of the People's Assembly had invalid membership. Some of those who had approved this extension had not really won the elections. The court referred to the decision of the minister of the interior, no. 8332/1989, repealing his earlier decision, which declared the electoral victory of those members and replaced them with others in accordance with a judicial ruling. Because those members did not enjoy parliamentary capacity, the People's Assembly's approval of extending the state of emergency was granted in violation of Article 148 of the constitution.

The court also ruled that Law 162/1958 on the State of Emergency, which allows the president of the republic to refuse to ratify rulings issued by state security courts and to call for a new trial, is a violation of the 1958 constitution, under which Law 162/1958 was issued and pursuant to which the state of emergency was declared, and a violation of the 1971 constitution. In addition, it decided that Law 162/1958 is unconstitutional because it was adopted in 1958 by presidential decree and not submitted for approval to the National Assembly at its first subsequent meeting. This was a violation of Article 53 of the 1958 constitution, under which the law was issued.[25]

The last two decades have seen a growing political, legal, constitutional, and social crisis in Egypt that has led to a structural failure and hesitation in the decision-making process. This has led government authorities, particularly the judiciary, to play a more important role in managing the political system. The judiciary's involvement has had positive consequences for the rights and freedoms of citizens, as well as for social and political groups.

## Recalling the Political Role of the Judiciary: Reasons and Actors

Calls upon the judiciary and its political role by different kinds of actors have increased in the last decades for several reasons.

### Reasons

As explained earlier, the reasons a political role for the judiciary is valued include the stagnation of the authoritarian system and the emergence of political and administrative corruption. These developments have led the ruling elite to use judicial mechanisms, referring major corruption cases to judicial authorities such as the general prosecutor, the socialist public prosecutor (see page 176), ordinary criminal courts, state security courts, and the courts of values to absorb the anger of the public and to stand up to the accusations of political corruption directed at them by some intellectuals and writers and the opposition. This phenomenon appeared in the Sadat era and has increased under Mubarak.

The structural stagnation of the regime, its institutions, and its symbols has also led to a slow-down in the decision-making process and an increase in the frequency of political crises. This has been followed by deterioration in the process of political, institutional, and legal modernization, which in turn has led the ruling elite to use the judiciary to postpone the adoption of political decisions for several years. An example of this is the electoral laws, which included unconstitutional provisions but nonetheless were used for parliamentary elections to achieve political aims.

The state has resorted to exceptional courts to prosecute radical political Islamist groups that were engaging in violence, in order to avoid ordinary courts, with all their guarantees for the accused and their victims. This choice of exceptional courts was a means consistent with the regime's official policy of establishing general deterrence and political stability.

### Actors

Actors that support a political role for the judiciary include the ruling political elite, the political regime, and opposition parties. Civil society organizations also resort to courts, especially to the State Council, to establish their legal existence in relation to the administrative entity (the ministry of social affairs) that controls them and the state security apparatus affiliated with the ministry of the interior. They also seek to challenge administrative decisions regarding their legality or to request that certain provisions of laws be declared unconstitutional. An example of this is Law 153/1999 on non-governmental organizations (NGOs), which was declared procedurally invalid and therefore unconstitutional because it had not been reviewed by the Consultative Council prior to its submission to the People's Assembly. The new law submitted by the government in 2002 nevertheless contained the same philosophy toward civil society organizations.

NGOs also resorted to administrative courts in their bid to be allowed to monitor the 2005 parliamentary elections. The courts declared this monitoring legal (see Chapter 15 in this volume, by Nathalie Bernard-Maugiron). Members of the Muslim Brotherhood used administrative courts to challenge detention orders and to contest the decisions of the president of the republic to refer its members to military courts. They argued that this referral is not legal because it violates the right of the accused to be tried before his or her natural judge. Other members filed actions before administrative courts challenging decisions that banned them from traveling and requesting that their names be removed from lists of those banned from traveling.

Activists of the political Islamist movement have resorted to courts in calling for the confiscation of books and works of art and for bans on the viewing of films and plays for what they deem to be religious reasons or for political reasons. Egyptian courts have become involved, therefore, in settling political conflicts disguised as conflicts over creative visions, research, or methodologies for analyzing creative texts in terms of critical and aesthetic views.

Coptic activists have filed actions calling for bans on films that touch on aspects of their belief. This attitude is consistent with the prevailing trend in the Orthodox Church and among its leaders.

Some individuals have played important roles by filing cases to free the public sphere from various legal, security, or administrative restrictions that prevent citizens from enjoying their political rights, such as the right to peaceful assembly, demonstrations, and peaceful marches. The Egyptian judiciary undoubtedly has played a role in removing obstacles in the public sphere and supporting basic rights and freedoms.[26]

Cases filed by individuals calling for a political role for the judiciary reflect interactions leading to the birth of the individual, in the philosophical, political, and legal sense, and the individual's role as an active participant in the public field. This is an extremely important matter in terms of the relationship between the individual and the state in Egypt, especially as many obstacles limit active social and political roles for individuals. According to some human rights NGOs and the American media, the ruling elite sometimes resorts to the judiciary in actions against members of the opposition for political reasons, such as in the cases of Saad Eddin Ibrahim and Ayman Nour.

Judicial supervision of elections is a political role for the judiciary that is constitutionally and legally recognized. However, it is done by a judiciary that must remain neutral in its relations with competing political parties and independent candidates. Judges' supervision and the reports of the Judges' Club are particularly important in the political arena. This is especially true in the case of their critical observations on the performance of some elements of the security forces, political violence, and acts of *baltaga* (hired thugs) who marred the 2000 and 2005 elections in order to affect the electoral process and its results. The observations of judges and members of the Office of Administrative Prosecution were one axis of the political debate that followed the parliamentary elections.

## Conclusion

Judges have responded to calls for them to take on a political role in a number of ways.

The implementation of the law and making judicial decisions are judges' main functions, as the constitution and laws require that they rule on the cases referred to them. Abstention from performing this role would be negligence in ensuring a venue for citizens to seek justice. The political role judges play by recognizing and supporting public and individual rights and freedoms is also part of their function. However, various forms of judicial discourse include aspects of political and ideological ways of thinking that affect the vision of judges when they address cases. This vision could be characterized as adopting a rather liberal stand within the Egyptian context, but with reservations. For example, some judges refer to the provisions and principles of Islamic *fiqh* in their rulings, particularly in cases dealing with alcohol and bank interest.[27]

Through the Cairo Judges' Club and clubs in other governorates, in particular in Alexandria, judges have played a major political role in promoting the position of the judiciary itself, the defense of its independence, and the interests of the club's members. They have sought full and effective supervision of elections. These activities have caused judges to have disputes with and meet opposition from the Supreme Judicial Council and the ministry of justice. The former opposed the various decisions of the general assemblies of the club that called for adoption of the club's 1991 draft amendment to the 1972 judicial authority law and proposed a different text. The ministry of justice, meanwhile, threatened to stop the financial support allocated for the judges' clubs.

The majority of judges support the board of the Judges' Club and the resolutions adopted by the club's general assembly. A minority supports the Supreme Judicial Council and the ministry of justice, claiming that the club is run by "satellite" judges. Judges who have called for the independence of the judiciary and for full judicial supervision of elections and who denounced the abuses committed during the 2005 elections were accused by the opposing minority of assuming a political role, in the negative sense of the word.

It is often difficult to make a distinction between the technical position of judges applying the law to a concrete legal dispute and their social and political position. This is particularly the case when legal provisions are vague or when there is a violation of the freedom of opinion and expression of public rights. It is also the case when political, social, and economic reality undermines the provisions of the constitution, as happened with the sale of the public sector and the privatization program, both of which were considered constitutional by the Supreme Constitutional Court despite the provisions of the 1971 constitution, as amended.

The different components of the Egyptian judiciary continue to play an important role in supporting the modern state, its structures, and its institutions. Nonetheless, the rulings of the judiciary affect political, social, constitutional, and legal developments in the country.

# 6

# The Political Role of the Supreme Constitutional Court: Between Principles and Practice

*Tamir Moustafa*

I was asked to prepare this chapter with the pre-selected title, "The Political Role of the Supreme Constitutional Court: Between Principles and Practice." The title puts me in the somewhat awkward position of having to pass judgment on the rulings of the Supreme Constitutional Court (SCC). As someone who admires the SCC for the role that it has played in attempting to bring the Egyptian government closer in line with constitutional principles, I hesitate to judge the jurisprudence of the court in the abstract. An isolated comparison of SCC rulings with constitutional provisions is of little use if one wants to understand the context of SCC decision-making and how the position of the court might be strengthened in the future.

This paper, therefore, adopts an explicitly political analysis of the SCC's jurisprudence, rather than an analysis that is strictly legal in orientation. The paper also moves beyond a framework that examines the political role of the court in constraining the government in isolation from other political actors. Opposition parties, human rights organizations, legal academics, the Lawyers' Syndicate, the Judges' Club, legal academics, and the Egyptian public all shape the political context in which the SCC makes its rulings. The gap between constitutional principles and their implementation is less the result of the SCC itself than the result of the broader political environment in which the SCC operates.

This chapter proceeds in four steps. First, I briefly review some of the celebrated rulings that the SCC has issued over the past twenty-five years in order to demonstrate the positive role the court has played. Second, I examine the limits of the SCC's ability to protect basic rights by looking at the hard cases of state security courts and military courts. Third, I examine government efforts to undermine the independence of the court. Finally, I sum up the most important elements of the Egyptian political context that undermine the court's ability to bring government practices fully in line with constitutional principles.

## The Celebrated Cases: SCC Rulings that Restored Political Rights

From the beginning of operations in 1979, the SCC did not shy away from challenging the government on a number of politically charged issues.[1] In one of its earliest rulings, the court enabled hundreds of prominent opposition activists to return to political life, including Wafd Party leader Fu'ad Serag al-Din and Nasserist Party founder Dia' al-Din Dawud.[2] In a 1988 ruling, it legalized the Nasserist Party against government objections.[3] The SCC even ruled national election laws unconstitutional in 1987 and 1990, forcing the dissolution of the People's Assembly, the establishment of a new electoral system, and the start of early elections.[4] Two similar rulings forced comparable reforms to the system of elections for both the upper house of parliament (Majlis al-Shura) and local councils nationwide.[5] Although the rulings on election laws hardly weakened the government's grip on power, they did significantly undermine the corporatist system of opposition control by opening the political field to independent candidates and enabling the Muslim Brotherhood to run independent candidates in the 2000 and 2005 People's Assembly elections.[6]

The SCC also issued a number of important rulings in the area of press liberties.[7] In February 1993, the SCC struck down a provision in the code of criminal procedures dealing with libel cases. The provision required defendants charged in libel cases to present proof validating their published statements within a five-day period following notification by the prosecutor. The SCC ruled that the time limit was too strict and that it interfered with the ability of the press to monitor the government, to uncover corruption and inefficiencies, and to encourage good governance. The ruling asserted that freedom of expression is an essential feature in a properly functioning democracy and that the five-day provision was a flagrant and unnecessary violation of Article 47 of the constitution.[8]

Following on the heels of this legal victory, the Labor Party successfully transferred a case to the SCC, contesting a provision of Law 40/1977 on political parties concerning the opposition press and vicarious criminal liability. According to Article 15 of Law 40/1977, heads of political parties were jointly responsible for all material in party newspapers along with the reporter and the editor in chief of the newspaper, in cases claiming libel of public officials.[9] This provision essentially formed a corporatist system of control over the opposition press. Since the heads of opposition political parties were held directly responsible for all publications, Law 40/1977 pressured them to practice self-censorship and to reign in their staff and writers.

Labor Party Chairman Ibrahim Shukri and the editor in chief of the Labor Party newspaper, Adel Hussein, filed the petition for constitutional review during the proceedings of their criminal trial in March 1994. Shukri and Hussein were standing trial on allegations of libel against a public official for accusations that were published in the Labor Party newspaper, *al-Sha'b*. The SCC ruling affirmed the Labor Party petition and struck down the provision of Law 40/1977 that enabled the government to press vicarious criminal liability charges against the heads of political parties. The SCC argued that Law 40/1977 violated Articles 41, 66, 67, 69, and 165 of the constitution, which collectively guarantee the presumption of innocence, the right of legal defense, and the right of the courts alone to adjudicate guilt and innocence.[10] The court initially took a cautious approach in its 1995 decision by limiting the ruling of unconstitutionality to the president of political parties. Just two years later, however, it extended its ruling to ban the application of vicarious criminal liability to libel cases involving the editors in chief of newspapers.[11]

The ruling set an important precedent, as it was the first time that a human rights NGO, the Center for Human Rights Legal Aid (CHRLA), successfully challenged legislation in front of the SCC. CHRLA represented a new breed of human rights organization that went beyond simply documenting human rights abuses to confronting the government in the courtroom. It quickly became the most dynamic human rights organization, initiating 500 cases in its first full year of operation, 1,323 cases in 1996, and 1,616 by 1997. In hopes of emulating the model provided by CHRLA, human rights activists launched legal aid organizations with different missions. The Center for Women's Legal Aid was established in 1995 to provide free legal aid to women dealing with a range of issues, including divorce, child custody, and various forms of discrimination.[12] The Land Center for Human Rights joined the ranks of legal aid organizations in 1996 and dedicated its energies to providing free legal aid to peasants.[13] The Human Rights Center for the Assistance of Prisoners similarly provided legal aid to prisoners and the families of detained individuals, investigating allegations of torture, monitoring prison conditions, and fighting through litigation, the phenomenon of recurrent detention and torture.[14] Opposition parties began to offer free legal aid as well, with the Wafd Party's Committee for Legal Aid providing free representation in over four hundred cases per year beginning in 1997.[15]

By 1997, legal mobilization had become the dominant strategy for defenders of human rights, in Egypt not only because of the opportunities that public interest litigation afforded but also because of the myriad obstacles to mobilizing a broad social movement. Gaser 'Abd al-Raziq, director of CHRLA for much of the 1990s, has explained that, "in Egypt, where you have a relatively independent judiciary, the only way to promote reform is to have legal battles all the time. It's the only way that we can act as a force for change."[16] A strong and independent judiciary was so central to the strategy of the human rights movement that activists institutionalized their support for judicial independence by founding the Arab Center for the Independence of the Judiciary and the Legal Profession (ACIJLP). ACIJLP set to work organizing conferences and workshops that brought together legal scholars, opposition party members, human rights activists, important figures from the Lawyers' Syndicate and Judges' Association, and even justices from the SCC itself. ACIJLP also began to issue annual reports on the state of the judiciary and the legal profession, extensively documenting government harassment of lawyers and exposing the government's interference in the everyday functions of judicial institutions. Like other human rights groups, ACIJLP established ties with international human rights organizations, including the Lawyers' Committee for Human Rights, in order to leverage international pressure on the Egyptian government.

Human rights activists engaged in public interest litigation began to understand that constitutional litigation in the SCC is potentially the most effective avenue for challenging the government. The change in legal tactics paid off handsomely when CHRLA successfully challenged Article 195 of the penal code, in cooperation with Egypt's main opposition parties.[17] Pleased with their swift success, CHRLA attorneys initiated a campaign to systematically challenge repressive legislation in the SCC, starting in late 1997. Their first target was Law 35/1976, which governs trade union elections. CHRLA initiated fifty cases in the administrative and civil courts, all with petitions to challenge the constitutionality of Law 35/1976 in the SCC. Ten of the fifty cases were successfully transferred and, within months, the SCC issued its first verdict of unconstitutionality against Article 36 of the law.[18] CHRLA also successfully advanced three cases to the SCC challenging sections of the penal code that dealt with newspaper publication offenses, as well as three additional cases dealing with the social insurance law.[19] The rulings of unconstitutionality and the additional fourteen pending decisions in a three-year period represented a tremendous achievement given the slowness of litigation in Egyptian courts and the relatively meager resources at the disposal of the human rights movement. Until this campaign, activists, opposition parties, and individuals initiated cases in an ad hoc fashion, but CHRLA's successful strategy of coordinated constitutional litigation prompted the rest of the human rights community to initiate similar litigation campaigns directed toward the SCC.[20]

This brief review of opposition and human rights activism illustrates how the new SCC provided institutional openings for political activists to challenge the state. For the first time since the 1952 coup d'état, political activists could credibly challenge the government simply by initiating constitutional litigation, a process that requires few financial resources and allows activists to circumvent the highly restrictive, corporatist political framework. Most importantly, constitutional litigation enabled activists to challenge the government without having to initiate a broad social movement, a task that is all but impossible in Egypt's highly restrictive political environment.[21]

## The Limits of SCC Activism: State Security Courts and "Insulated Liberalism"

Although the SCC took a bold stand on many political issues, there were important limits to SCC activism. At odds with its strong record of rights activism, the SCC ruled Egypt's emergency state security courts constitutional. It also delayed issuing a ruling on the constitutionality of civilian transfers to military courts. Given that Egypt has remained in a perpetual state of emergency for all but a year and a half since 1967, the emergency state security courts and, more recently, the military courts have effectively formed a parallel legal system with fewer procedural safeguards, serving as the ultimate government check on challenges to its power.[22]

By 1983, dozens of cases had been transferred to the SCC that contested a legal provision denying defendants the right to appeal rulings of emergency state security courts in the regular judiciary. Plaintiffs contended that the provision violated the right of due process and the competency of the administrative courts, as defined in Articles 68 and 172 of the constitution.[23] The following year, the SCC ruled the courts constitutional.[24] It reasoned that because Article 171 of the constitution provided for the establishment of state security courts, they must be considered a legitimate and regular component of the judicial authority.[25] The SCC rejected the plaintiffs' claim concerning Article 68 protections guaranteeing the right to litigation and the right of every citizen to refer to his competent judge. The SCC also reasoned that the provision of Law 50/1982, which gives the emergency state security courts the sole competency to adjudicate their own appeals and complaints, was not in conflict with Article 172 of the constitution. Finally, the SCC contended that the procedures governing emergency state security court cases were in conformity with the due process standards available in other Egyptian judicial bodies, such as the right of suspects to be informed of the reasons for their detention and their right to legal representation.

Although this ruling was based on legal reasoning that many constitutional scholars and human rights activists found questionable at best, the SCC never looked back, refusing to revisit the question of emergency state security courts' competency. Six months after this landmark decision, the SCC summarily dismissed forty-one additional cases contesting the jurisdiction of the courts.[26] The SCC dismissed another thirty cases petitioning the same provision over the course of the following year.[27] The flood of cases contesting the competency of the emergency state security courts in such a short period reveals the extent to which the government depends on this parallel legal track to sideline political opponents. The large volume of cases transferred to the SCC from the administrative courts also underlines the determination of administrative court judges to assert their institutional interests and to fend off encroachment from the emergency state security courts. Finally, the

SCC's reluctance to strike down provisions that deny citizens the right of appeal to regular judicial institutions, despite the dozens of opportunities to do so, illustrates the SCC's reluctance to challenge the core interests of the government.

In the 1990s, the SCC faced a similar dilemma with even more profound implications when it received petitions requesting judicial review of the government's increasing use of military courts to try civilians. Despite the control that the president holds over the emergency state security courts, in isolated cases, these courts handed down rulings that were quite embarrassing for the government in the late 1980s and early 1990s.[28] These occasional inconveniences in the emergency state security courts prompted the government to begin using military courts to try terrorism cases in the 1990s.[29] Military courts provide an airtight avenue for the government to try its opponents, as all the judges are military officers appointed directly by the minister of defense and the president for two-year renewable terms and as the courts have almost no procedural safeguards, with trials held in secret and with no right to appeal.

The first cases transferred to the military courts concerned defendants accused of specific acts of terrorism. Within just a few years, however, the government began to try civilians for mere affiliation with moderate Islamist groups such as the Muslim Brotherhood.[30] The government's use of military courts to try civilians was hotly contested, and opponents of the government attempted to wage a legal battle over the procedure in the early 1990s. Both liberal reformers and Islamist activists argued that Military Law 25/1966 might, at most, give the president the authority to transfer whole categories of crimes to the military judiciary, but that it did not permit the president to handpick individual cases for transfer.[31] A ruling from a lower administrative court on 10 December 1992, supported these critics' contention.

In response, the government launched its own legal offensive. First, state attorneys appealed the lower administrative court decision to the Supreme Administrative Court. On 23 May 1993, the Supreme Administrative Court issued an authoritative ruling overturning the lower court's ruling and affirming the right of the president to transfer any crime to the military courts during the state of emergency. The court based its decision on Articles 73 and 74 of the constitution and an earlier ruling by the executive-dominated Supreme Court, which had operated from 1969 to 1979.[32] Next, the government attempted to establish an air of legal legitimacy around the transfer of cases to the military judiciary by asking the SCC to exercise its power of legislative interpretation and give a definitive reading of Law 25/1966.[33] The SCC obliged and, in January 1993, confirmed the broadest interpretation of the law.[34]

Unsuccessful in the administrative courts, opposition activists attempted to challenge the constitutionality of Military Law 25/1966 in the SCC. The defense panel for a Muslim Brotherhood case being tried before a military court requested the right to challenge the constitutionality of the military law before an administrative court. On 7 November 1995, its request was granted.[35] The petition of unconstitutionality was filed with the court within a month, but until the time of this writing, the SCC had not issued its ruling. Given the extreme political sensitivity of the case, the court probably will never rule against these core interests of the government.

The Supreme Administrative Court ruling, the SCC's interpretation of Law 25/1966, and the failure of the SCC to produce a timely ruling on the constitutionality of civilian trials in military courts clearly illustrate the limits of political reform through judicial channels. SCC justices must look after their long-term interests vis-à-vis the government and pick their battles appropriately.[36] Although the court has had ample opportunity to strike down provisions that deny citizens the right of appeal to regular judicial institutions, it almost certainly has exercised constraint because impeding the functioning of the exceptional courts would likely have resulted in a futile confrontation with the government.

Moreover, even outside the military courts, the government effectively detains its political opponents for long periods through a procedure known as recurrent detention. Under Article 3 of the emergency law, prosecutors can detain any citizen for up to thirty days without charge. When a subject of administrative detention is released within the required thirty-day period, he is sometimes transferred to another prison or holding facility and then registered for another thirty-day period—a practice that essentially allows state security forces to lock up anyone they wish for months or even years at a time. Human rights organizations first brought the phenomenon of recurrent detention to light through extensive documentation in the 1990s. The Egyptian Organization for Human Rights (EOHR) noted that the problem became particularly prevalent after 1992, when the government began to wage a protracted campaign against militant Islamists.[37] Between 1991 and 1996, EOHR documented 7,891 cases of recurrent detention, but the actual number of cases is almost certainly much higher.[38] Ninety percent of EOHR investigations revealed that detained subjects suffered from torture. Most were denied the right to legal representation or family visits.

Article 3 of the emergency law permits the president of the republic, or anyone representing him, to "detain persons posing a threat to security and public order." The law does not define the terms 'threat,' 'security,' and 'public order,' leaving it to prosecutors to apply the provision with its broadest possible interpretation. Administrative courts issued a number of rulings attempting to define and limit the application of Article 3, but their rulings landed on deaf ears.[39]

Ironically, the government's ability to transfer select cases to exceptional courts and even to detain political opponents indefinitely through the practice of recurrent detention facilitated the emergence of judicial power in the regular judiciary. The SCC was able to push a liberal agenda and maintain its institutional autonomy from the executive largely because the government was confident that it ultimately retained full control over its political opponents.[40] SCC activism may therefore be characterized as 'insulated liberalism.' To be sure, SCC rulings have had an effect on state policy, but the court ultimately has been bound by a profoundly illiberal political system.

## Threats to Court Independence
Since 1998, and particularly in the past few years, the SCC has suffered from a number of setbacks. Here, I briefly review these setbacks and place them in the broader political context of state-society contention.

The first direct challenge to the court occurred in late 1997, when Hamed al-Shinawi, a member of the ruling National Democratic Party (NDP), submitted a bill to the Complaints and Proposals Committee of the People's Assembly that was designed to strip the SCC of its powers of judicial review and to make its decisions non-binding. The bill was transferred to the Constitutional Committee of the Shura Council, which is the last stop before debate in the People's Assembly, when a draft was leaked to the press. Opposition newspapers slammed the bill for days and human rights organizations unanimously condemned the draft law. The NDP leadership denied responsibility for the bill and explained that al-Shinawi had proposed the legislation on his own, without consulting

NDP leadership. A popular consensus emerged among reformers, however, that the bill and the press leak itself were thinly veiled warnings to both the SCC and opposition activists that the powers of the court could be curtailed if it continued to push its reform agenda. While it only made veiled threats to the SCC in early 1998, the government soon changed course and placed concrete constraints on court powers.

The government's first concrete assault on the SCC came just months after the uproar over al-Shinawi's bill. In July 1998, President Mubarak issued a presidential decree amending the law of the SCC, effectively limiting compensation claims in taxation cases to plaintiffs with cases then pending in front of the SCC and denying compensation to all future plaintiffs seeking retroactive compensation for the same unconstitutional legislation. Past SCC rulings on taxation (not to mention compensation rulings for Nasser-era sequestration and nationalization laws) had drained state coffers of billions of Egyptian pounds, and pending cases on the SCC's dockets had the potential to make these early rulings pale in comparison. Most significantly, ninety-two petitions on the SCC dockets contested a variety of provisions of the sales tax law. The minister of justice, Seif al-Nasr, estimated that rulings of unconstitutionality on this law alone could cost the state up to approximately US$2.3 billion. The government was quite bold in stating that its objective was to shield itself from these and future claims.

As after its previous threat to the SCC, the government faced a storm of protest. Opposition newspapers were filled with editorials insisting that the decree was unconstitutional on both procedural and substantive grounds.[41] Organizations such as ACIJLP joined the fray, printing extensive critiques in opposition papers.[42] Prominent members of the legal profession, such as the head of the Cairo branch of the Lawyers' Syndicate, also criticized the decree.[43] Al-Nasr and government supporters insisted on the legitimacy and legality of the amendment.[44] Outside of written reports and extended critiques in the opposition press, however, little resistance was given to Mubarak's decree. The executive authority's pressure on the SCC would increase dramatically after two of its boldest rulings were issued in 1999 and 2000.

## The Rulings on the Associations Law and Judicial Monitoring of Elections

At the same time that the government was beginning to pressure the SCC, it continued its assault on the most important advocate for the court's independence, the human rights movement. In just over a decade, the movement had grown to over a dozen organizations, many of which had established strong links with the international human rights community and achieved observer status in a number of international human rights regimes, such as the United Nations Economic and Social Council. The human rights movement was increasingly able to leverage international pressure on the Egyptian government through these channels. Domestically, human rights organizations had begun to cooperate more closely with opposition parties and professional syndicates, as demonstrated most effectively in their monitoring campaign in the 1995 People's Assembly elections. Moreover, the most dynamic human rights organizations increasingly used the courts to challenge the government. In response, the government began to turn the screws on the human rights movement as early as 1995, through intimidation, smear campaigns in the state press, and discouraging donor organizations from contributing to local human rights organizations. By the late 1990s, the government had launched a full-fledged campaign to undermine the human rights movement.

In 1999, the government issued a new law regulating NGO activity, tightening the already severe constraints imposed by Law 32/1964. Law 153/1999 eliminated the loophole that had allowed organizations to operate as civil companies. All human rights organizations were forced to apply for a license with the ministry of social affairs (MOSA) or face immediate closure. The new law forbade civil associations from engaging in any political activity and gave MOSA the right to dissolve any association "threatening national unity or violating public order or morals." The new law also struck at the Achilles' heel of the human rights movement by further constraining its ability to receive foreign funding without prior government approval. In addition, NGOs were prohibited from communicating with foreign associations without first informing the government. These new regulations were clear attempts to place new constraints on human rights groups that were effectively leveraging international pressure on the Egyptian government. The greatest asset of the Egyptian human rights movement had became its greatest vulnerability.

The human rights movement mobilized considerable opposition to the new Associations Law in a short period. Within a week, human rights groups organized a press conference in which they contended that Law 153/1999 violated the constitution. They vowed to fight it in the SCC if it was not repealed. At the same time, they met with the major opposition parties and professional syndicates and secured their support. Days later, a national NGO coalition was convened, bringing together over one hundred associations from across the country. NGOs committed to mobilizing domestic and international pressure on the government through a demonstration in front of the People's Assembly, a week-long hunger strike, and litigation in the courts. International pressure came quickly in the form of statements from Human Rights Watch, Amnesty International, the International Federation of Human Rights, the Lawyers' Committee for Human Rights, and the United States State Department.

The Egyptian government proved its resolve to rein in human rights NGOs when the State Security Prosecutor announced in February 2000 that the ongoing case against human rights defender Hafez Abu Seada would be reopened and that he would be tried before the Emergency State Security Court under Military Decree 4/1992 for accepting money from foreign donors without governmental approval. The charges cast a shadow not only over Abu Seada and his Egyptian Organization for Human Rights but also over the entire human rights movement, which depended almost entirely on foreign funding.

A ray of hope emerged in April 2000 when the commissioners' body of the SCC recommended that the new NGO law be ruled unconstitutional. On 3 June 2000, the court issued its final ruling in the case, striking down the single most important piece of legislation governing associational life in decades.[45] The ruling came at a critical time for human rights activists and pro-democracy reformers because national elections for the People's Assembly were just months away and human rights activists planned to document electoral fraud across the country, which would enable opposition candidates to fight election results in the courts, as they had done following the 1995 elections.

In the lead up to the 2000 elections, the SCC issued another bombshell ruling, this time requiring full judicial supervision of elections for the first time in Egyptian history. The ruling stated unequivocally that Article 24 of Law 73/1956 on the Exercise of Political Rights was unconstitutional because it allowed public sector employees to supervise polling stations despite the guarantee in Article 88 of the constitution that "the ballot shall be conducted under the supervision of members of the judicial organ."[46] Once again, what opposition parties were unable to achieve through the People's Assembly over the previous three decades, they were able to bring about through constitutional litigation.

Success in battling the government's restrictive NGO law and the ruling forcing full judicial supervision of elections illustrated how rights groups and opposition parties had become increasingly adept at using judicial institutions to challenge the government and defend their interests. However, both rulings also exposed the downside of using litigation as a primary strategy for confronting the government. The government circumvented the full impact of the ruling on judicial monitoring of elections through a number of quasi-legal and extralegal measures, including more aggressive coercion outside of polling stations, multiple voting, and ballot-box stuffing. Moreover, the government dampened the impact of the SCC ruling on judicial monitoring by interpreting 'judicial authorities' as inclusive of the State Litigation Authority (SLA) and the Office of Administrative Prosecution, both of which are under the control of the executive-dominated ministry of justice. The government also issued a new associations law, Law 84/2002, to replace Law 153/1999, which had been struck down by the SCC two years earlier. Law 84/2002 proved to be just as draconian, maintaining the power of the ministry of social affairs to reject or dissolve any association threatening 'public order or public morality.'

## Reining in the Supreme Constitutional Court

With the retirement of Chief Justice Muhammad Galal in late 2001, the government saw its opportunity to rein in the SCC. To everyone's surprise, including that of the justices, President Mubarak announced that his choice for the new chief justice would be none other than Fathi Nagib, who held the second most powerful post in the ministry of justice.[47] Opposition parties, the human rights community, and legal scholars were stunned by the announcement. Nagib was the person who had drafted the vast majority of the government's illiberal legislation over the previous decade, including the oppressive Law 153/1999 that the SCC had struck down only months earlier. Moreover, by selecting a chief justice from outside the justices sitting on the SCC, Mubarak broke a strong norm that had developed over the previous two decades. Although the president of the republic always retained the formal ability to appoint whomever he wished for the position of chief justice, constitutional law scholars, political activists, and justices on the court had come to believe that the president would never assert this kind of control over the court and that he would continue to abide by the informal norm of simply appointing the most senior justice on the SCC. Mubarak proved them wrong.

The threat to SCC independence was compounded when Nagib announced that he would increase the number of justices on the SCC by 50 percent, or five judges — four from the Court of Cassation and one from the Cairo Court of Appeal.[48] Nagib justified the new appointments by arguing that almost all of the justices sitting on the SCC came from the administrative courts and that their expertise should be balanced by that of other justices with backgrounds in criminal and civil law.[49]

With Fathi Nagib's sudden death from a heart attack in August 2003, the question of SCC autonomy in appointments resurfaced. Instead of reverting to the prior norm of seniority as many had hoped, President Mubarak surprised political activists again by appointing Mamduh Mar'i, the current head of the Cairo Court of Appeal. Not only had Mar'i spent much of his career in the inspection department of the ministry of justice, a post informally charged with exerting government control over judges, but most lawyers, judges, and political activists also did not think of him as a candidate with sufficient experience and education to head the most important court in Egypt.

## A New Political Role for the SCC?

In the past few years, the government has obtained favorable rulings in several highly politicized cases. Take, for example, the SCC's interpretation of the term 'judicial authorities.' As noted earlier in this paper, in the aftermath of the June 2000 SCC ruling demanding full judicial supervision of elections, the government sought to circumvent the full impact of the ruling by interpreting 'judicial authorities' as inclusive of the State Litigation Authority (SLA) and the Office of Administrative Prosecution, which are under the control of the executive-dominated ministry of justice. The SLA is a body that represents the state in litigation, while the Office of Administrative Prosecution is in charge of investigating disciplinary cases in which public servants are involved. Opposition activists contested the status of the SLA and the Office of Administrative Prosecution and their ability to participate in election monitoring. In June 2003, the Court of Cassation ruled the election results in the Cairo district of Zaytun void because polling stations there were supervised by members of the SLA and the Office of Administrative Prosecution, who must be considered employees of the ministry of justice and not members of the independent judiciary.

Faced with this fundamental blow to the integrity of the electoral process, President Mubarak requested that the SCC issue a definitive interpretation of the term 'judicial authorities' in the law governing political rights. The SCC responded in less than two months that the SAL and the Office of Administrative Prosecution must be considered a part of the 'judicial authorities' because the law governing political rights refers to the Higher Council for Judicial Authorities, of which the SLA and the Office of Administrative Prosecution are members.[50] With this ruling, the court severely limited the impact of its own June 2000 ruling. In practical terms, this was arguably the single biggest legal rollback for opposition parties because it expanded the government's ability to tamper with election outcomes.

A second controversy stemming from the 2000 elections that was resolved in the government's favor through the SCC concerned the 2003 by-elections. In this case, it came to light that a considerable number of People's Assembly members had managed to avoid their military service illegally. Since most were NDP members, opposition parties shamed the government through the press and forced irregular by-elections for open People's Assembly seats in December 2003. The Wafd Party led the charge by claiming that candidates who had not participated in the 2000 elections should not be permitted to enter the race, but the government dismissed this claim because it would essentially mean losing a considerable number of seats. The NDP ran new candidates in the elections, which resulted in another round of political struggles in the courts. Thirteen administrative courts decisions declared the by-elections invalid, while two administrative courts sided with the government's position. The Supreme Administrative Court came down on the side of the opposition, declaring the participation of new NDP candidates illegal. At this point, Mubarak requested that the SCC interpret the intent of the law regulating the People's Assembly, and the SCC found in favor of the government's position, stating that there was nothing written in the People's Assembly regulations that precluded the participation of new candidates in a by-election.[51] Once again, the government enjoyed the benefits of ending political controversies and disempowering the administrative courts through the SCC.

A third example comes from the 2005 presidential elections. In February of that year, Mubarak announced that Egypt would hold its first-ever multi-candidate presidential election. The decision was a strategic move to placate the United States and to appease domestic critics. By early May, it was clear what Mubarak had in mind. The People's Assembly issued a draft amendment to Article 76 of the constitution specifying in precise detail the rules that would govern multi-candidate presidential elections. Candidacy would be restricted to those who could muster the support of at least 250 members of the People's Assembly, the Shura Council, and local councils nationwide, making it virtually impossible for independent candidates to enter the race and effectively sidelining the Muslim Brotherhood.[52] Political parties with at least 5 percent of the seats in both the People's Assembly and the Shura Council would also be able to field one candidate each if they satisfied a number of additional requirements.[53] No opposition parties met the 5 percent threshold, but the draft amendment specified an exception for the 2005 elections by allowing each party to nominate a candidate regardless of its current strength in the People's Assembly. By opening the election to opposition candidates, the government appeared to make a bold gesture in the direction of political reform.[54] The government risked little, if anything, because of the weakness of formal opposition parties and the difficulty of any party in satisfying the entry requirements in future elections.[55]

In order for the government to further control the process, the draft amendment called for a Presidential Elections Commission with complete control of the election process and adjudication of all petitions of fraud. This commission would be composed of five members of the judiciary and five "public figures known for their impartiality" who would be nominated by the (NDP-dominated) People's Assembly and Shura Council.[56] Essentially, the amendment would undermine the ability of judges to adequately detect and deter election irregularities. More importantly, it would sideline the ability of citizens to contest election results before an independent judicial body. The government clearly sought to circumvent the embarrassing barrage of litigation that opposition activists launched after every election in order to shame the state in front of the Egyptian public and the international community.

Even more troubling was a provision in the draft amendment that required the SCC to review the legislation governing the new multi-candidate system of elections within fifteen days to determine its constitutionality. If any aspect of the draft was found to be unconstitutional, then it would be returned to the People's Assembly for modification. In other words, the court would be asked to perform *abstract* (prior) review of legislation before its promulgation, despite the fact that the law of the court only provides for *concrete* review of legislation.[57] The move was meant to protect the referendum against any future constitutional challenge.

The SCC was faced with a politically loaded request. The draft constitutional amendment was deeply flawed, contradicting both the spirit and the letter of multiple articles of the constitution. The procedure by which the request for judicial review reached the court was unprecedented and without legal basis, as well as an extremely troubling indication of how the court might be abused in the future.

It is important to note at this point that the shift to prior review of legislation was a threat that was leveled at the court during the high mark of SCC activism under Chief Justice 'Awad al-Murr. In a lengthy interview published in *al-Musawwar* magazine in 1996, Fathi Surur, Speaker of the People's Assembly, claimed that the SCC was imposing deviant interpretations of the constitution that diverged from the interests of the nation. He also said that these rulings destabilized the legal framework of the state.[58] Surur's proposed solution at that time was to switch to a process of abstract review of legislation in its draft stage and only upon the request of the president, the speaker of the People's Assembly, or the prime minister. After examination at the draft stage, laws would be immune from future review. Al-Murr responded to Surur's proposal with an extensive interview of his own in which he articulated the fundamental role that the SCC played in upholding constitutional protections on civil and political rights and how prior review would undermine the work of the court.[59] When asked about the prior review proposal during a lecture at Cairo University, al-Murr stated bluntly that prior review would be used as a tool "to get the seal of approval of the Constitutional Court, and the result would be that the constitutionality of these bills could not be challenged later on." He added, "If you want to destroy the Constitutional Court, let's shift to prior revision."[60]

Opposition to the government on such a sensitive political issue would not have been a viable option even in the heyday of SCC assertiveness. The leadership of Chief Justice Mamduh Mar'i further complicated the ability of principled SCC justices to take a stand. The court performed the task as requested and facilitated the government's efforts to project a façade of competitive political life while firmly controlling the process every step of the way. Mar'i went on to chair the Presidential Elections Commission, implicating the SCC even further in the fraud that Egyptians associate with every election cycle.[61] The day after the presidential elections, *al-Ahram* ran front-page quotes from Mar'i confirming that elections supervision ran smoothly and that there was no cause for concern.[62]

## Conclusion

I began this essay by stating that the gap between constitutional principles and their implementation is less the result of the actions of the Supreme Constitutional Court itself than the result of the broader political environment within which the SCC operates. This is no different from any other court on the planet. As institutions charged with mediating between conflicting interests, constitutional courts are asked to perform roles that are undeniably political in nature. Courts are most effective in bringing government practice in line with constitutional principles when there is a balance of power between competing actors. When there is a stark imbalance, courts become vulnerable to political punishment.

Given the overwhelming strength of the Egyptian government, the SCC should be commended for its strong stand on important human rights provisions. At the same time, it should be no surprise that the SCC did not rule against the constitutionality of the emergency law, the emergency state security courts, and civilian transfers to military courts. To do so would have been institutional suicide, and the same hard realities hold true in other authoritarian states.[63] Troubling new developments in what are referred to as 'consolidated democracies' illustrate the fact that civil liberties and basic rights protections are constantly fought over and renegotiated, and can unfortunately face dramatic setbacks. Only weeks before we convened for the conference in April 2006, former American Supreme Court Justice Sandra Day O'Connor reminded Americans that "statutes and constitutions do not protect judicial independence—people do."[64] If Justice O'Connor is right, we need to look beyond the relationship between the Egyptian government and the SCC to how opposition parties, human rights organizations, the Lawyers' Syndicate, the Judges' Club, academics with a law focus, and the Egyptian public all shape the political context in which the SCC makes its rulings.

The SCC has become a crucial avenue for political activists over the past twenty-five years because nearly all formal avenues for political participation have been closed by the Egyptian government. Litigation has afforded strategic advantages to political activists because it has provided an avenue for challenging the government without having to initiate a broad social movement. Ironically, this ability to initiate litigation in lieu of a broad social movement also had distinct disadvantages in terms of sustaining a thoroughgoing reform movement. When the SCC began to face pressure from the government, no credible countervailing force emerged to defend the court. Opposition activists, human rights organizations, and academics could only print newspaper articles and attempt to rally international support for judicial independence. They were detached from the broader Egyptian public and unable to mobilize grassroots support for SCC independence. When President Mubarak abandoned the custom of appointing the chief justice from among the sitting justices on the court, no credible resistance was offered. The introduction of prior review of legislation is cause for further concern, and it may signal a turning point in the political role of the court.

Political activists cannot expect judges to take aggressive political stands. At best, courts can take only calculated risks because they must preserve their long-term institutional integrity. What activists can do is attempt to shape the political context in which judges make their decisions, in order to make calculated risks viable. They can do this by focusing on the critical tasks that courts cannot do by themselves, such as providing research and documentation of government malfeasance; raising legal consciousness through coverage of court cases in opposition newspapers; organizing national and international conferences; and mobilizing international resources in support of the legal battles that judges decide to wage.[65] Many of these tasks are already being performed by rights groups and opposition parties. The most critical task, which has not been performed and which happens to be the most difficult to achieve, is for opposition parties and human rights groups to form a popular base of support for judicial independence and rule of law in the general public. Statutes and constitutions do not protect judicial independence—people do.

# 7

# The Role of the Judges' Club in Enhancing the Independence of the Judiciary and Spurring Political Reform[1]

*Atef Shahat Said*

Two sets of questions are particularly crucial for understanding the role of the Judges' Club in defending the independence of the judiciary in Egypt and the democratic reform it is promoting. First, why do the many judges who represent one of the fundamental state authorities insist on calling for democratic reform, which they see as linked to their independence? In addition, if judges are indeed concerned about their independence, why do those who insist on comprehensive legal reform do so despite the adverse effects their participation in legal reform activities might create? Second, have we reached a crisis of constitutional legitimacy in Egypt, given that the credibility of the constitution has been questioned? Has the principle of separation of powers collapsed? Have the executive and legislative powers lost their legitimacy, given the challenges to the transparency of the 2005 parliamentary and presidential elections?

In this chapter, I do not claim to offer comprehensive answers to these important questions. I argue that any plausible understanding of the role played by the Judges' Club, whether in defending democracy or in supporting the independence of the judiciary, should be situated in the larger context implied by the two related sets of questions above. This paper is divided into four sections, the first and the last of which are devoted to this larger context. The first section discusses the position of the Judges' Club in the structure of judicial authority in Egypt.

The second discusses the club's struggle to increase the independence of the judiciary in relation to its defense of democracy. The third section examines the role played by the Judges' Club in the events of 2005. The last section is dedicated to exploring the limits of the role of the Judges' Club and the meaning of its political role.

## The Judges' Club within the Structure of the Judiciary
### The Status of the Club

The Judges' Club was established in 1939 in Cairo to enhance solidarity among members of the judiciary, look after their interests, establish a cooperative and saving fund for its members, and help the families of deceased members. It is run by an administrative board whose members are elected by the general assembly of the club. All judges' ranks are represented on the board.[2] Another club was created in 1941 in Alexandria, after which several clubs were established throughout the country.[3]

The club's membership is open to all members of the Office of Public Prosecution and of the ordinary judiciary. Membership is not compulsory, but most judges and members of the prosecution are keen to become members in view of the various social services offered to its members. Former counselors and judges also can join the club. The Judges' Club now has approximately nine thousand members, meaning about 90 percent of all judicial personnel in Egypt.[4] It gathers all judges from the ordinary judiciary, whatever their level, rank, court, and competence. This feature renders the club a unique place where hierarchical relationships vanish between senior and junior judges and between judges and members of the Office of Public Prosecution. All members have an equal vote in the general assembly, which provides the club with a distinctive democratic environment. Since general assemblies of the courts have lost most of their powers, except for the courts of appeal and the Court of Cassation, the club remains a unique place where judges can practice freedom of expression in a context where hierarchy disappears, at least formally.

The financial independence of the club relies considerably on the support received from the ministry of justice, which has been used as leverage to pressure the club.[5] The government has consistently pushed to reduce the role of the club to a social gathering that offers some social services to its members but does not include discussion of the comprehensive issues that concern judges and the judiciary and that affect the performance of their functions. According to Counselor Tarik al-Bishri, however:

It is not a mere social club that provides social and cultural services to its members; nor is it concerned with affairs similar to those of syndicates, which defend their members' rights; nor is it like syndicates that look after the professional and legal ethics among their practitioners and protect their scientific and technical standards. The Judges' Club is concerned with all such issues plus another more vital role. It is a distinctive entity whose members' rights and independence are of identical nature to the larger public's interests, that is, independence of judges and the judiciary.[6]

The Judges' Club considers itself the true representative of judges, as its board is elected by its general assembly, unlike all other administrative bodies of the judiciary in Egypt. The Supreme Judicial Council claims that it is the legal representative of the judiciary because it is the most important administrative entity within the judiciary, for which it provides instructions in such fields as transfers and seconding. Another major entity that competes for the authority to represent and intervene in the affairs of the judicial authority is the ministry of justice. The ministry rules on many judicial issues, including medical support for judges and their families. It is also the hand of the ruling regime in the judiciary.

Consequently, we are confronted with three entities, two that represent the judicial authority and one that represents the executive authority. Given the likelihood of a representational crisis in the judicial authority, it is only logical to admit that there should be some degree of consistency or at least coordination between the two parties representing the judiciary, namely the Supreme Judicial Council and the Judges' Club. Because the council is composed of members sitting *ex-officio*, however, it looks more like an administrative organ and a council of appointees than a representative body. The conflicts between the Supreme Judicial Council and the Judges' Club increased when Counselor Fathi Khalifa took office as president of the Court of Cassation in 2002.

## The Struggle for the Independence of the Club

Since its establishment in 1939, the Cairo Judges' Club has fought many battles to ensure its independence. It has been through several difficult stages, especially during the Massacre of the Judiciary in 1969. On 28 March of the previous year, the club had issued a statement objecting to the requirement that all judges join the one-party Arab Socialist Union and arguing that the absence of judicial independence was one of the main reasons behind the June 1967 defeat. The statement also indicated that recovery of the occupied territories depended upon freedom, the rule of law, and the independence of the judiciary. On 31 August 1969, several decree laws were passed that required dissolution of the board of the Judges' Club and its replacement by a non-elected board. This board was chaired by the president of the Cairo Court of Appeal and composed of the general prosecutor, the most senior vice-president of the courts of appeal, the president of the Cairo Court of First Instance, and the most senior chief prosecutor in Cairo. Many judges condemned the decree laws. Judge Yahya al-Rifa'i was among the most prominent leaders of the judicial battle for the restoration of the club and the abrogation of the decisions pertaining to the Massacre of the Judiciary. Many judges were involved with the litigation of the case in the Court of Cassation. On 29 December 1977, the court annulled Decree Law 84/1969, which had dissolved the elected board of the club, and repealed all of its effects.[7]

The Judges' Club has no legal status. It is not registered as an NGO or as a professional syndicate. The government repeatedly attempted to subject the club to the law on civil associations in the 1960s. In 1999 and 2000, the club's board of directors decided to register the club as an NGO and put it under the supervision of the ministry of social affairs, but in 2000, the Law 153/1999 on civil associations was declared unconstitutional. In June 2001, the board was changed. As confirmed by Counselor Zakarya 'Abd al-'Aziz in an interview with me on 8 April 2004, the conduct of some judges and their attempt to impose judicial custody on the club and to subject it to the law on associations was always for electoral reasons. The club's general assembly convened on 21 June 2002, and decided that the club was a purely judicial entity and should not be made subject to the Law on Associations.

Shortly after that assembly meeting, an attempt was made to replace the ministry of social affairs with the Supreme Judicial Council as supervisor of the club. The Judges' Club issued a decision in its general assembly on 12 March 2004, that the club, being a private entity, could not be made responsible to any body except its general assembly. As expressed by Counselor Farid Fahmi, former president of the Alexandria Judges' Club and ex-member of the Supreme Judicial Council, before the general assembly meeting on 12 March 2004:

The general assembly of the Judges' Club should be exclusively responsible for all the club's affairs. There is no sense in the proposal to replace one administrative entity with another in running the club's business, even if this body were the Supreme Judicial Council itself. Being no longer under the control of the ministry of social affairs, the club shall only be subject to its general assembly.[8]

As Counselor Zakarya 'Abd al-'Aziz points out, the club's independence is part of the independence of the judiciary.[9]

## The Judges' Club and the Independence of the Judiciary

The Judges' Club considers no democratic reform conceivable in the absence of an independent judiciary. The independence of the judiciary as an institution and as an authority is irrevocably tied to the independence of judges. Since the adoption of the judiciary law in 1972, the club has been calling for its amendment. The club succeeded in 1984 in having the law modified, but it has been struggling since for further amendments. (For the amendment introduced in 2006, see Chapter 3, by Mahmud al-Khudayri, in this volume).

### The Amendments of 1984

The abolition of the Supreme Judicial Council was one of the most detrimental decisions of the 1969 Massacre of the Judiciary. The Judges' Club, together with its successive assemblies, has been emphasizing since then that the independence of the judiciary cannot be attained without it having full control over its own affairs. Early in 1980, a large majority of the club backed the amendment of the 1972 judicial authority law, with special emphasis on restoration of the Supreme Judicial Council. On 11 October 1980, President Anwar Sadat visited the Judges' Club, and in light of the club's criticism of his establishment of the courts of values (see Chapter 10 in this volume, by Hafez Abu Seada), he promised to reinstate the Supreme Judicial Council. Although other bodies were involved in the controversy and in activities intended to bring back the council, including the general assembly of the Court of Cassation in 1982, the Judges' Club never stopped pressing ahead with dialogue with the ruling regime on the desired amendment.

In March 1983, the ministry of justice prepared a draft amendment of the judicial authority law that lacked any provision for restoration of the Supreme Judicial Council. The club resorted to *al-Ahram* newspaper and to publish a strongly worded criticism of the ministry's draft, which did not fulfill Sadat's promise to reinstate the council.[10] In response to the persistence of the ministry of justice in resisting the return of the council, the club made a concerted effort to criticize the ministry's viewpoint legally while corresponding directly on the subject with the prime minister in 1983 and 1984. In 1984, after President Hosni Mubarak assumed power, in view of an alleged democratic breakthrough and under the pressure exerted by the Judges' Club, Prime Minister Fu'ad Muhi al-Din interfered to strike a balance between the drafts of the ministry and the club.

The result was the return of the Supreme Judicial Council and the start of immunity for the general prosecutor and other members of the Office of Public Prosecution. The other amendments were no more than a compromise between the two drafts, and thus failed to give substantial authority to the Supreme Judicial Council and retained the ministry's vast powers of appointment of presidents of courts of first instance and its supervision over the Judicial Inspection Department.

## Preparation of Amendments to the Judicial Authority Law

Judges were well aware that the 1984 amendments did not bring full independence to the judiciary.[11] All these amendments achieved was the recovery of the council, which was nevertheless stripped of any real competence. After the Justice Conference in 1986, serious steps were taken toward working out a draft law on judicial independence. At the general assembly of the Judges' Club on 25 November 1988, judges specified the main features that ought to be included in the draft law to guarantee their independence. Among them was real competence for the Supreme Judicial Council. The club gave a mandate to the president of the Court of Cassation to form a committee to draft that law, but he did not take any serious steps to do so. The club's efforts were hindered in 1989 because of the elections. When Counselor Yahya al-Rifa'i assumed the presidency of the club once again in 1990, the club decided on 7 October 1990 to invite its general assembly to support the drafting of a new judicial authority law. After this draft law was approved, it was forwarded to the club's extraordinary general assembly on 18 January 1991, which approved the draft.[12]

The ministry of justice exerts several types of pressure on members of the judiciary. One is frequent direct interference in trials. Another is the lack of criteria when judges are delegated to work in ministries and governmental organizations, which affects their impartiality, as well as flaws in the rules and conditions of secondment of judges abroad. Another factor that cannot be overlooked is the insistence of the government, that is, the ministry of justice and members of the Supreme Judicial Council, on extending judges' retirement age. Older and junior judges calling for judicial independence argue that this measure would affect junior judges in terms of promotions and salaries, as well as have a detrimental psychological effect.[13] Finally, incidents of government interference in the work of the Office of Public Prosecution, particularly regarding investigations of heads and members of the police force, have shaken the people's confidence in the prosecution.

The most important features of the 1991 draft law of the Judges' Club were:[14]

Emphasis on an independent budget for the judicial authority

Reinforced composition and competence of the Supreme Judicial Council

Affiliation of the Judicial Inspection Department with the Supreme Judicial Council

Consolidation of the powers of the general assemblies of courts

Canceling the secondment of judges to non-judicial positions

The independence of the judiciary and of the Judges' Club

Putting rules on judicial secondment and secondment abroad

Support of the National Center for Judicial Studies

Penalizing any violation of judges' immunity

Benefiting from the experience of retired judges

What may seem paradoxical in the controversy between the Supreme Judicial Council and the Judges' Club is that the draft prepared by the club called for the consolidation of the competences of the council at the expense of the ministry of justice. The club's draft was built on the philosophy that "the affairs of the judge must be entrusted to the good hands of his colleagues," as stated in its explanatory note. The draft was intended to strengthen the democracy of the council by bringing in elected elements beside the general prosecutor, the president of the Court of Cassation, and the president of the Cairo Court of Appeal. The draft also expanded the competence of the general assemblies of courts.

In other words, the law intended to achieve in-house 'democratization' of courts and the judicial authority and to guarantee and consolidate their independence in the face of the executive authority. The draft was meant to be balanced: it had not dropped the appointment of members of the council and had accorded a degree of administrative competence to the ministry of justice to coordinate between the government and the judiciary. Therefore, the draft can be said to have put matters on the right track. The Judges' Club had demonstrated its dedication to the consolidation of the independence of the Supreme Judicial Council.

Although no serious steps have been taken toward the adoption of this law since 1991, the club has continued to promote it. In 2003, the club's general assembly decided to set up a committee to promote the long-advocated adoption of the draft. The drafting committee introduced some revisions to the 1991 draft, finalized it in April 2004, distributed copies to all courts for judges' contributions, and published it in *Qudah*. The 2004 draft broadened the scope of elected members in the Supreme Judicial Council, with emphasis, as in the 1991 draft, on the independence of the judiciary.[15] The features of the 1991 and 2004 draft laws deserve more study because, despite their importance, they have not received much attention from legal professionals and academics.

## The Judges' Club and the Defense of Democracy

Judges have contributed to the defense of democracy by introducing a vision for comprehensive legal reform that would ensure respect for the rule of law. They also have contributed to that aim through positions adopted by their club and by preparing draft amendments to the Law on the Exercise of Political Rights.

### The 1986 Conference on Justice

The National Conference on Justice, convened on 14 and 15 April 1986, still stands out as the most important and comprehensive effort of the Judges' Club for legal and judicial reforms. Preparations for the conference took several months. The conference sessions included the work of five committees: a legislative committee, a committee on criminal procedure, a committee on civil procedure, a committee of judicial affairs, and a committee on the affairs of judges' auxiliaries.

More than its details, the reason for the conference needs to be singled out, as it highlights the extremely sensitive nature of issuess of justice for the club and of threats to the ordinary judiciary and to the sovereignty of law under the state of emergency. When the government called for total reliance on the emergency law to curb terrorism and stated that the ordinary judiciary was incapable of carrying out "effective" justice, the idea of the conference came to maturation.

The conference was held two weeks after the aggressive uprising of the central security forces.[16] Even though the government turned to the ordinary judiciary to face the situation, judges feared the government would extend the state of emergency. At the opening session of the conference, the president of the Judges' Club and the conference called for the state of emergency to be ended. Judges' fears proved correct when, on the first day of the conference, the government decided to extend the state of emergency. The conference adopted a general statement on the rule of law and a collection of recommendations for improving procedure and administration. It also condemned exceptional courts.

## The Club and International Issues

On several occasions, the club has taken a nationalist position on issues of international relations and has expressed its opinion regarding international double standards vis-à-vis major national questions. For instance, the club issued two famous statements on Iraq, in January 1991 after the Iraqi invasion of Kuwait and in March 2003 after the American invasion of Iraq.

The first statement not only accused Iraq of wrongly invading Kuwait but also criticized the double standards of international law. The statement, issued on 18 January 1991, by the club's general assembly, underlined the absence of the rule of law and freedom in the Arab world.[17] In the second statement, issued on 24 March 2003, the club clarified that lack of democracy, forging of election results, and dictatorial Arab governments are the major reasons behind the crisis of the Arab nation. It stated, "the most prominent reason behind the current crisis is a frail nation deprived and denied, respectively, of its dignity and right to real democracy. The hindering of real democracy is a grave breach nearly equivalent to homicide and vulnerability to its enemies."[18]

The statement said that the goal of reform was "to free the nation from oppressive rulers who stay in office for as long as they live, falsifying election results, enforcing emergency laws, and handing the country down to their heirs. Judges have examined the great stance of the peoples of this nation, as well as the stance of governments, which denounce any aggression verbally, while exercising actual oppression of these peoples." The significant point here is not the reiterated statements, but the creation of some healthy legal and constitutional debate.

The statements constituted moral support for all demands for democratic reform in Egypt.

## A Draft Law for the Exercise of Political Rights

Judges hold that one of the fundamental components of political and democratic reform is transparent elections under judicial supervision. This supervision must be real and not simply formal. True supervision means that the electoral process is overseen by judges in its entirety, starting with the preparation of electoral lists and ending with the sorting of votes. Other constant parameters of this reform are pinned on comprehensive legislative reform to bring about the rule of law and the end of the state of emergency.

Separation of powers is achieved when the balance of power among the three authorities is established and each authority acts as a check on the others. The executive authority is traditionally in full control of all coercive forces. The legislative authority gains its strength from its ability to mobilize the masses that entrusted their representatives with enacting legislation to safeguard individuals' rights and freedoms. The power of the judiciary hinges on the balance struck between the other two authorities, as well as on the keenness of the legislative authority to restrict and watch the executive. If the executive authority overrides the legislative authority by falsifying the will of electorates or interfering to impose candidates, the parliament is turned into a powerless organ affiliated with the executive authority and subject to its directives. History teems with examples, including Emperor Caligula, who won a seat for his favorite horse in the Roman Senate!

Permeation by the executive authority invalidates the capacity of the judiciary to protect citizens' rights against the other two authorities. The judiciary loses power when there is no balance between the legislative and executive authorities. Seizure by the executive of the legislative authority facilitates the promulgation of laws intended to undermine the rights of individuals and to limit the jurisdiction of the judiciary for the purpose of discrediting it. Therefore, it can be concluded that actual redress for lack of justice must begin with fair elections.[19]

The judges' recent demands for genuine judicial supervision over the electoral process are not new. Since the 1986 National Conference on Justice, whose recommendations were ignored by the government, the Judges' Club has insisted on true judicial supervision in conformity with judges' constitutionally mandated role. The 13 November 1987 general assembly of the club issued a significant statement on judicial supervision of elections:

> It has long been propagated by the executive authority and some media that the electoral procedure and proclamation of the results are supervised by the judiciary. This aimed at raising confidence in that procedure, on the basis of the people's confidence and reliance on the impartiality of the judiciary. If the judiciary is proud of and cherishes this confidence, and would like elections to enjoy the same confidence, they have to acknowledge, however, that judges' supervision has been merely symbolic, as they have only supervised the general and main stations in the various constituencies. Thus, judges have merely been allowed to perform vote counting and announce the final results, whereas actual voting took place in auxiliary polling stations outside their supervision. Out of true concern for the neutral performance of their national role in the actual supervision of the general elections, they have requested the amendment of the laws organizing the elections in a way to place the overall electoral process in the hands of the judiciary. They want to head the polling stations, whether general, auxiliary, or main, where voting occurs and where the scrutiny of votes and announcement of results take place.

The statement closed with a declaration: "Until this demand is fulfilled, judges insist on being exempted from this symbolic supervision. Either the entire electoral process is delegated to them, and they are trustworthy, or they are entirely relieved from it today."[20]

The judges' demands having been disregarded, the club decided to introduce a draft law to amend the 1956 Law on the Exercise of Political Rights to ensure true judicial supervision of elections. The club organized a symposium, "Integrity of the Elections of 27 June 1990," in order to investigate the Law on the Exercise of Political Rights. Participants gave recommendations at the end of the symposium that constituted the basis for the draft amendment of the law. Among the proposed amendments were the necessity for judges' supervision over both general and auxiliary polling stations, for proving the presence of the elector (by means of an identity card, passport, driving license, weapon license, or the like), for controlling electoral lists, and for requiring that the supervisory organ be entirely judicial. The draft law set severe punishments for electoral crimes and granted the injured party the right to turn to direct prosecution for electoral crimes, even if the accused is a government employee, a civil servant, or a person responsible for maintaining order.

Immediately after the symposium, the recommendations were submitted to the president along with a letter carrying the date of the symposium. The importance of the symposium and its resultant draft law should not be underestimated, as it became an essential part of every list of demands for any opposition force or civil rights organization calling for the amendment of electoral laws and seeking to ensure the integrity of the electoral process. The government disregarded the recommendations until 2000, when the Supreme Constitutional Court issued a ruling invalidating all elections that were not fully supervised by judicial bodies. However, the 2000 amendments of the Law on the Exercise of Political Rights that followed the decision of the Supreme Constitutional Court granted the task of electoral supervision to the ministry of the interior and maintained the status of the State Litigation Authority and the Office of Administrative Prosecution as judicial authorities, which allowed them to supervise the judicial process. Judges supervised the parliamentary elections of 2000 and complained afterward that they were asked not only to supervise elections with no guarantees but also to keep quiet about violations that took place.

The new amendments of the law introduced in 2005 adopted several suggestions of the judges' draft law, such as the requirement to prove electors' presence and the use of phosphorescent ink. However, the Presidential Elections Law was passed to grant supervision to a commission headed by the chief justice of the Supreme Constitutional Court. The Law on the Exercise of Political Rights and the People's Assembly Law were amended to grant supervision of parliamentary elections to a commission headed by the minister of justice. Despite the involvement of judges, both active and retired, and law professors in the two electoral commissions, the real meaning of judicial supervision of elections was not respected.

It seems that the government and the legislature, regardless of the opposition of human rights groups, some members of the parliament, and citizens in favor of democracy, define judicial supervision merely as supervision of general and auxiliary polling stations and not of the electoral process as a whole. Moreover, the State Litigation Authority and the Office of Administrative Prosecution are still identified by law as judicial bodies, even though they lack neutrality.[21]

## The Role Played by the Club in 2005

Historically, the Judges' Club has used different methods to perform its role. These methods include its general assemblies, fact-finding committees, and other mobilization and educational mechanisms. Using examples, I will demonstrate how these methods were particularly important in the events of 2005.[22]

### General Assemblies

General assemblies are one of the club's vehicles for encouraging debate about election supervision, as well as discussion and adoption of draft laws that ensure the independence of the judiciary. The Cairo Judges' Club held three important general assemblies in 2005 and one at the beginning of 2006.

### 13 May 2005

This extraordinary general assembly adopted decisions requiring both the government and the Supreme Judicial Council to adopt the draft law on the judiciary prepared by the Judges' Club in April 2004. The judges declared that there was a link between their supervision of the elections and the issuance of a law that guarantees their independence. The discussions in the general assembly focused on the means to pass the draft law amending the judicial authority law, which had been presented to the ministry of justice but had been shelved. The most important point discussed in that meeting was that five thousand attendee-judges linked their participation in electoral supervision to the adoption of the draft law. The general assembly issued four major decisions:

To abstain from supervising the upcoming presidential and parliamentary elections if the club's draft law on the judiciary were not fully adopted and if its demands regarding full judicial supervision of the elections were not accepted.

To stick to the draft law on the judiciary prepared by the Judges' Club for financial and administrative independence from the ministry of justice.

To have an emergency general assembly on 2 September 2005, to evaluate the situation and take a final decision on whether or not to supervise the elections, in light of the government's response to their demands.

To delegate to the club's board the responsibility to make the necessary contacts, to follow up on the implementation of the decisions, and to invite judges to attend open meetings designed to brief them on the club's activities on the issue.[23]

Despite these decisions, the judges agreed to participate in the supervision of the referendum on 25 May 2005 on the amendment of Article 76 of the constitution.

The Supreme Judicial Council repeatedly raised doubts about the validity of the decisions taken by the club's general assembly and questioned the real number and quality of the participants. It insinuated that it had received many complaints that a large portion of those in attendance did not belong to the judiciary. The club denied these claims.

## 2 September 2005

This second extraordinary general assembly agreed to supervise the presidential elections on 7 September despite the government's obstruction of adoption of the draft law on the independence of the judiciary. The judges held to their right to evaluate balloting.

The general assembly also decided to form a committee to observe the presidential elections and to prepare a report. The assembly called on the Presidential Elections Commission to convene to reassign 1,700 judges excluded from supervising the elections, to abrogate the designation of auxiliary prosecutors to head auxiliary stations, and to consider judicial seniority in assigning judges to the polling stations. The assembly decided to give the Supreme Judicial Council an ultimatum, giving it until 15 October 2005, to offer its final opinion on the draft judicial authority draft. The assembly arranged to have a sit-in on 21 October if the council did not reach a decision. During the voting process, some judges threatened to boycott the presidential elections if their demands were not met.[24]

## 16 December 2005

The main goal of this regular meeting of the general assembly was to elect new boardmembers of the Judges' Club. Judge Zakarya 'Abd al-'Aziz and his list of candidates were reelected by an overwhelming majority, which meant that the majority of judges supported the club's stance, specifically in relation to adopting the 2004 draft law. The assembly charged the club's board with the task of sending a telegram to the president of the republic asking for termination of the state of emergency and abrogation of exceptional laws.

An opinion poll affirmed that 3,656 judges would refuse judicial supervision of the elections in light of present procedures for presidential and parliamentary elections. The opinion poll also showed that 3,706 judges objected to extending the age of retirement. At the same time, 4,374 judges agreed to supervise general elections on the condition that their demands for full judicial supervision and for judicial police be satisfied.[25]

The committee in charge of following up on the judicial supervision of the parliamentary elections declared that its report would be released on 17 March 2006, during a general assembly of the club.[26]

## Fact-finding Committees

One of the most important reports issued by the fact-finding committee formed by the club's general assembly was about judicial supervision of the referendum on the constitutional amendment on 25 May 2005. The strongest feature of the report was that it relied on testimony of judges who supervised the elections. It held two closed hearings to compare verbal testimony with the written testimony of judges who supervised the referendum, and ruled out unsigned testimony. The government exerted pressure on members of the prosecution and on judges not to cooperate with the committee. The matter escalated to the point where two members of the Office of Public Prosecution were summoned for judicial inspection. The committee respected the secrecy of the investigation and took into consideration the possible embarrassment of judges. Therefore, the names of judges and members of the prosecution who testified were not mentioned in its report.

The report embarrassed the regime and put it in an awkward situation by revealing the following findings:

The government's claim that more than 11,000 judges supervised the referendum was far from true.

The heads of general polling stations did not monitor or supervise auxiliary stations.

Ninety-five percent of the auxiliary stations were suprevised by employees who enjoyed neither independence nor immunity and who were terrorized by the police. These stations, which had no judicial supervision whatsoever, witnessed many violations of the law, including the falsification of turnout figures and the forging of ballot cards.

Some presidents of courts of first instance constrained judges' efforts to supervise auxiliary stations and helped in breaching the law as far as supervision of these stations was concerned.[27]

## Other Methods

The club uses additional means to perform its function, including preparing draft laws, such as the 1991 and 2004 draft amendments of the Law on Judicial Authority and the 1990 draft amendment of the Law on the Exercise of Political Rights. The formulation of draft laws demonstrates the participation of judges in the drafting of legal texts relevant to them and to judicial matters. It is also an attempt to offset the slowness of the government and the ministry of justice in issuing such legislation.

The club also holds seminars and conferences, in addition to several regular workshops. The first Justice Conference in 1986 is still regarded as a watershed in the history of the contemporary judiciary in Egypt.

The Judges' Club corresponds with a number of other entities concerned with the judiciary, such as the president of the republic, the minister of justice, and the Supreme Judicial Council. It notifies these entities of its draft laws and the recommendations of its general assembly. Examples of its correspondence include briefing the head of state on the recommendations of the Justice Conference, filing a request with the general prosecutor to inquire into the cases of those implicated in the assault on judges in the 2005 legislative elections, and sending messages to the head of the Presidential Elections Commission and to the minister of justice with regard to the parliamentary elections.

The club had also established a permanent platform for discussion in *Qudah*, which has many objectives, including providing news on the club's services and activities.[28] It issues press releases. Because government media and the national newspapers are biased in favor of the ministry of justice and the Supreme Judicial Council, the club's president is compelled to deal with the government media to refute lies about the club.

The club has formed special committees, where numbers are chosen either by the general assembly or the board of directors, to follow up on the club's recommendations. Examples include the fact-finding committee set up by the assembly to take stock of the judges' participation in the referendum on the constitutional amendment and the committee charged with assessing judges' involvement in the presidential and parliamentary elections. The club also has organized protests and sit-ins.[29]

The club makes in-house bulletins available at its premises to inform members of all developments relating to their affairs and those of their club. It has also published subsidized books.

## Limits on the Role of the Club: The Meaning of Working in Politics

Since becoming highly vocal, the Judges' Club is the most democratic expression of the ordinary judiciary in Egypt. It has been criticized by other members of the judicial family, but in most cases it is criticized by the government, often through pro-government newspapers. Some of the most common criticisms are that the club does not represent the majority of judges and that the leaders of the club are in the minority with their opinions. There are secondary accusations in this matter, such as doubts concerning the number of participants in the general assemblies of the club. Critics say that the club's leaders or the leaders of the judicial independence movement look out only for their personal interests. They suggest that by approaching the media, they have forsaken the customs of judicial work and become involved in politics, which impinges on the integrity of the judges. They argue that the club's involvement in politics means that its members are conspiring with or being influenced by members of the Egyptian opposition. Accusations of this sort have escalated to the point of implications of national treason. This was brought up in April 2006 when a human rights monitoring organization asked to meet with the board of the Judges' Club to become acquainted with the club's viewpoint regarding independence of the judiciary.

The criticism that the movement for the independence of the judiciary was led by a group of individuals from the opposition and is not representative of the majority of judges is dishonest. There are many valid indications of the support of a majority of judges for the movement, starting with the large turnout of judges at the club's recent general assemblies and the 2005 reelection of Zakarya 'Abd al-'Aziz and his list of candidates, who won with an overwhelming majority. The logical interpretation of the increase in the number of judges and prosecutors participating in the club's general assemblies is that the club offers a democratic environment, especially for young judges and prosecutors, who are ordinarily dominated by their superiors and by the Judicial Inspection Department. With the government's ever-increasing control over the general assemblies of the courts, the democracy offered by the Judges' Club and its general assembly becomes more meaningful.

The second criticism is the most severe, and it is the core criticism directed at judges and propagated by the government-owned media. The accusation that judges are engaging in politics has only been directed at the supporters of the independence movement. Its aim was to silence the movement for the independence of the judiciary. As Counselor Ahmad Mekki said:

> Upon reading the 28th March Statement [of 1968], one realizes that it is similar to statements issued by judges either today or that might be issued tomorrow. But supporters of the ruling regime interpreted the 1968 judges' statement as an attack on socialist gains. Today they interpret the judges' discourse as a criticism of privatization. The supporters of the 1968 statement interpreted it as a criticism of the role of the armed forces and of getting the state prepared for war. Today, the supporters of the ruling regime interpret the judges' discourse as a criticism of the peace process and a call to involve the armed forces in politics. The very restrictions that blew away the citizens' freedoms on the pretext of protecting transformation to socialism are still ongoing and firmly in place, on the pretext of protecting privatization and the sale of the public sector. The agents of the ruling regime in both eras are the same people, and this is their constant pursuit, since the fall of the Khalifate, allegedly to build a correct democratic life.[30]

In one of the electoral documents of the club's board of directors in 1981, Yahya al-Rifa'i said:

> We, judges, have nothing to do with politics; we won't involve either ourselves or our club in its struggle. . . . Reciprocally, politics has nothing to do with us either. As a matter of fact, politics imposed itself on the club's affairs; and we all remember the 1968 and 1969 events.[31]

This issue deserves greater scrutiny. From a theoretical viewpoint, there are many responses to the accusations directed at the Judges' Club. First, all United Nations documents, including the 1985 Basic Principles on the Independence of the Judiciary, clearly and expressly state that there should be no restrictions on judges' freedom of opinion, expression, or assembly, as long as they conduct themselves in such a manner *as to preserve the dignity of their office and the impartiality and independence of the judiciary*. In this context, does not the Egyptian judges' insistence on a law that guarantees their independence fall under their legally acknowledged freedom of expression? Is it not a matter of legitimate freedom of expression that the judges refuse to be involved in elections that lack integrity, in order to protect their own impartiality? Is defending judges' impartiality the practice of politics?

Second, the judges' discourse on electoral supervision is interrelated with their constitutional duties. As explained by Counselor Tarik al-Bishri:

> Judges' demands cannot be considered as working in politics, as implied by the Supreme Judicial Council. If these demands were considered as such, then we should consider electoral supervision, mandated by constitutional Article 88, as working in politics. Supervision has been the reason behind such demands; electoral supervision is a duty assigned by the legislative power to organize elections and consequently obliges judges to supervise them. The executive power should not obstruct the process or the efficiency of supervision, which must ensure impartiality, independence, and integrity.[32]

Finally, would keeping silent in the face of fraud and police assaults on judges not be a political stance?

Speaking in practical terms, the government has burdened the judiciary beyond what is supportable. In the 2005 elections, for example, it requested that the judiciary accept not only its disregard of the draft law on judicial authority, but also presidential and parliamentary supervision of elections with no guarantees. It asked that judges keep quiet about the violations that took place during the elections, which escalated into assaults on some judges.

## Conclusion

So, why would a group of judges who represent a significant branch of the state insist on the independence of the judiciary and a democratic state when such a stance requires sacrifices of them? According to Counselor Ahmad Mekki:

> Although the judiciary is one of the three state authorities, it is distinguished from the other two by people's trust in its efficiency and position—the core of its existence. Confidence in the judiciary

is what makes people appeal to it in their litigation and bear no grudge in complying with its rulings. Other state authorities might seek the use of money, power, and submission of the ruled; the judiciary is almost the only authority that rules through people's love for justice and their trust in judges.[33]

In his speech before the club's general assembly on 17 March 2006, Judge Mahmud al-Khudayri addressed the members of the Supreme Judicial Council, as follows:

You should know that history will record that you stand as the main obstacle to the desired reform, especially when the executive authority uses you as a pretext to delay adoption of the law that will achieve the hope of reform. You, elders, should know that you are squandering the neutrality and impartiality of the judiciary, deeply rooted in people's hearts, when you refuse to fight corruption and fraud and attempt to terrorize reformers. What do you want from us? Do you want us to say that we are ready to supervise elections unconditionally and with no restrictions, as you did? Are we requested to disregard, in humiliation and shame, the crimes that take place in elections and pretend that they are mere trespassing, that they do not invalidate the election results? We will not speak except to tell the truth of these crimes committed by serious criminals, which amount to high treason against the people.[34]

There are many elements that contribute to the persistence of the judges, through their club, in demanding independence, including their role as leaders in Egyptian society, the country's liberal judicial heritage, and the economic and professional pressures applied by the government, through the ministry of justice and the presidents of courts, on judges in general and junior members of the judiciary in particular.

I raised a question at the beginning of this paper regarding what might be called the "constitutional legitimacy crisis" in Egypt. In the face of domestic and international pressure for constitutional and political reform, the ruling regime finds itself in a conflicted position. On the one hand, it aspires to maintain the remaining trace of democracy, or even to increase it, by boosting the marginal independence of the judiciary. On the other hand, it does not want a real independent judiciary. Now, more than ever, it is evident that the current political regime wants neither a real democracy nor a real judiciary. Many analysts indicate that its latest, trivial reforms were merely a way to absorb people's demands for reform. What really happened is that the old dictatorial system was clothed in a new mantle. In this context, the regime simply could not put up with the judges' demands for integrity in the elections. According to Dr. Hasan Naf'a:

Because the government fully realizes that its closed authoritarian regime could be opened by force or be broken if elections were truly fair, it will exert its utmost efforts to abort the draft law on judicial authority prepared by the Judges' Club. If the judiciary fully supervises elections, the ruling regime will become incapable, in any legislative elections, of getting the majority needed to pass laws. Everyone knows that government candidates always fail in any free elections, whether it is bar association elections, or the journalists' syndicate elections, or even sports club elections. Had our government been impartial and genuinely keen on an independent judiciary, it would have immediately welcomed the Judges' Club draft law. Instead, it tried to manipulate that law at first, and then, when it failed, it decided to decline it altogether and to pass another law that would not ensure necessary guarantees of independence.[35]

Given recent suggestions that the regime is illegitimate, can the judges of Egypt and those calling for democratic reform afford to keep silent about the "assassination" of the judiciary? There is no better way to close these concluding remarks than Dr. Hasan Naf'a's call to action:

The battle for the independence of the judiciary deserves that all sectors of civil society be mobilized to stand behind the Judges' Club, even if this means to organize a million-person demonstration march, a public strike, or civil mutiny. The independence of the judiciary is the only battle remaining to save the regime from itself by peaceful means. Will the people of Egypt win this battle?[36]

# 8

# Reining in the Executive: What Can the Judiciary Do?

*Nathan J. Brown*

The domination of the executive over the state structure, and over political society as a whole, has emerged as a central, if not the central, issue in Arab governance. This is true in most Arab states, but it has become especially notable in Egypt. With the number of other imposing economic and social problems facing Egyptian society, the centrality of constitutional issues to political discussions is remarkable. A decade ago, constitutional and legal scholars and specialists discussed the domination of the executive authority, but such discourse rarely attracted broader public attention.

In the past few years, however, advocates of constitutional reform have won major intellectual battles. Constitutional discourse is no longer restricted to the quiet rooms of academic conferences and non-governmental organization (NGO) workshops; it has seeped out to the mass media and even greatly affected electoral politics. In the recent parliamentary elections in Egypt, most major opposition parties rallied around a detailed and well-designed program of constitutional reform. While the alliance of opposition parties, Kifaya, fared quite poorly at the polls, the surprisingly strong showing by the Muslim Brotherhood (Ikhwan) was based largely on an election program that focused on constitutional reform. It is not an exaggeration to say that the Ikhwan won many seats by running on Kifaya's platform. Even the governing National Democratic Party (NDP) promised constitutional reform that seemed designed to mimic, in appearance if not in spirit, some of the opposition demands.

Although they have won intellectual battles, advocates of constitutional reform have made no progress in the broader war. The presidency still dominates political life and almost all organs of the state. Whether one views Egyptian politics from the perspective of the press, political parties, the bureaucracy, parliament, the security services, or virtually any of Egypt's institutions, the influence of the executive in general, and the presidency in particular, never seems far away. Indeed, the Egyptian constitution, which places the presidency as an institution above all other authorities, legislative, judicial, and even the executive, is a frank expression of this situation.

However, Egypt is not a totalitarian society in which a single authority controls all aspects of public life. The executive is everywhere, but it is not everything. Indeed, in recent years, there have been openings, limited to be sure, in the media, parliament, and intellectual life that suggest different possibilities for Egyptian public and political life. Important institutions can never escape executive influence but they do retain some autonomy.

The judiciary traditionally has been an institution that enjoys greater autonomy than most state structures. In the past few decades, it has at times used this autonomy to articulate a vision of even fuller autonomy and to push for measures that would realize the ideal of judicial independence more fully. The judicial struggle for independence has slowly attracted the attention and respect of other political actors. Starting with 2005, it also has attracted their enthusiastic support. Yet the tools that judges wield are few in number and often quite clumsy. Can the judiciary remold its relations with the executive branch, and, if it does so, can this have any influence on the constitutional structure and political environment in the country?

In this paper, I will explain why the struggle for judicial independence attracts such high hopes from advocates of political liberalization and constitutional reform; explore the various tools that judges have, acting individually and collectively, to pursue the path of constitutional reform; examine the degree to which judges have been successful; and explain the limits and potentialities of judicial activism by focusing on the electoral process. I will conclude by showing why judicial accomplishments, while significant, are unlikely to lead by themselves to a fundamentally different political order. Indeed, there are severe risks that an overly ambitious agenda will backfire.

In many writings on the judiciary, especially on that in Egypt, judges are portrayed as highly principled actors and as heroes in the quest for political liberalization, democracy, and constitutional reform. Some have indeed played that role, but others have failed to try, or, just as ominously, have tried and failed. As a political analyst, I wish to focus as much on the limitations of the judiciary as on its potentialities. I seek to write not a celebratory tale of resistance to oppression but rather a political analysis of the genuine prospects for change.

## Relying on the Judiciary

At first glance, the judiciary seems an unlikely institution to work for political and constitutional reform. Even in democratic countries, the judiciary is the least democratic branch of the state because its members are not elected (except in a small number of countries) and they are politically accountable to elected officials. In civil law countries in particular, judiciaries historically have been discouraged from intervening in constitutional questions. Judges themselves often jealously preserve a non-political ethos; if they work for constitutional reform, their work often takes the form of specifically judicial concerns (such as stronger guarantees of independence) or implementation of constitutional standards that they did not originate. Even in cases in which they do support broad political reform, judges frequently seek to cast their efforts as nonpolitical and narrowly judicial.

All these factors are present in the Arab world in general and in Egypt specifically. Judges are not elected and they often come from elite backgrounds. They have been given few tools with which to engage in constitutional questions, and they seek to preserve their nonpolitical status. Yet judges have been drawn into the struggle for constitutional reform, most dramatically and consistently in Egypt but also occasionally in other Arab countries.

Part of the reason for this is the weakness of democratic institutions. Formally, Arab republics are democratic. Egypt has regular elections, a pluralist political party system, and a constitution that contains guarantees of basic democratic rights. These formal mechanisms are hollowed out, however, by a variety of techniques that render the executive authority unaccountable to the people. This makes the judiciary a surrogate or perhaps a refuge for those seeking political reform as they work to use the tools given by the law and the courts to pursue their agendas.[1] Egyptian administrative courts and the Supreme Constitutional Court have become sites for individual and organized efforts to breathe life into Egypt's formal democratic practices and institutions. Political parties seeking to gain recognition, individuals seeking political rights,

NGOs challenging restrictions, and activists seeking to eliminate unfair electoral procedures all have found the courts far friendlier places than the other institutions of the Egyptian state.

A second reason that judiciaries attract the attention of those pursuing political reform is that they offer an opportunity to enhance horizontal accountability. If vertical accountability—in which senior officials and institutions are accountable to the people—is the hallmark of democratic government, then horizontal accountability—in which various organs of the state hold each other accountable to clear legal standards—is the hallmark of constitutional government. The autonomy of the judiciary, limited though it might be, offers possibilities to those who seek to ensure that state officials follow the rules they have promised to live by. Administrative courts can be an important instrument in this regard, but constitutional courts also can enhance the same sense of horizontal accountability.

## How Many Divisions Do the Judges Have?

Can the judiciary possibly meet the tremendous demands that are placed upon it? The question suggests comparisons with Joseph Stalin's cynical observation on the moral influence of the Catholic Church: "How many [military] divisions does the Pope have?" Judges have tools to act individually and collectively, but the tools are few in number and sometimes clumsy and easy to deflect.

The first and perhaps most obvious tool that judges have is the issuance of rulings in particular cases. Indeed, there is probably no area where the regular judiciary has more autonomy from the executive. The ability of judges to issue rulings that disappoint or even confront the executive is what has led the executive to avoid the regular courts by constructing exceptional courts and granting specialized courts exceptional jurisdiction. While some of that exceptional authority remains in Egypt, the use of exceptional courts has declined gradually over the past two decades. In addition, the existence of a strong administrative court system, as well as of a constitutional court, allows many fundamental issues of governance to be brought before the judiciary.

While a judicial ruling may be the surest tool in judicial hands, it is characterized by three features that suggest it would annoy rulers more than substantially restrict them. First, for the most part, judicial rulings are limited to individual cases. The ability of the administrative courts to cancel regulations and decisions and the authority of the constitutional court to invalidate legislation lend more substantial weight to some judicial decisions. Second, judicial decisions only restrain the executive to the extent that there is a legal basis for such restraint. The legislative process is still dominated by the executive: most legislation is drafted within ministries, and the executive is able to obtain parliamentary approval even to fairly controversial proposals. Thus, judges do not always find the laws they need to rein in the executive authority. Third, the executive's control over the legal framework often allows it to manipulate the jurisdiction of the courts. Sometimes this can be done crudely, as in the case of exceptional courts. It also can take the more subtle form, admittedly used less in Egypt in the recent past than in other countries (such as the United States), of tinkering with court jurisdiction to place certain kinds of cases in friendlier courts or removing certain kinds of authorities from the review of the judiciary.

Judicial decisions may be an important tool for individual cases of abuse of executive authority, but they are an uncertain tool even in such instances. Judges have other, more collective ways of facing an imperious executive. Perhaps the most important is the judicial council. In many civil law systems, judicial councils oversee many critical aspects of the administration of justice. Most Arab countries have adopted the structure of the judicial council to manage judicial affairs. Some countries, particularly Egypt, have a notable history of reasonably strong judicial councils. In other Arab countries, such as Iraq and Palestine, potentially strong judicial councils have been created only on paper.

Arab states' experiments with judicial councils show their limits in allowing the judiciary to constrain executive power. First, the composition of the council often includes several members of the executive branch, and in a few countries, the council is formally led by the head of state or by his representative, the minister of justice. That is why the composition of the judicial council is often a critical political battle, one that was fought and fought again in Egypt, with a fairly autonomous judicial council only being firmly established (by law, not by constitutional text) in 1984. Second, the jurisdiction and competencies of the judicial council are often limited. Even in cases in which judicial councils are granted authority over the most significant administrative issues—hiring, assignment, and promotion of judges—other seemingly secondary matters (such as secondment of judges to non-judicial positions) are not the exclusive concern of the councils. This leads to the third problem: judicial councils can facilitate certain kinds of executive influence. Even judicial councils that are formally independent might do the executive a favor by concentrating collective judicial power in a few hands. In such a case, it no longer becomes necessary to coopt each individual judge, as a few senior judges at the apex of the system might be sufficient.

Fourth, autonomous judicial councils are created because of the claim that the judiciary can best manage its own affairs, but this is not always the case. Judges may possess wisdom and legal knowledge, but they are not selected and promoted for their administrative ability. To place the oversight of judicial administration in the hands of part-time and untrained administrators has been an unhappy experience in some countries.[2] It is also the case in the Arab world that some judicial councils have been accused of becoming part of the problem rather than the solution. By offering judges autonomy within their own sphere, councils open the door to temptations such as nepotism in hiring, which have devastating effects on the judiciary's reputation for integrity. Finally, judicial councils are limited because they can address only judicial issues. A judicial council may be able to draft a strong law on judicial organization, lobby for adequate budgets, and develop proposals for judicial staffing and training, but it will have far more difficulty if it wanders away from core judicial issues. In short, the judicial council is a critical, though hardly flawless, tool for protecting judicial autonomy, but not for reigning in the executive authority in other fields.

Another collective judicial tool, a judges' club or union, can sometimes fill this gap. While judges' unions have been integrated successfully into the legal order in some European states, judges' clubs are far more common in the Arab world. Indeed, with unions and professional associations often becoming highly politicized and occasionally falling under direct executive domination, few Arab judges are likely to be interested in moving to the union model. A judges' club has very different origins, as it generally is founded simply to pursue social or other needs for judges. In societies that allow few opportunities for autonomous organizations, however, such a club always has the potential to develop into far more than a social body. Few Arab states have strong judicial clubs, though most Arab judiciaries have expressed strong interest in developing them. The Egyptian Judges' Club stands out as an exception. At times, such as in the late 1960s and again, starting in 2005, the club showed remarkable boldness in confronting the executive authority. It is instructive to note that in both cases, the confrontations began over specifically judicial issues, such as judges' inclusion in the Arab Socialist

Union in the late 1960s and a new judicial law and election monitoring in 2005. Because of the nature of the political system, the disputes took on far greater significance. The club showed the promise of judicial activism against the dominance of the executive authority and its dangers, presenting the executive with a strong and principled challenge. At both times, the club found itself politically exposed, divided, and facing an adversary with many different tools and a strong political will.

## What Has the Egyptian Judiciary Accomplished?

The record of much of the twentieth century indicates that the judiciary can be an important actor in opening political space. If the judiciary is either called upon or attempts to accomplish too much, however, it risks political isolation, defeat, internal division, and politicizing itself. On two occasions in the past, in the mid-1950s and the late 1960s, Egyptian judges confronted the regime and lost, and in both cases it took decades for the institution to recover. This should not be taken to suggest that the judiciary cannot accomplish anything, only that it should not be called upon to move without clear objectives and an accurate assessment of the political context.

Over the past six decades, Egypt has seen a remarkable concentration of political authority in the hands of the executive. At critical stages of that process, elements of the judiciary have worked to counter or limit the process. The judiciary has scored some significant victories, but when judges were politically isolated or questioning core regime interests, it also suffered some disastrous defeats.

In the 1940s and early 1950s, the judiciary was behind some significant changes that established the basic framework for judicial independence in the country. During that period, the judiciary secured the creation of a fairly autonomous judicial council to oversee its affairs; secured the establishment of the State Council, which allowed judges to review administrative actions; and established the principle of judicial review of the constitutionality of legislation. These steps were accomplished through a combination of judicial decision and collective action by the judicial leadership. Individual judges and courts were important in establishing the principle of judicial review and in reviewing administrative acts. Indeed, Egypt is one of a small number of countries where judicial review was established through court decision rather than through explicit constitutional provision. Judges acting through their collective structures were influential in securing the necessary legislative changes to establish an autonomous judicial council and a powerful state council.

Yet, this period also demonstrated how critical the general political context can be in aiding and undermining judicial accomplishments. The judiciary's impressive achievements were possible at the legislative level only through the actions taken by the parliament and the cabinet. The law would not have changed without such support, and obtaining that support had a cost, as the struggle over the State Council, for example, dragged the judiciary into political rivalries between the Wafd Party and other parties.[3]

While the judiciary generally managed to navigate such rivalries in the pre-1952 period, the environment became far more difficult after July 1952. In 1954 and 1955, in the absence of parliamentary life and in the face of a regime that was consolidating its authority, the judiciary found its past successes something of a liability. The newly powerful judicial structures were sometimes regarded with considerable suspicion by the new regime, and the involvement of some leading judges in attempts to restore constitutional life deepened the concerns of Egypt's new rulers. In 1954, in the face of a major confrontation among factions of the new regime, elements of the judiciary were perceived as implicitly allied with the losing group. The result was a purge in the administrative courts, followed by a series of legislative changes that removed major areas from the jurisdiction of the courts. What independence the judiciary retained was primarily in areas that lacked political importance or sensitivity. Most elements in this series of defeats were probably unavoidable, but they illustrate that even fairly important and apparently stable accomplishments can become vulnerable when the political circumstances supporting them rapidly shift.

In the late 1960s, the situation seemed to change in ways that made it more favorable for judicial assertiveness. In the previous period, individual court decisions played less of a role and the legislative framework in Egypt became so favorable to executive power that courts had few tools to use against a determined leadership. In the aftermath of the 1967 defeat, however, the country's leadership came under severe pressure to govern both more democratically and more effectively. In this context, the victory of reform-minded leaders in the Judges' Club was an important political barometer. While the country's leadership hinted at the establishment of new tools to rein in the judiciary, most notably requiring judges to join the Arab Socialist Union, judges not only resisted such measures but also, speaking through the Judges' Club, supported calls for general political liberalization. In so doing, they seem to have deeply disturbed a regime that faced much discontent but little organized opposition. After some hesitation, the regime began the 1969 Massacre of the Judiciary. The starkest measure of the Massacre was the dismissal of a significant number of judges, including much of the leadership of the Judges' Club. Other steps included the creation of a new executive-dominated body to oversee the judiciary and a new Supreme Court to sit at the apex of Egypt's judicial order. In August 1969, Egyptian judges lost the ability to act individually and collectively, and it would take over a decade for them to recover from the blow.

Beginning in the 1970s and early 1980s, judicial actors began to reemerge slowly from the setbacks caused by the 1969 measures. Unlike in the 1950s and the 1960s, there was no dramatic confrontation between the executive and the judicial branches. Instead, advocates of judicial independence managed to obtain a series of concessions that had the cumulative effect of placing the Egyptian judiciary in perhaps the most powerful position it had ever occupied. There was some fragility to these accomplishments, however, and Egypt now is living through a period of contestation that may determine whether the achievements of the past two decades will be extended or reversed.

The first significant change came with the restoration of many of the judges dismissed in 1969. This step only reversed some individual effects of the 1969 measures without addressing more far-reaching institutional changes. In 1979, a far more significant institutional step was taken, though its significance was not realized at the time. The Supreme Court, created by decree law in 1969 and given a constitutional basis as the Supreme Constitutional Court in the 1971 constitution, was recreated by statute. Perhaps the most significant reform was that justices were given a significant role in appointing the court's members. Because the judges of the Supreme Court carried over to the Supreme Constitutional Court, the immediate effect was not great, but the long-term effect was profound. The court gradually changed from an institution created to allow the executive authority to oversee the judiciary into perhaps the boldest judicial actor Egypt has ever seen. The appointment procedure allowed the court to establish itself over time as an independent body.

This role reached its height under Chief Justice 'Awad al-Murr, whose presidency lasted throughout most of the 1990s. Al-Murr's individual role was impressive, but he did not act alone; the court was staffed by a number of justices who worked to expand the ambiguous provisions of the 1971 constitution to its liberal limits. In the process, the court sometimes antagonized the executive branch, but it was usually cautious concerning core executive interests. Thus, the court required changes in Egypt's taxation, property, party, and electoral systems, but it generally avoided decisions on security measures even when fundamental constitutional issues were involved. It is difficult to avoid the conclusion that the court carefully judged not only the cases before it but also what the broader political context would permit.

A second institutional change, the 1984 amendments to the 1972 Law on Judicial Authority, was made not to enforce the 1971 constitution but to contain its effects. The 1971 constitution, like most Arab constitutional documents, combines general promises of judicial independence with few procedural or institutional guarantees of these promises. Most significantly, perhaps, it recognized the Supreme Council of Judicial Bodies, which effectively placed most of the judiciary under executive oversight. In 1984, however, the judiciary law restored the authority of a largely judicial Supreme Judicial Council. The Supreme Council of Judicial Bodies could not be eliminated without amending the constitution, but its precise responsibilities were determined by statute and the 1984 law transferred many of them to the Supreme Judicial Council.

Again, the effects of the 1984 law were not immediately apparent. Indeed, the Judges' Club in 1986 set in motion, with the Conference on Justice, a process that called for further revisions in the law. Even with its flaws, however, the 1984 law made possible a judiciary that did not fear negative repercussions for specific decisions and granted the judiciary autonomy that, while incomplete, is rivaled by few judicial institutions in the region. Not surprisingly, these institutional changes made it possible for judicial actors, most notably the Supreme Constitutional Court and the Supreme Administrative Court but also parts of the regular judiciary, including the Court of Cassation, to take latent provisions in legal and constitutional texts and give them practical meaning. The authority of the executive was very strong at the core, but the judiciary began to have some effect on limiting executive authority at the margins; that is, the judiciary was often able to require the executive to live according to the rules the executive had laid down rather than its whims of the moment. The Supreme Judicial Council and a restored Judges' Club were able to obtain a host of concessions from the executive on more mundane matters related to judicial prerogatives and infrastructure. Judges worked in better conditions and for higher salaries as a result of Supreme Judicial Council pressure and lobbying.

The accomplishments of the 1980s and 1990s seemed to show the benefits of a more conciliatory approach toward the executive. The 1969 confrontation was not repeated, and after some time, the judiciary showed it could achieve more than many thought possible. It must be emphasized that the judiciary did not remake the Egyptian political order by rendering the executive wholly accountable to legal and democratic mechanisms. But, after years of judicial action, the country saw a notable increase in the ability of citizens to challenge some executive actions and of the judiciary to carve out a considerable degree of autonomy. Even when the regime showed its most authoritarian face, as it did toward Islamist groups in the 1990s, it tended to do so not by reining in or abusing the courts but by avoiding them.

The slow expansion of judicial autonomy came to an end in the early 2000s in a far less dramatic and decisive way than in 1969. Few of the accomplishments of the 1980s and 1990s have been reversed, but it has become clear that these accomplishments, while real, have limitations. First, the judiciary never really attempted full constitutionalism and accountability, but focused on the elimination of some of the most egregious aspects of executive power. Second, the judiciary could only go as far as the law would allow. In the face of legal provisions that enable the executive to exercise its authority in judicial matters, the judiciary rarely can do more than complain unless executive actions are unconstitutional. Third, the judges' accomplishments may have increased the importance of critical positions, some of which fall under executive control. The leadership of the Supreme Constitutional Court, the leadership of the Supreme Administrative Court, the composition of the Supreme Judicial Council, the leadership of the Judges' Club, and the general prosecutor do much to determine how the judiciary actually operates. While most of these are established positions that do not follow direct orders from the executive, the concentration of authority in a few judicial positions makes the judiciary more susceptible to cooption than it might otherwise be. Thus, a replay of 1969 is not necessary, as the executive authority can reassert control by persuading a few actors and allowing rivalries and divisions to do the rest.

## The Potentialities and Limits of Judicial Activism: The Electoral System

Another way to assess the ability of the judiciary to rein in the executive authority is to examine a single field over time. Perhaps the most indicative of both the potential and the limitations of judicial action is the country's electoral system.

Although Egypt has a long history of parliamentary life stretching back into the nineteenth century, the rules for parliamentary elections have always been contested and often are shaped to guarantee a particular outcome, generally one designed by the executive branch. Since the regime launched a limited liberalization program in the 1970s, it has carefully crafted electoral rules to allow for real opposition representation in parliament but in insufficient numbers to embarrass the government or significantly affect policy. It also has manipulated the kind of opposition allowed, working at times to exclude the more strident voices.

The regime has deployed a wide variety of tools before elections to serve these ends, closely controlling licensing of political parties, monitoring NGOs, harassing previously legalized groups and parties, and carefully devising electoral rules to entice opposition elements to participate while depriving them of the possibility of winning more than a smattering of parliamentary seats. On election day, the regime leaves oversight of balloting to the ministry of the interior, which it can trust to serve its ends.

Over the past twenty years, however, a series of court decisions has forced the regime to shift its methods constantly. Parties denied a license sometimes have successfully appealed to administrative courts to win legal recognition. Egypt's Supreme Constitutional Court ruled that political independents have a right to compete for office, thus invalidating an electoral system based on party lists. This ruling undermined the ability of the regime to keep some parties out of electoral competition, and it weakened the control of the regime's NDP over its own members. Those denied party nomination have regularly sought election as independents and successfully gained readmission to a party anxious to retain its parliamentary majority.

The effect of such judicial decisions, however, should not be overstated. The Ikhwan have not applied for recognition as a party, doubtless because of their ambivalence about changing into a purely political movement and because of strong suspicion that they would not be accorded approval. This suspicion seems justified. In 1995, a group of Ikhwan activists left the movement to form their own party dedicated to melding liberal and Islamic values. The resulting Wasat (Center) Party is still waiting for its status to be resolved. Convinced that the rules were stacked against them, most opposition parties lost interest in parliamentary elections, with boycotts becoming common over the past decade. Ikhwan members, however, can and do run and are elected as independents under present election rules.

For the 2000 parliamentary elections, the regime was hit with a particularly inconvenient judicial ruling: the Supreme Constitutional Court held that the constitution mandated full judicial supervision over balloting. Article 88 of the Egyptian constitution provides, "The law shall define the necessary conditions that the members in the People's Assembly must fulfill. It shall specify the provisions for elections and referenda, providing that the balloting take place under the supervision of a judicial body." The reach of this judicial supervision is ambiguous in three ways. First, the judicial body referred to is nowhere defined. Second, it is unclear which elections are included. The article is placed in the section dealing with the parliament, but the reference to referenda suggests that perhaps non-parliamentary elections are to be included. Third, the nature of the supervision is not specified.

For decades, most controversies have centered on this last ambiguity. Complaining that there were not enough judges to place at every polling station, the government had judges involved only at the stations where ballots were counted. Critics claimed that this did not meet the constitutional requirement. In 2000, they won a victory when the country's Supreme Constitutional Court struck down the election law because it did not provide for judicial oversight of each polling station. The government responded quickly by drafting legislation that spread the balloting out over several days, so that judges could move around the country to be present at all polling stations, and included all judicial and quasi-judicial personnel, including prosecutors and members of the State Litigation Authority, responsible for advising and representing the official bodies in litigation. Some complained that those who were not firmly within the judicial branch did not have the independence required and that their participation violated Article 88's stipulation that a "judicial body" be involved.

The more trenchant criticism of the 2000 election law was that it simply moved electoral manipulation outside of the polling stations, sometimes by just a few feet. Opposition candidates and movements complained of official harassment, such as disconnected telephone lines, intimidation by security forces that often surrounded polling stations, and other steps designed to deny them the opportunity to communicate with and mobilize potential supporters. The result in 2000 was favorable to the government but only after a large number of NDP members running as independents rejoined the NDP. The government's methods were so extreme that the elections did little to enhance the regime's democratic credentials.

Under heavy domestic and international pressure to devise a more credible system, the government nominally entrusted the 2005 elections to a newly formed electoral commission. This step far from reassured opposition elements, but a changed international and domestic atmosphere combined to create a sense of opportunity among Egypt's diverse opposition groups, as well as a perception that the regime, which had so carefully manipulated the electoral game in the past, was momentarily off balance. It was in this context that the Judges' Club threatened to boycott its constitutionally mandated oversight role.

The initial impetus for the boycott call came from a confrontation between lawyers and judges in Alexandria, in which a judge was physically attacked. The Alexandria branch of the Judges' Club linked its grievances in this case to a broader critique of the government's failure to protect judicial independence. More outspoken members of the judiciary charged further that their integrity was being used to lend credibility to a process over which they had only limited control. They therefore insisted that the government's electoral reforms go further to place all election oversight within the judiciary. Significantly, judges did not support calls for independent, much less international, monitoring. They asked for the judicial authority to conduct the oversight itself, but not for any assistance in the task.

Resentments over the electoral system were deepened by judicial complaints about the government's dawdling on issues of judicial independence. A project begun in the mid-1980s to draft a new law for the judiciary seemed to be making the slowest possible progress. When an opposition member of parliament agreed to introduce the draft, the government responded that it was studying the matter but would not be able to act before the upcoming elections for the presidency and the parliament. Linking the proposal to elections may have been a tactical mistake by the government, as it suggested to the judges a very different linkage of their own. With the proposed law in limbo, and with some senior judges lukewarm at best in their support for the law, the Alexandria branch of the Judges' Club decided to press the issue. On 8 April 2005, the branch called for a boycott of its oversight role in the elections. Only if the government acted on the proposal and gave the judiciary a full supervisory role over elections would the judges reconsider their stand. The boycott threat resulted in the national Judges' Club calling for an emergency meeting of all of its members on 13 May 2005.

The boycott threat could not have come at a worse time for the government. Not only was it facing an upsurge in domestic opposition but it was also falling under increasing international criticism for its autocratic nature. For the opposition, the boycott's implicit criticism of the existing electoral system, made explicit by some judges, offered vindication of their demands for more thorough reform. In the period leading up to the 13 May meeting, therefore, both the government and the opposition maneuvered to ensure a favorable outcome. Opposition elements claimed the judges' cause as their own. The government, by contrast, enlisted various groups of judicial personnel, such as members of the State Litigation Authority and the Cairo Court of Appeal, to declare their willingness to monitor elections.

The meeting was held in a tense atmosphere, but both the government and the judges held back from full confrontation. Judges, mindful of the 1969 events and professionally averse to any partisan political activity, phrased their demands in general terms related to the rule of law and judicial independence. The government tended to ignore the brewing crisis in its public statements. On the day of the meeting, government officials prevented al-Jazeera journalists from filming the proceedings. For their part, the judges declined to invite representatives from Kifaya to enter the meeting hall. Outside, government and opposition supporters were less restrained.

The meeting resulted in a full endorsement of the boycott call. The club decided that it would revisit the matter in September to assess whether it would indeed follow through with the boycott. That left time and room for maneuvering. The government responded by reacting in a restrained manner in public. Indeed, it presented the judges' call for full supervision of the election as a nationalist rejection of United States President George W. Bush's call for international monitoring, barely commenting on the boycott threat itself. Opposition leaders were elated at the outcome, perhaps excessively so.

Despite such statements, the outcome of the confrontation was far less than decisive. In the end, the judges did not follow through on their boycott threat. The Judges' Club did, however, set up its own system for monitoring electoral violations. The NDP had its expected victory, but it had to resort to clumsy tools to guarantee this outcome. Independents who had defeated NDP candidates were once again rushed back into the ruling party. In districts where opposition candidates were strong, police surrounded polling stations to prevent voters from entering. Journalists covering voting were physically attacked. Supervising judges who publicly criticized official behavior were threatened with prosecution, while the perpetrators of violence were allowed to act unimpeded. The result was something of a schizophrenic election. The campaign itself saw freer discussion and media coverage, limited but real willingness to accept some domestic monitoring, discrete arrangements for international observers, and the creation of at least the form of an independent election commission. As the extent of the Ikhwan's popularity became clear, however, the gloves came off and the regime used only its crudest tools. Far more thuggery and manipulation were necessary to ensure the regime's dominance in the elections than was healthy for its reputation.

In the end, the judiciary hardly brought about a transformation of the political system. By forcing the executive authority to use a different set of tools, however, the judges helped to move the election process out into the open. In the process, they exposed themselves to charges of politicization and initiated a conflict between the Judges' Club and the Supreme Judicial Council.

## Conclusion

A survey of the political record of judicial-executive relations in Egypt shows what the judiciary can and cannot accomplish in terms of reining in executive power. It is clear that the judiciary is generally a respected institution with a strong inclination toward supporting the rule of law. For that reason, it will be a natural focus of attempts to strengthen constitutionalism. While the judges might be inclined to view constitutionalism sympathetically, their power to enforce a constitutionalist vision are hardly unlimited.

In general, the judges are most likely to be effective under three conditions. First, the law must be on their side. In an authoritarian political order, authoritarian laws generally abound, so the judiciary will encounter some limits to its capabilities, but these limits are not absolute. Even an authoritarian regime needs laws to operate, and those laws may be used in many different ways. Second, the judges are far more effective when they focus on areas that are specifically judicial in nature. They may be less effective when they venture into broader political issues, though they have met with some success in this realm when they have had a sound legal and constitutional basis for their position. Third, judges are more effective when not acting alone, but they must be careful in forming alliances. An isolated judiciary is easily defeated, as happened in 1969. Even when the judiciary is operating in the context of a broader political movement for reform, it faces a number of risks. The collective judicial structures that do exist—the Supreme Judicial Council and the Judges' Club—were not designed for political strategizing. To the extent that judicial activism involves members of the judiciary in political struggles, they risk becoming politicized themselves. In addition, a legitimate concern exists that supporting a broader political agenda for reform will endanger, rather than support, the narrow judicial gains the judiciary has achieved.

The Egyptian judiciary as a body is likely to support the rule of law, constitutionalism, and an end to executive domination of the political order, but if it acts rashly or in isolation, it could pay a heavy price. This should not deter all action. The judiciary cannot remake the political order on its own, but it might provide some political space to those who wish to pursue such an agenda. It also might shore up the political space that liberalizing movements create.

# 9

# Judges and Elections: The Politicization of the Judges' Discourse

*Sherif Younes*

Regardless of how the conflict over the 1972 Law on Judicial Authority and the laws governing election monitoring ended, judges have succeeded for the first time since 1954 in transforming the question of their full independence into a public political issue.[1] The political environment in which judges operate has created a movement that could be described as close to trade unionist. However, the close association of the judiciary with the infrastructure of the political regime has largely determined their discourse concerning these issues.

Since 1986, when the first Justice Conference was inaugurated by the president of the republic,[2] Egyptian judges have been putting forward their two main requests: amendment of the 1972 Law on Judicial Authority and amendment of the 1956 Law on the Exercise of Political Rights, which sets up, *inter alia*, balloting procedures for parliamentary elections. In 2005, the debate on these requests moved from the corridors of the regime and broke through into the public sphere in memos presented by the Judges' Club to the president of the republic and other senior government officials, in books written by judges, and in the magazine issued by the Judges' Club, *Qudah*.

Judges have demonstrated that their independence is inadequate and that this has adversely affected their performance in election supervision, which is in violation of the provisions of the constitution.[3] The constitution vests the judiciary with the authority to monitor balloting,[4] but in practice, until 2000, this supervision was restricted to seconding some members of judicial bodies to general committees to keep

151

them away from direct rigging operations.[5] In reality, a limited number of judges was chosen by the minister of the interior so that their job was an honorary component of a basic security plan. Their mission was effectively confined to the receipt of ballot boxes from auxiliary committees, vote counting, and announcement of election results.

Judicial groups and leaders have been working for a long time on the question of judicial supervision of elections. The Justice Conference in 1986 addressed the issue of the organization of judicial supervision by proposing that judges preside over all electoral committees, general as well as auxiliary. In June 1990, a seminar for judges issued recommendations emphatically stating that judicial supervision as then organized was no more than a dummy control and impaired the prestige of the judiciary and public confidence in it. The seminar also recommended that electoral procedures be placed entirely under the supervision and within the jurisdiction of the judicial authority, from the division of circuits, through the organization of voter registration, and to the announcement of results. In accordance with the seminar's recommendations, the board of directors of the Judges' Club, led by Counselor Yahya al-Rifa'i, a symbolic figure of judicial independence,[6] prepared and submitted a memo to the president of the republic,[7] but these efforts failed to achieve a breakthrough.

In 1991, a plea of unconstitutionality based on an electoral challenge was referred to the Supreme Constitutional Court. In its decision of July 2000, the court ruled as unconstitutional the provision of the 1956 Law on the Exercise of Political Rights that provided for the appointment of heads of auxiliary committees from non-members of judicial bodies.[8] The ruling defined judges' supervision as exclusively connected with the balloting process,[9] but stipulated that judges should oversee all general and auxiliary committees. The amendment of the 1956 law to implement that ruling for the 2000 elections prompted the ministry of the interior, which was in full control of the multifaceted management of elections, to besiege election premises, to harass citizens suspected of being affiliated with the opposition, and to prevent them from entering polling stations. During the 2000 parliamentary elections, judges were eyewitnesses to the uselessness of their participation in supervision, which, besides, caused them loss of prestige, as public opinion considered them a party to electoral abuses. In addition, some judges were physically harmed.

In 2005, transformations in the political atmosphere contributed to bringing the judges' demands close to the forefront of public debate. The country was the scene of a mounting democratic discourse by several political powers and social blocs that had international support, with many formerly hidden groups coming into the public eye, including the Movement for the Independence of Universities and the Democratic Engineers. Political demonstrations involving leftist and national forces as well as the Muslim Brotherhood began raising democratic slogans as a regular practice in various ways. These events took place against a backdrop of the approaching end of the term of office of the president of the republic and the legislative term of the People's Assembly and the intention of the president of the republic to amend Article 76 of the constitution, as stated in his address in February 2005. Within six months, the Egyptian population had to vote on the referendum for the constitutional amendment and in both the presidential and the People's Assembly elections. Consequently, the judges' demands became a subject of public interest.

This paper deals with the issue of the participation of the judiciary in the elections from the point of view of the judges' public discourse in defense of their demands within the context of the referendum and the two elections. I will discuss the limits of these demands, the opposition to them, and, most importantly, the features of the political infrastructure that allowed this distinctive role of the judiciary to emerge in public. I will demonstrate how the judges' positions have been politicized and will then analyze the structural roots of the judges' movement in the political infrastructure.

## Politicizing the Judges' Positions
Although judges tried to escape the politicization of their positions by referring to their need for independence, their discourse ended up being politicized. I will discuss their sources of legitimacy before analyzing the consequences of this politicization.

### Judicial Independence as a Way to Increase Election Transparency
Since the convocation of the second general assembly of the Alexandria Judges' Club on 15 April 2005,[10] judges have dealt unequivocally with the two correlated requests of judicial independence and election transparency. They have demonstrated in various ways how the domination of the executive over the judiciary has played a major role in election rigging. They have emphasized how the interference of the executive in the

affairs of the judiciary has been effective, influential, and aimed, *inter alia*, at bringing under control the judges' oversight of elections, subjecting the judiciary to the executive's will, appropriating elected councils politically, and hindering the movement for judicial independence. Moreover, they have revealed that judges are divided into a majority concerned about judicial independence and fair monitoring of elections and a minority that has been won over to the side of the regime.

This correlation of the issues of judicial independence and election transparency originated in the stipulation set forth in the constitution requiring judges' supervision of elections, particularly after the issuance of the decision of the Supreme Constitutional Court in 2000. It is clear that the regime has had a strong interest in maintaining pressure on judges, or on some of them, to proclaim results that benefit the government, as manifested in the by-elections in 2003. The regime has thus needed to orchestrate the distribution of judges to general and auxiliary committees so as to strengthen regime security by tightening its grip on election results. Accordingly, coopting some judges has become a pressing necessity for the regime and was made possible by keeping in place or even expanding mechanisms that ensured interference in judges' powers and ranks. Judges, of course, have feared that the effects of this corruption might extend to the consideration of cases as well, because of the mutually supportive ties between some judges and the executive authority. This is why judicial supervision of elections raises the issue of the control of the executive authority over the judiciary.

The publication of reports by the Judges' Club on the constitutional referendum and the presidential elections, as well as the general assemblies of the club, eventually culminated in a better orientation for active public opinion regarding the relationship between the two issues. This produced broad-based support for the demand for the independence of the judiciary. Counselor Zakarya 'Abd al-'Aziz, president of the Judges' Club, mentioned this public support, saying, "Your demands have become the hope of the nation, which supports and even defends them." This public pressure resulted in the inclusion of the judges' requests in the platforms of all the candidates running in the presidential elections, including President Hosni Mubarak.[11]

## Politicizing the Judges' Positions

Since the beginning of the judges' protest movement, the official media has deliberately imposed a news blackout on their requests.[12] However, opposition newspapers, neutral broadcasts, and satellite television channels, in addition to assiduous follow-up by opposition political forces and widespread support from new social groups, largely defeated the government's efforts to control information on the judges' movement. As usual, the official media published the statements of the Supreme Judicial Council exclusively, without referencing their context, which ended up calling attention to the very issue that was meant to be kept in the dark.

Because of the failure of the news blackout and the strength of the judiciary at the time of the elections, political assaults were initiated aimed at dividing the judges. Their requests were presented as interest-oriented demands. The official media criticized the judges' revelation of election rigging in the newspapers, calling it a breach of judicial tradition and an intrusion of judges in politics. In their general assemblies, judges characterized this discourse as mere accusations meant to penalize them, individually and collectively. They argued that their requests, though involving personal interests, were also for the benefit of society as a whole. As Ahmad Saber, boardmember of the Judges' Club, said in his speech, "The independence of the judiciary does bring integrity and assurance for the citizen."[13] With the increasing attacks of the supporters of the government and its institutions, the discourse of the Judges' Club was gradually directed at openly defending their right 'to talk politics.'

Initially, the president of the Judges' Club assured the government that the use by some young judges of tough language was but an indication of "further adherence to real and effective supervision, not a relinquishment of, or a refrain from it. He added that judges did not intend to assail the authorities in place, but rather that they "hold the government in esteem inasmuch as it trusts the wisdom of judges and their unquestionable interest in stability and the reform process." He repudiated the accusation that the opposition backed the judges, saying, "Judges have nothing to do with politics and its fluctuations. They were, still are, and will remain part of the state authorities. They are a power concerned with its influence, independence, and dignity insofar as it is concerned with the influence and dignity of the two other powers." He noted that all judges "strive for their independence, their neutrality, and their desire to transcend political differences."[14] More than one judge stated that his stance was motivated by the desire to achieve stability and solidify legitimacy—a stand that required the end of the judiciary's clash with the executive authority. The judges insisted that their demands be met while also considering the power dispute an internal matter.

At the second general assembly of Cairo Judges' Club, in September 2005, Counselor Zakarya 'Abd al-'Aziz asserted that "judicial reform is a reform of the state . . . [and] election system reform is the cornerstone of the reform process," which made the judges' discourse part of the political reform discourse. He said, "The judges' requests are the requests of the nation," noting that court deliberation among judges in the run-up to the issuance of judgments "constitutes the basis of democracy" and added, "Our unity [as judges] is Egypt's safety valve."[15] He thus placed the judges' movement at the heart of the democratic and national movements. In response to the accusation that judges blackmailed the regime, he was quoted as saying, "Our request is not blackmail but it is long-lasting. We are claiming a right, not a personal or group interest. We call for the independence of the judiciary, not for the increase of our salaries."[16]

Critics said that judicial supervision of elections was a constitutional and legal obligation that judges should respect in their capacity as men of law, without restraint or condition. They added that the judges' calls for amendments to laws relating to their work or the Law on the Exercise of Political Rights were nothing but a violation of the prohibition on judges entering the political field and an aggression against other state authorities, as the judiciary was not authorized to legislate but only to enforce laws in accordance with the principle of separation of powers. Counselor Zakarya 'Abd al-'Aziz, at the third general assembly, openly defended the judges' right to interfere in politics, saying, "They accuse us of talking politics; it is not forbidden; it is a right of citizenship. We have only talked about our work. They want to stop us from thinking of our homeland. In that case it is is terror." Furthermore, he noted a difference between engagement in politics, which he defined as affiliation to parties, and talking politics, saying, "Where do we actually stand with regard to the reform advocacy launched by the President? Regrettably, it is all just talk, nothing more." He concluded, "Suffice it to say, we [the judiciary] still have our high position and do not want this kind of work [election supervision]."[17]

Judges' supervision of elections is in a way a political role. The regime has used the judiciary's insufficient supervision, subject to regime interference, to confer legitimacy on successive elections run by the ministry of the interior, at the expense of judges and their reputations, which is closely linked to their profession, as they have often stated.[18] The conflict, in fact, does not turn on whether or not judges have a political role to play but rather on the nature of this role. It could be said that the escalating politicization of the judges' movement is a reaction to this original politicization. On the basis of the link between the government's manipulation of judges to cover up rigging of elections and its undercutting of judicial independence, any decline in the regime's hegemony over judges has developed into a political issue because it leads to political losses for the regime and therefore to a redoubling of its efforts to control the judiciary. After installing judges in electoral auxiliary committees in accordance with the Supreme Constitutional Court decision, the government placed its security forces outside the committee premises to attack citizens with the world as a witness, thereby also creating antipathy toward the security forces.

The judges' relationship with politics is not exclusively associated with elections. Deciding on cases can be a political act because ordinary laws and constitutional legislation imply political issues. The judiciary can avoid political issues only under stable political conditions, where a balanced relationship between the powers can be taken for granted. The judiciary has increasingly taken to deciding political issues. The habitual rejection of political parties by the Parties' Committee has been followed by the recognition of most official parties by means of court judgments based on appeals from the committee's decisions.[19] In professional syndicates where opposition currents prevail, judicial committees have been set up in place of elected leaders. Islamist opposition groups also use the judiciary for political gains. The most famous case is the ruling of separation from his wife imposed on Nasr Hamid Abu Zayd because he published a work deemed blasphemous (see page 229). Here, the judiciary was used to penalize an individual for publishing his ideas. The judicial process thus has became an arena for litigating against dissenting political opinions.

## The Sources of Legitimacy of the Judges' Movement

Obviously, the parameters of the judges' discourse have by no means been predominantly religious. The principle of separation of powers is a modern principle enshrined in Montesquieu's famous book, "The Spirit of the Laws," published in 1748. Unlike their legal memos, the judges' political writings teem with Islamic expressions, which increased in their addresses at general assembly meetings. The general assembly held on 16 December 2005, started only after a judge recited sections of the Qur'an. Most judges began and ended their speeches by reading out Qur'anic verses and making reference to the Prophet's hadiths.

In addition to this general religious atmosphere, the perception spread that religion was as a source of power for which the judges had to fight. Counselor Mahmud al-Khudayri, for example, stated that "justice is a characteristic of Allah, the Almighty, whom men of the judiciary materialize on earth." Counselor Ashraf al-Barudy said that judges had to abstain from election supervision because "it is only Allah whom we fear and we have to dread on the Day of Judgment."[20] Counselor Zakarya 'Abd al-'Aziz started his speech before the next general assembly by saying, "Blessed greetings from Allah, who selected you from His creation to establish justice among the people." Another member addressing the judges said, "Beware election rigging, it is a sturdy vice. . . . Go back to Allah . . . redeem your guilt and repent for salvation."[21] Several judges' speeches combined statements implying that judges were the representatives of Allah in their struggle for the establishment of justice with others implying that their conscious commitment to their struggle was specifically rooted in their faith.[22]

This does not mean that the judges' movement is attached to the Islamist movement. Its leaders have a number of different political inclinations. The religious discourse is only one of the judges' sources of legitimacy. The others include democracy in its modern conception, the national discourse that addresses the "great people of Egypt," and international legislation and its standards for fair elections,[23] as well as a direct legal discourse based on the sovereignty of law and consistency of legislation.

Counselor al-Khudayri, one of the more radical members of the judges' movement, or simply the most inclined to open counterattacks, called on "the people" to support the judges' demands, stating that "we want to live like free people, without a state of emergency or detention camps." He also addressed judges in the name of the people, noting, "the people request that you keep it up until their purposes are met and their fetters loosened to become free to choose their own rulers without patronage." All popular forces were invited to start moving because the "battle is not one of judges alone, but it is actually the battle of the entire people."[24] Al-Khudayri called upon judges who had been victims of assault to consider their injuries "a decoration of pride and honor" that they wore for the sake of making the people's dream come true by winning freedom and dignity. He said, "Casualties should not be considered insults but rather a sacrifice for the triumph of the people."[25] The judges were, in one way or another, portrayed as representatives of the people.

It is important to note that the judges have never put forward their discourse from a liberal perspective based on individual, citizens', or voters' rights, as do most political actors.

## The Consequences of the Judges' Politicization

Being required to involve themselves in political conflicts has disturbed many of the judges. In the three general assemblies of the Judges' Club held in 2005, almost all of the participating judges took the floor in favor of the club's demands but expressed mixed feelings about the actions to be taken.

One counselor thought that taking part in the elections had put the issuance of judgments on hold, halting the main task of judges. In the end, he added that the elections did not turn out the way many had hoped and the judges were subjected to scurrilous statements in newspapers and even accusations of involvement in vote rigging. The counselor's statement was not intended as a call for surrender to the regime but rather as a recommendation that judges refrain altogether from involvement in elections in the absence of guarantees, pending the amendment of the constitution.[26]

The judges' struggle with the executive authority was coupled with an escalating confrontation with the Supreme Judicial Council, which began with the judges' request that the judicial authority law be amended to provide for elected members in the council.[27] The disagreement cemented the alliance between the executive authority and the Supreme Judicial Council, which may explain the increasingly aggressive reaction of the council to the judges' movement.

Judges were divided on the increasing politicization of their movement. The report of the committee in charge of implementation of the decisions adopted at the general assembly meeting of 13 May 2005, explains how the judges changed their minds and agreed to supervise the elections even though no guarantees had been provided. The report shows that the judges were not unanimous about refraining from election supervision, which implies that a decision to this end was bound to divide judges at a time when their unity was critical to achieving the independence of the judiciary and to doom the club's mission of consolidating ties among judges.[28]

The report also listed the reasons put forward by judges who were against abstention from election supervision. These judges argued that it is the duty of judges to enforce laws, however oppressive, and that the way to oppose such laws is to seek their amendment within the framework of the existing regime. They also suggested that participation in supervision is better because it might reveal violations within the context of the fight against the regime's policies. Moreover, they said that state authorities had responded to some of the judges' demands and had "respected their anger and adopted some of their interpretations." According to these individuals, judges have to heed the "status, prestige, and jurisdiction of the other two authorities, being part of the regime," and to be patient until the regime itself becomes convinced that fair elections are the "sole vehicle to combat terrorism and counter attempts to change the regime by force." In their view, young judges would have to bear the consequences of the decision not to monitor the elections because they are subject to judicial inspection and to the supervisory authority of their presidents. Most significant, these judges argued that a boycott decision would be "harmful without being useful, unless at least the majority of judges go for it. Therefore, its adoption by the majority of those attending the General Assembly is insufficient; otherwise the unity of the judiciary would be imperiled and the club itself put at risk."[29]

The justifications for not implementing the boycott decision varied from respect for the limits of the judicial authority as part of the regime, to the judges not being able to reach a consensus, to the ability of the executive authority to adopt sanctions against some of the judges. This position within the political infrastructure needs further analysis.

## The Structure of the Judges' Movement in the Political Infrastructure

The regime is founded on an unstable balance of power, which undermines the work of numerous professional categories, among them the judiciary, and continually gives rise to conflicts within state institutions. This phenomenon began in the Nasser era and has only increased under the current constitution.

### The Judiciary in the Nasser Era

Under the law occasioned by the July 1952 coup d'état, judges formed a pocket of 'legal legitimacy' within the regime. The regime reserved for the judiciary a great deal of independence by considering this independence, within certain limits, one of the pillars of public order. The coup officers found it sufficient to curtail judicial competence by establishing political and exceptional courts and by immunizing some of their decisions against the control of the administrative judiciary,[30] in addition to controlling the Office of Public Prosecution. Unlike the administrative judiciary, whose jurisdiction was fettered, the ordinary judiciary remained mostly beyond direct interference from the regime until the adoption of the 1971 constitution. Accordingly, Egyptian judges preserved their own culture, which was based on the idea of the sovereignty of law and was different from the ideology of the regime. They abided by the law within the scope of the jurisdiction conferred on them but were aware of the constraints in their work environment.

As far as the regime was concerned, this pocket of judicial practice was a necessity on the one hand and a problem on the other. This could be because the regime established by the officers was built around two kinds of organizations. The first type of organization was official public institutions with different functions, such as ministries, specialized agencies, syndicates, civil associations, and universities, all governed by regulations and laws. The ordinary judiciary and the State Council belonged to this category, with their competence to decide cases concerning individual rights relating to disputes between citizens and between citizens and civil servants, and relating to internal disputes between civil servants. The second type of organization was high security organs, such as the state security investigative police, the national security forces, and public and military intelligence bodies. This type of institution was given certain roles that ruling political parties normally play in democratic systems, mainly adjusting public institutions in the best interest of the regime.

These high security organs were responsible for straightening out the political and social systems in an unofficial way, which required interference, through their own means, to ease social and political tensions, starting with labor problems within the public and private sectors and the level of freedom allowed in economic activities and ending with the appointment of pro-regime staff to various posts. Their means involved barring certain individuals from legal activities or fabricating legal pretexts to justify the dissolution of a particular party or association. They also included punishing individuals for their failure to respect the pervasive organization of power. An atmosphere of terror was one of the control mechanisms. Their activity was not limited to the repression of opposition groups—it extended to the organization of the country as a whole.

The political role of high security organs was not based on law but achieved either by direct repression or control over public institutions or by influence over the heads of these institutions and control over appointments to critical posts. Accordingly, these bodies coordinated the activities of public institutions with the security considerations of the regime. For example, while a university dean or the minister of higher education decided who would be hired to a teaching post, the decision was based on security instructions. Under these circumstances, the regime was characterized by a lack of synergy between security requirements and the regular operation of state institutions, which adversely affected all employees in these institutions and the individuals dealing with them, although some benefited from their links with security organs. This lack of synergy was the outcome of the impossibility of codifying broad-based security requirements precisely because those in charge of security had no rules other than their own estimations of variable situations.

Historically speaking, this duality arose because the 1952 coup brought an isolated group of officers without political background to a position of power. The officers ruled by building bridges with different forces and organizations in society and placing them under the control of the state's security mechanism. The problem with this power arrangement always has been the political vacuum it generated, which is the reason ideological hegemony had to be maintained and the transformation into a 'normal' political system never occurred. The officers' authoritarian regime sought to solve this problem by establishing administrative institutions with limited powers, some of which were called authorities, such as the 'authority of the press,' while ensuring their compliance with the requirements of what became more or less a corporatist state.

The regime was not in a position to commission security organs to undertake the roles of engineers, attorneys, judges, or university professors. The most it could do was to try to interfere with the decisions of such professionals. Thus, these professional categories enjoy a greater degree of independence and influence than any elected body. It is no coincidence that the most influential protests against the regime's oppressive tactics have been by non-elected professionals who owe their influence to their competences. In order to ensure control over such individuals and their institutions, the regime has retained the ability to interfere in their affairs.

Another aspect of the 'coup-based' regime is the need to retain the ability to stage mini coups from time to time to reinforce its declared legitimacy and the legitimacy of official institutions. This capacity requires a system of 'lawful defects' and 'tailored laws,' no less pressing than the law itself, to make this duality as functional as possible. For the regime to continue operating in this manner, the law must not obstruct interference by its underground organs in the activities of its institutions. Consequently, the executive authority and its security machinery use the law and the constitution for their own ends. The judiciary, as an exclusively law-based institution, developed into an instrument for the regime to substantiate its policies, and the regime uses any means to interfere, one way or another, in the judiciary's affairs in crucial cases.

In the 1960s, the government tried to incorporate judges into the single-party organization, the Arab Socialist Union, but judges resisted the attempt by issuing a statement in 1968 calling for the independence of the judiciary and for respect of the rule of law. The regime retaliated by issuing republican decrees in 1969 that hit the relative independence of the judiciary in the so-called Massacre of the Judiciary. The regime deemed the judges' resistance a 'reactionary' political stance, in the wording of that period.

## The Judiciary under the Current Constitution

The constitution concentrates power in the hands of the president of the republic, who exercises it via different administrative bodies, primarily high security organs. The constitutional system does not provide for the separation of powers, which also is not applied in practice. The president of the republic is vested with vast competence and can be given exceptional powers by the People's Assembly. The president combines the positions of chief executive and head of state. The latter renders him the arbitrator between authorities, according to Article 73 of the constitution, which states that "he observes limits separating authorities to guarantee performance of respective roles in national action." This formula presumes the existence of a comprehensive, defined, and unified "national action" under which the different authorities have specific roles. This implies that the constitution prescribes a division of labor among authorities rather than a separation between them, whereas the principle of separation of powers derives from the philosophy of ensuring individual freedoms. The constitutional provision that charges the president of the republic alone with managing the performance of these roles in a systematic, unified manner places the 'nation' rather than its citizens at its core. Therefore, the position of the president in this "national action" scenario is much like the position of the director of a theater performance.

The goal of the regime is no longer the incorporation of judges into the "regime's party," as the regime itself has given up this mobilization approach. In its post-Nasser public discourse, the regime strove to reinforce the status of judges as one of its pillars. The economic liberalization processes of the time were increasingly in need of an independent judiciary to act as a safeguard for the different parties to disputes, especially because of the urgent need to bring in capital from abroad. This is why the executive authority continuously expressed its "appreciation" of judges and extended in-kind and financial benefits to them,[31] in addition to the protection the judiciary enjoys against attacl by the media. The judicial authority occupies a position that is best described as crucially sensitive. For this institution/power to achieve its mandate, its members require a great deal of independence and built-in immunity, which makes it impossible for the government to resort to direct repression in dealing with them.

The law provides for the president's exercise of his powers in respect to the judiciary in his capacity as head of state, by means of the executive power as represented by the minister of justice. The latter is vested with manifold competences by the judicial authority law.[32] In practice, the judiciary, like any official or unofficial institution in society, is subject to pressures from the high security organs through indirect interference and the referral of politically sensitive cases or issues of interest to the ruling power to certain court circuits.[33] Such referrals come from the regime's desire to avoid the issuance of a court decision likely to embarrass it. The executive authority similarly courts the favor of some judges, on a discriminatory basis and according to their degree of allegiance, by offering wage differentials, conferring the power of delegation in and out of the country to the minister of justice, and affiliating the judicial inspection department with the minister of justice. It attempts to win over loyal members of the judiciary and to punish the rebellious.

However, interference in the judiciary by the regime exceeds the limits of tolerance in many ways. Judges are indirectly requested to enforce laws that seem contradictory or defective or that have loopholes that allow security interference. The centralization of the Office of Public Prosecution and the appointment of the general prosecutor by the president of the republic serve to separate the prosecution from the judiciary and enable the executive authority to impose checks on inputs to the judicial system. The effective domination by security organs over the execution of judgments enables them to control the results, which explains the judges' request for judicial police.

The legal and constitutional ideology of judges is categorically different from the state's corporatist, security-based views. The differences became even more pronounced with the state's attempts to benefit from the independence accorded to the judiciary to strengthen its position as a regime allegedly founded on the rule of law and state institutions, including, until 2000, the judges' fictitious supervision of elections. However, the sanctified judiciary turned against the regime when the latter took a confrontational stance toward the judges' movement.

Judges' immunity and status may be the reason for the public's interest in the issue of judges' supervision of elections. The people need a privileged and powerful body to protect them from the security authority. Very few bodies in Egyptian society perform this task.

## Conclusion

In light of the special place of the judiciary within the Egyptian political system, any discourse on the independence of the judiciary, whatever its source, is a profound political discourse because it represents, more or less, a challenge to the infrastructure of the regime and to state security. The distinctive immunity that judges enjoy is incompatible with the security system, which may explain the assaults on judges by some political security officers. Therefore, "talking politics," to which each citizen presumably is entitled, according to Counselor Zakarya 'Abd al-'Aziz, is "more political" if done by a large group of judges than by one of the opposition parties, because the entire party system, while it has the potential to be politically effective, is still weaker than the judges, whom the regime needs to maintain its power.

However, the judges cannot extend their protest-like discourse because they are part of the state and must confirm the legitimacy of the regime, its constitution, and its laws, which they apply daily in courts. The 2007 amendment of the constitution that revoked the judges' supervision of elections may have relieved most of the protesting judges by detaching them from the political arena of elections. One might have expected that the judges' movement would place the regime in direct conflict with internal and external political actors over election monitoring and fairness. The cooling off of its confrontation with the judges, however, did not lead the regime into serious confrontations with other political forces in Egyptian society, even though they had been clinging to the issue of the judges' supervision of elections.

# 10

# Exceptional Courts and the Natural Judge

*Hafez Abu Seada*

According to the Egyptian constitution of 1971, the right to litigation is inalienable, and no one shall be deprived of his natural judge.[1] Several exceptional courts have been established by the legislature, however. The creation of exceptional courts goes back essentially to the 1952 Revolution. The first one was the Court of Treason (Mahkamat al-Ghadr), established after the revolution to try former politicians and officials of the royal era, including public servants, ministers, members of parliament, members of municipal, village, or directorate councils, and any person who had been assigned to a public service post or was a public representative and who, after 1 September 1939, had committed one of the actions specified in Article 2 of the 1952 decree.[2] This provision contained a list of the acts that were considered treason, including personal corruption, exploitation of one's influence, and abuse of authority.

Article 3 of the decree stipulated the transferal of whoever was charged with one of the acts specified as treason to the Court of Treason, which was composed of a judge from the Court of Cassation (as head of court), two judges from the Cairo Court of Appeal appointed by the minister of justice, and four senior officers of a rank not less than major appointed by the commander in chief of the armed forces. Article 6 prohibited appeal of the court's rulings by any ordinary or extraordinary methods of appeal.

The Court of the Revolution (Mahkamat al-Thawra) was established in 1953 to judge cases of high treason when the internal and external security of the country was threatened or any action was taken against the regime or the fundamental principles of the revolution.[3] The court also judged any act that contributed to corruption of power and enforced imperialism in the country or constituted an abuse of power. The court was made up of three members of the Revolutionary Command Council.[4] No appeal of its decisions was possible.

Another Court of the Revolution was established by Decree Law No. 48 of 1967. It was competent to rule on cases transferred by the president of the republic regarding acts specified in Book 2 of the penal code or the military code, or any crime that had to do with the internal and external security of the country or was an infringement of the principles of the revolution. It was composed of a president and two judges appointed by the president of the republic. Its rulings could not be appealed in any ordinary or extraordinary way. Moreover, they had to be presented to the president of the republic for approval.

The major characteristic of exceptional courts is that they try political opponents of the government in courts that lack the guarantees of a fair trial. The justifications advanced by the Egyptian authorities for referral to exceptional courts are the country's state of emergency and the presence of armed groups or those committing violence. However, some Egyptian citizens who have committed no acts of violence and adopted no methods aimed at pulling down the regime by force have been referred to these courts on the basis of fabricated accusations.

The current Egyptian judicial system identifies four kinds of exceptional courts: state security emergency courts, military courts, courts of values, and the Court of Party Affairs. Permanent state security courts established by Law 105/1980 were canceled in June 2003.

## State Security Emergency Courts

State security emergency courts (*mahakim amn al-dawla—halat al-tawari'*) were reinstated in October 1981, when the state of emergency was renewed after the assassination of President Anwar Sadat.[5] They are temporary courts and should disappear whenever the state of emergency ends. They are organized by Law 162 of 1958 on the State of Emergency.

### Structure

State security emergency courts are of two types: summary state security courts (*mahakim amn al-dawla al-juz'iya*) and high state security courts (*mahakim amn al-dawla al-'ulya*). Each type enjoys a special field of competence according to the severity of the crime it has to examine. Summary state security courts operate within courts of first instance and are composed of a judge of that court. As an exception, the president of the republic may decide to add two officers to the court (Article 7 of the 1958 Law on the State of Emergency). He also may decide that the court will be formed of officers only (Article 8). These courts are competent to examine crimes punishable by short-term imprisonment and/or fines. High state security courts operate within courts of appeal and consist of three counselors of that court. As an exception, the president of the republic may decide to add two officers to the court (Article 7). He also may order that the court be formed of three officers only (Article 8). These courts examine felonies *(jinayat)*, as well as any crime assigned to them by the president of the republic.

The president of the republic appoints members of summary and high state security courts after seeking the opinion of the minister of justice and of the minister of defense for officers about potential judges and counselors. In practice, military figures have not been appointed to these courts since their establishment.

## Competences

According to Article 7 of the 1958 Law on the State of Emergency, state security courts rule on crimes committed in violation of decrees issued by the president of the republic pursuant to the law on the state of emergency. According to Article 9, the president of the republic may decide to refer crimes penalized by ordinary laws. For instance, Presidential Order 1/1981 referred to state security courts several crimes under Chapters 1, 2, and 2 bis of Book 2 of the penal code (dealing with internal and external security), under Law 394/1954 on weapons and ammunition, under Law 14/1923 on meetings and demonstrations, and under Law 40/1977 on political parties. The president of the republic may refer any crime perpetrated in violation of these laws to the state security courts without having to justify his decision, even if the crime has nothing to do with the state of emergency.

High state security courts are also competent to rule on complaints of administrative detainees challenging their detention at least thirty days after the date of their arrest or detention (Article 3 bis). The court must give its decision within fifteen days of the complaint's submission and after hearing the testimony of the detainee. If the court decides to order the release of the detainee, the minister of the interior can object within fifteen days. In that case, the complaint is heard anew by another district of the court within fifteen days of the date of the objection. If the second district confirms the decision of release, the ruling goes into effect. If the court rejects the complaint, the detainee is entitled to submit a new petition after thirty days. In the meantime, there is no judicial control over these detentions, even though people are arrested on the request of the executive authority.

In practice, detainees released by the state security courts often are rearrested immediately after their release and many people arrested pursuant to the state of emergency law remain in prison for years. The decisions of the courts have to be approved by the president of the republic (Article 12), who can commute the sentence, change it to a lighter penalty, cancel some or all of the penalties, suspend its execution, or order a retrial before another district of the court. If the second district declares the accused innocent, he or she must be released even if the first district has declared the accused guilty. If he or she is declared guilty by the second district, the president of the republic may decide to commute the penalty, suspend its execution, or suspend the sentence (Article 14).

The decisions of these courts are not subject to any appeal before any court (Article 12). They are not even subject to review by the Court of Cassation.

## Procedure

Any person arrested should be informed immediately, in writing, of the reasons for his or her arrest and has the right to contact whoever he or she might wish. These individuals also have the right to a lawyer and to be treated in the same manner as any other administrative detainee (Article 3 bis).

State security courts should follow the procedure established by ordinary laws, unless stated otherwise by the state of emergency law or in the presidential order that referred the case to them (Article 10). State security courts offer restricted procedural guarantees to the accused. The fact that presidential orders can determine the procedure to be followed means there are no fixed rules and principles. The prosecution enjoys both the right of investigation and of accusation (Article 10).

## Military Courts

Military Law No. 25 of 1966 *(qanun al-ahkam al-'askariya)* organizes the competences and structure of military courts.[6] This law is considered a heritage of the martial laws established during the British occupation of Egypt. It has been amended several times, the last time being April 2007, when several provisions were modified and the name of the law was changed to the Law on Military Judiciary *(Qanun al-qada' al-'askari).*[7]

## Structure

Military courts *(mahakim 'askariya)* are composed of members of the armed forces. Until April 2007, the military law did not require military judges to have legal qualification, except for the director of the department of the military judiciary (Article 47). Article 2 now requires that judges of military courts fulfill the conditions stated by Article 38 of the 1972 Law on Judicial Authority, meaning that they must be law graduates or the equivalent. Until April 2007, judges were appointed for a two-year period that was renewable (Article 59) by decision of the minister of defense on the proposal of the director of the military judiciary (Article 54). They could not be transferred to other positions, except for reasons of "military necessity" *(darura 'askariya)*. Since April 2007, judges are not removable, except for disciplinary reasons (Article 3), and cannot be arrested except in cases of *flagrante delicto*, with the authorization of the Committee of the Military Courts Body.

Military judges are subject to all regulations prescribed by the military law (Article 57), important characteristics of which are discipline and obedience, which is in contradiction with the requirements of judicial work. Since 2007, Article 1 of the law pretends that these courts are an "independent judicial body" and Article 3 adds that military judges are independent and that no authority will be exercised over them in their decisions except law. The question is how they can be independent while under the direction of the ministry of defense.

## Competences

Military courts are competent to rule on crimes committed by or against members of the military forces during the performance of their functions (Article 7) or within the premises of the armed forces (Article 5, paragraph 1), and crimes that infringe on their equipment or secrets (Article 5, paragraph 2). The courts can also decide on crimes provided for in Chapters 1 and 2 of Book 2 of the penal code and referred to them by presidential decree (Article 6, paragraph 1), or on any crime punishable in the penal code or in any other law referred to them by the president of the republic, if committed during a state of emergency

(Article 6, paragraph 2). Some competences of military courts, therefore, are contingent on a decree of the president of the republic. By virtue of this provision, if a state of emergency is declared, military courts may hear all crimes over which the ordinary judiciary normally has jurisdiction. Military courts decide if the crime lies within their jurisdiction or not. No other judicial authority has the right to dispute their authority concerning this matter (Article 48).

The provisions of the military law deprive citizens of their right to appear before their natural judge.

## Procedure
### Rights of the Defense
According to Article 10 of the military law, ordinary procedural law and penalties apply unless a special provision is included in the law. According to Article 35 as amended by Law 5/1968, preventive detention ends after fifteen days. It can be renewed, however, by a lower military court once or several times for a maximum of forty-five days. If the investigation is not yet finished, a higher military court can renew preventive detention. The military law does not specify the maximum length of preventive detention, unlike the code of criminal procedure, which specifies six months as the maximum detention period (Article 143). Any person accused of a felony *(jinaya)* is meant to be provided with a lawyer (Article 74). The decision of the court is a majority opinion, except in the case of the death penalty, which requires unanimity (Article 80).

The military law does not allow retrial in case of trials *in absentia*, which is allowed by the code of criminal procedure (Article 77).[8] A special Office of Public Prosecution exists for military cases (Article 25), and it is vested with wide-ranging powers. The rulings of the military courts have to be ratified by the president of the republic in his capacity as chief of the armed forces or by the armed forces officer to whom this power has been delegated (Articles 97 to 100). Until 2007, the courts were not subject to challenge before any administrative or judicial body. Article 43 bis, added by Law 16/2007, established a Supreme Military Appeal Court composed of military judges who decide appeals of the final decisions of all military courts on ordinary crimes. This appeal court rules on points of law, like the Court of Cassation.

In practice, these courts do not provide enough time for defendants to prepare their defense and for defense lawyers to consult case documents and meet with their clients and witnesses. They also deprive defendants of their right to seek the assistance of personally chosen lawyers. Courts in some cases refuse lawyers' demands to meet their clients in private. They ignore defendants' frequent claims of having been exposed to torture and attempts to extract information from them by force. In addition, they deliberately burden lawyers' and defendants' families by convening trials in distant locations. For example, in some cases, trials were held in Alexandria and Marsa Matruh even though the defendants and lawyers were Cairo residents.

## Example: Referral of Civilians to Military Courts
### The Decision of the Supreme Constitutional Court

The referral of civilians to military courts was legitimized by a decision of the Supreme Constitutional Court regarding the legality of Presidential Decree 373/1992, which transferred defendants referred to as "returnees from Afghanistan" and "the jihad organization" to military courts. A case was brought before the Court of Administrative Litigation against the president of the republic, asking that the referral decision be stopped. On 8 December 1993, the Court ruled that the decision should be stopped. The government challenged that ruling before the Supreme Administrative Court and asked that it be canceled. The government also submitted to the Supreme Constitutional Court a request for interpretation of Article 6 of the state of emergency law,[9] according to which, during a state of emergency, the president of the republic may transfer any crime punishable by the penal code or any other law to the military judiciary.

The controversy between the rulings of the Court of Administrative Litigation and the Supreme Administrative Court lay in the meaning of the words "any crime" *(ayyi min al-jara'im)*. The Court of Administrative Litigation interpreted the word crime as the categories of crimes so specified by the legislature. The Supreme Administrative Court and the military courts expanded the interpretation of the word crime to mean individual crimes discretionarily specified by the president, even after the crime had been committed. In response to the request for interpretation, the Supreme Constitutional Court interpreted "any crime" as meaning both a whole category of crimes and an individual and specific one.[10] This interpretation provided momentum for the government to expand the scope for transferring civilians to military courts, as the president was allowed to hand pick individual cases for transfer to military courts.

**Practice**

With the escalation of armed violence by Islamist political groups in the early 1990s and specifically in 1992, civilians started being transferred to military courts. Most of them were related to radical Islamist political movements. In 1995, members of the Muslim Brotherhood started being transferred to such courts even though they were not accused of any violent act or of instigating acts of violence, but rather of undermining the political order and subverting the constitution.

From early November 1992 until November 2000, the authorities referred cases of terrorism and other cases against 1,023 defendants to military courts. These courts handed down 92 death sentences and 644 other verdicts ranging from life imprisonment with hard labor to one year of imprisonment. Although 297 defendants were declared innocent, only a small number of them were set free, and the others were imprisoned again through an administrative decision. The prevailing characteristic of decisions by military courts is the high instance of the death penalty, with those convicted unable to challenge the rulings.

If one had followed the violent events during the 1990s, one would have discovered that the transferal of civilians to military courts did not put an end to violence. On the contrary, it stirred up violence. When violence indicators and military trials are compared, the highest rates of recorded victims occurred after extensive referral to military courts. Moreover, violence indicators went down after the Luxor massacre in November 1997. This reduction in violence indicators was not a result of military trials or the increase in the number of death sentences but rather a direct consequence of security policies, coordination on security matters at home and abroad, a government initiative for ending violence, and other domestic factors related to armed groups.

## Courts of Values

The courts of values *(mahakim al-qiyam)* were established by Law No. 95 of 1980 for the Protection of Values against Shameful Conduct *(Himayat al-qiyam min al-'ayb)*, which forbade criticism of the regime and repressed the president's opponents. Law Decree 141/1981 entrusted the courts of values with considering the resolution of situations deriving from the imposition of sequestration, with the competence to rule on all litigation regarding this matter. In December 2006, the president of the republic announced in his request for constitutional amendments that these courts should disappear with the abrogation of the socialist public prosecutor. In November 2007, however, Law No. 95 of 1980 had not yet been abrogated, and the courts were still working.

## Structure

Through Article 27 of the 1980 law, the courts of values are organized on two levels. At the first level are the summary courts of values *(mahakim al-qiyam al-juz'iya)*, which consist of seven members headed by a vice-president of the Court of Cassation. Three counselors of the Court of Cassation or courts of appeal and three public personalities *(shakhsiyat 'amma)* also sit on the court.

At the second level, the high courts of values *(mahakim al-qiyam al-'ulya)* consist of nine members headed by a vice-president of the Court of Cassation. They include four counselors of the Court of Cassation or courts of appeal and four public personalities. Thus, these courts mix judicial and non-judicial elements.

The court structure is established at the beginning of each judicial year by a decree of the minister of justice with the approval of the Supreme Council of Judicial Bodies (Article 27). The public personalities are chosen from a list compiled by the minister of justice, after approval by the Supreme Council of Judicial Bodies (Article 28). Members are appointed for a two-year, non-renewable term (Article 29) and are irremovable during that period. Any person referred to the courts of values must be provided with a lawyer (Article 36). Prosecution before these courts is done by the socialist public prosecutor. The rulings of the summary courts of values can be appealed before the high courts of values within thirty days of the ruling (Article 39). The rulings of the high courts of values can be challenged before the Court of Cassation (since 1997).

## Competences

Values were defined by Article 2 of the 1980 law as the ethical values set forth by law and by the constitution and aimed at protecting people's rights, religious values, and political, economic, social, and ethical assets. The definition included the protection of Egyptian family authenticity, that is, values, traditions, national unity, and social harmony. Therefore, courts of values were entrusted with a broad scope of competences, including political, economic, social, religious, and ethical aspects, all broadly defined. For instance, violations of moral values included incitement to deny or act in violation of heavenly injunctions, encouraging youth to abandon religious values, lack of loyalty to the fatherland, and publication or spreading of false rumors with evil intent. Such violations were treated as generating a kind of *political* responsibility for their authors. Article 2 was abrogated by Decree Law 221/1994.

According to Article 34 of the 1980 law, courts of values have jurisdiction to decide all cases filed by the socialist public prosecutor. They can impose sequestration according to Law 34/1971, decide on the cases mentioned in Article 2 of Law 53/1972 concerning settlement of sequestration, and decide on litigation regarding compensation of victims of sequestration, according to Law 141/1981 on the settlement of sequestration. The courts used to be empowered to disqualify candidates from parliamentary and local elections or trade union elections and from establishing political parties on the basis of a violation of public morality. This competence also was abolished by Decree Law 221/1994.

### Investigation and Prosecution: The Socialist Public Prosecutor

The socialist public prosecutor *(al-muddaʿi al-ʿamm al-ishtiraki)* was first established by President Sadat in Law No. 34 of 1971 on the Organization of the Sequestration and Security of the People *(bi-shaʾn tanzim fard al-hirasa wa taʾmin salamat al-shaʿb)*. The office's powers were increased by Law No. 95 of 1980 on the Protection of Values against Shameful Conduct. The Law on the Protection of the Internal Front and Social Peace of 1978 also gave the socialist public prosecutor important powers, for instance, in the political field, but this law was abrogated by Decree Law 221/1994. Until the constitutional amendments of March 2007, the position was mentioned in Article 179 of the Egyptian constitution.[11] This is not the case anymore. However, the above-mentioned laws had not been abrogated by June 2008, nor had the position of socialist public prosecutor disappeared.

Article 5 of the 1980 law stipulates that the president of the republic shall propose the name of the socialist public prosecutor to the People's Assembly, which shall accept this proposal by a two-thirds majority. This prosecutor is chosen from among current or former members of judicial bodies, law professors, and attorneys who have exercised these functions for a certain minimum number of years (five, eight, and ten years, respectively) (Article 8). He is responsible before the People's Assembly. The prosecutor's term ends with the legislative term of the People's Assembly or with its dissolution (Article 6). One-tenth of the members of the People's Assembly may request that the prosecutor be relieved of his functions, if the prosecutor has lost the confidence and consideration required for such a position. After a debate in which the socialist public prosecutor would be invited to participate, the Assembly would vote, with the majority of its members present, on the request (Article 6). According to Article 15, the prosecutor must submit an annual report to the president of the republic and the People's Assembly by the end of March. The report describes the tasks, investigations, and procedures the office has undertaken and presents proposals for the protection of the political regime or to amend laws and regulations regarding the protection of national unity and social peace and strengthening the rule of law. The People's Assembly discusses the report, informs the socialist public prosecutor of its remarks, and invites him to express his views during a session convened for this purpose.

According to Article 16 as amended by Decree Law 221/1994, the socialist public prosecutor's competences are those stated in Law 34/1971, as well as in other laws. According to Article 2 of Law No. 34 of 1971 on the Organization of the Sequestration and Security of the People, the prosecutor is in charge of investigating and charging persons responsible for actions that may threaten the internal or external security of the country, the economic interests of the socialist society, the socialist benefits of peasants and workers, as well as investigating and charging persons who have corrupted political life or put national unity in danger. In all these cases, the prosecutor may ask for the properties of the accused to be sequestered. Since the amendment of the 1980 law in 1994, his main powers concern the prosecution of those involved in corruption, drug trafficking, the black market, or financial manipulations. The socialist public prosecutor examines and investigates issues related to citizens' public interest, according to an assignment from the president of the republic or the People's Assembly or a request from the prime minister (Article 17 of Law 95/1980). The prosecutor is vested by Law 34/1971 and Law 95/1980 (Article 18) with wide-ranging powers of investigation and interrogation. He is allowed by Law No. 95 of 1980 on the Protection of Values against Shameful Conduct to prevent individuals from traveling abroad. His office's findings may be referred for trial to the courts of values.

The socialist public prosecutor is one of the serious defects in the judicial system. That system uproots the jurisdictions of both investigation and accusation from the Office of Public Prosecution, in addition to enjoying absolute competences in taking protective measures concerning properties and individuals. Complaints concerning decisions of the socialist public prosecutor cannot be made except before the courts of values, which are composed of judicial and non-judicial members. These exceptional courts deprive citizens of their natural judge.

## Court of Party Affairs

Article 5 of Political Parties Law No. 40 of 1977 *(Qanun bi-nizam al-ahzab al-siyasiya)* established a so-called Court of Party Affairs.[12] People seeking to found a new party must ask for a license from the Committee for Party Affairs (Lajnat Shu'un al-Ahzab al-Siyasiya) (Article 8). This administrative committee is composed of three ministers, three retired judges, and three public personalities chosen by the president of the republic.[13] The committee's decisions may be challenged within thirty days of the decision before the first district of the Supreme Administrative Court, which is headed by the president of the State Council and composed of five judges and the same number of public personalities. The public personalities are chosen by the minister of justice with the approval of the Supreme Council of Judicial Bodies.[14] They must have good reputations, be at least forty years old, and not belong to the legislative authority.

The court rules on the appeal within four months of the date of the submission of the appeal. Its decisions are final and cannot be challenged. It also rules on appeals from decisions taken by the Committee for Party Affairs to freeze a party (Article 17, section 3) or its newspaper. On the request of the committee, the court may decide to dissolve a party for violation of Law 40/1977 on political parties. In such a case the socialist public prosecutor is in charge of investigating the violation.

The mixed structure of the Committee for Party Affairs and the courts of values is considered a violation of the principle of separation of powers, which guarantees the independence of the judiciary. The judiciary as an authority and judges as individuals should have the sole authority to decide cases submitted to courts, whatever the case.

## Conclusion

Even if it were acceptable for the Egyptian regime to demand exceptional procedures such as arrests and preemptive measures against violence, little justification can be given for removing jurisdiction from natural judges and courts of the judiciary and for referring cases to exceptional courts that lack any kind of fair trial standards. Many characteristics qualify a judge to be a natural judge, including impartiality, independence, immunity, and judicial qualifications. Exceptional courts and their members lack most or all of these minimum standards and guarantees.

# 11

# Judges and Acts of Sovereignty

*Mohamed Maher Abouelenen*

Judges are vested with broad powers vis-à-vis the legal provisions they have to apply. They have to give meaning to these rules and may themselves have to infer a legal rule when current laws are silent regarding a legal dispute put before them. This creative role played by judges is even more important when public bodies are involved, as with cases before administrative and constitutional judges. Rulings adopted in this field influence the political, economic, and legal life of the society to a great extent, for almost all basic rules in administrative law are derived from decisions of the administrative judiciary. The constitutional judiciary is also a source of law.

The legislature has intervened to withdraw some kinds of cases from judicial control by designating them as involving political acts *(a'mal siyasiya)* or acts of sovereignty *(a'mal al-siyada)*. These concepts mean that certain actions are not subject to judicial control not only because it would be difficult for the judiciary to deal with such issues but also in order to allow the executive authority to exercise a broader discretionary power. Despite the wide range of judicial control over all activities exercised by the modern state, many of the practices of the executive authority in Egypt are not included in the jurisdiction of the judiciary. Such actions are known as 'acts of the state' in England and as 'acts of the government' in France. In Egypt, they are known as 'acts of sovereignty' or 'political acts.' The wider the scope of such issues, the broader the discretionary power of the executive authority becomes, until it could eventually jeopardize human rights and freedoms and even the public interest. Despite the continuing work of legal scholars against this theory, it still exists.

It has been impossible for the legislature in Egypt and in most other countries to draw a demarcation line between actions of the executive authority that are subject to judicial control and actions outside such control. Therefore, the nature and scope of acts of sovereignty can be known only through an analysis of court rulings dealing with such issues. The position of administrative and constitutional judges on this notion of acts of sovereignty in Egyptian history will be presented in this study, followed by concrete examples of its implementation.

## Acts of Sovereignty in Egyptian History

Before the 1949 judicial reform that led to the abrogation of the mixed courts, a difference had occurred between the mixed and the national jurisdictions in the development of the theory of acts of sovereignty.

### Before the Mixed Courts

The theory of acts of sovereignty in the mixed courts went through three phases. The first phase started in 1875, when no provision was stipulated in the regulations of the mixed courts. Then, in 1900, Article 11 of the regulations was amended to provide that the mixed courts were not entitled to adjudicate cases involving the ownership of public property. They also were not entitled to judge acts of sovereignty or actions undertaken by the government to enforce laws and administrative regulations.

On the occasion of the abrogation of the foreign capitulations at the Montreux Conference on 8 May 1937, the Egyptian government submitted a draft judicial regulation to replace the old mixed courts regulations. This became Law No. 49 of 1937, of which Article 43 provided for the immunization of acts of sovereignty and stipulated that such actions do not fall within the jurisdiction of the mixed courts, either directly or indirectly. In practice, the mixed courts always had tried to limit the scope of application of the concept of acts of sovereignty in order to preserve foreigners' rights.

### Before the National Courts

The 1883 Regulations of the National Courts did not provide for acts of sovereignty; therefore, such actions were not immunized before the national courts. Law No. 90 of 1937 amended Article 15 of the 1883 regulations to provide in Article 15, paragraph 10, for the immunization of acts of sovereignty: "National courts are not entitled to rule, directly or indirectly, on acts of sovereignty." This amendment was introduced on the occasion of the cancellation of the foreign capitulations. As mentioned above, Article 43 of the mixed courts regulations also was amended, thus each would be consistent with the other. After the dissolution of the mixed courts, Judiciary Law No. 147 of 1949 was promulgated to regulate and specify the jurisdiction of the various degrees of the national courts. Article 18 of that law provided that courts should not consider acts of sovereignty, either directly or indirectly.[1]

The state's attorneys in the Government Cases Administration (Idarat Qadaya al-Hukuma) have used the concept of acts of sovereignty excessively. The position adopted by the national courts differs from that developed in the mixed courts. Article 17 of the 1972 Law on Judicial Authority provides that courts are not entitled to examine, either directly or indirectly, acts of sovereignty.

## Before the State Council

Immunity of acts of sovereignty was provided for by the first law (Law 112/1946) on the State Council, which established the council. Article 6 of that law stipulated that the following claims are unacceptable: claims filed regarding decisions related to actions regulating the relations between the government and the two parliamentary assemblies, domestic and foreign state security measures, political relations or military actions, and all other claims related to acts of sovereignty.

Article 7 of Law 9/1949 continued in the same vein regarding acts of sovereignty. Article 12 of Law 165/1955 on the reorganization of the State Council provided that the council, as an administrative judicial authority, is not competent to rule on claims related to acts of sovereignty. Law 55/1959 on the State Council used the same wording before being amended in 1963 to stipulate that the decisions of the president of the republic to pension off or dismiss public servants are acts of sovereignty, although they are purely administrative decisions and thus free from any political considerations. A number of examples of such acts were specified in Article 6 of Law 112/1946 and Article 7 of Law 9/1949, but in Law 165/1955, the legislature remained silent about those examples. Article 11 of Law 47/1972 on the State Council provided that the council courts are not competent to rule on claims related to acts of sovereignty.

## Acts of Sovereignty before Egyptian Courts
I will analyze the decisions of the State Council on acts of sovereignty before moving on to the rulings of the Supreme Constitutional Court.

### The Administrative Judiciary and Acts of Sovereignty
### Acts of Sovereignty under Previous Laws

In a 1947 decision, the Court of Administrative Litigation considered acts of sovereignty to be those exercised by the government on the basis of its supreme authority. The court decided that Article 6 of the State Council law provided a number of examples.[2] In 1948, the court was of the view that most acts of sovereignty relate to the high politics of the state.[3] It also decided that measures related to internal and external state security matters, considered acts of sovereignty by Article 6 of the State Council law and consequently prohibited to the Administrative Court, were procedures taken by the government by virtue of its supreme authority to preserve security.[4]

In a 1951 decision, the court continued to elaborate, stating that acts of sovereignty are those acts exercised by the government in its capacity as a ruling authority, as opposed to an administrative authority. Such acts are characterized by an objective standard, where reference is made to the nature of the actions themselves rather than to the circumstances surrounding them.[5] In a significant ruling, the court decided that the demarcation line between acts of sovereignty and administrative acts, be they administrative orders or concrete actions, is based on the nature of the action. However, it is impossible to give a specific definition or draw a precise list of such acts, as an act considered administrative at one time could, under certain political circumstances, become an act of state sovereignty. Likewise, an action considered an act of sovereignty could, under other circumstances, become an ordinary administrative act.[6] According to the Supreme Administrative Court, when the legislature has excluded some particular acts from judicial control, it is up to the judge to determine the nature of the acts brought before him or her.[7]

For example, decisions by the government to propose laws and regulations and to refer them to the Chamber of Deputies should be considered acts of sovereignty.[8] Acts of sovereignty could be acts organizing the relations between the government and the two parliamentary councils, or political relations with foreign countries. They also could be measures taken to defend public security against internal disorder or to secure the state against foreign enemies, such as the announcement of martial law, a state of war, or issues related to military actions.[9]

Measures viewed as necessary by revolution leaders and by the existing regime to protect the state come under acts of sovereignty. The decision to dispense with a number of officers who do not conform to revolution principles should thus be deemed an act of sovereignty.[10] This decision was confirmed in another ruling, according to which, since the revolution succeeded and became the legitimate authority in the country, the regime is allowed to take measures necessary to secure its safety, proceed with the achievement of its goals, and prevent whoever tries to stop the implementation of these goals from doing so. Accordingly, the decision of the chairperson of the Supreme Revolutionary Council to pension off a number of officers is a measure taken to protect the revolution and the regime that sustains it and to help it achieve its goals. Therefore, such a decision does not fall within the jurisdiction of the State Council because it is an act of sovereignty.[11]

The Supreme Administrative Court decided that Law 31/1963, which amended the law on the State Council to include the decisions adopted by the president to pension off or dismiss certain public servants by ways other than disciplinary measures, was adopted in conformity with the mandate of the legislative power. The legislature could decide to immunize certain acts from judicial control because the constitution gives it competence to regulate judicial bodies and to specify their jurisdiction.[12]

On the contrary, decisions to censor,[13] suspend, or suppress a newspaper were considered by the Court of Administrative Litigation to be administrative acts, not acts of sovereignty.[14] Decisions and decrees issued by the government to enforce laws and regulations also were not considered acts of sovereignty. The courts decided that these acts fell within the scope of ordinary governmental work and were not so significant that they should be on equal footing with acts of high politics. The administrative decree issued for the enforcement of a law or regulation, therefore, had nothing to do with the acts of sovereignty.[15] This was the case even for individual decisions taken in application of martial law or a decision to withdraw a weapons license.[16]

### Acts under Law No. 47 on the State Council

According to the Supreme Administrative Court, certain acts by their nature are acts of sovereignty and thus fall outside court jurisdiction, including relations between states, relations between the executive and legislative authorities, and acts of war. However, when it comes to relations between the state and its nationals under ordinary circumstances, acts of sovereignty are limited to higher measures taken to defend the state or its security.[17]

The Court of Administrative Litigation decided that the presidential decision to appoint the prime minister and other ministers is issued by the president in his capacity as state president, that is, in his capacity as the ruling authority rather than as an administrative authority. Therefore, it is an act of sovereignty and any appeal filed against it for cancellation or compensation does not fall within the jurisdiction of the court.[18] The same applies to the appointment of governors.[19] The decision to appoint or not appoint a vice-president also is considered by the court to be an act of sovereignty.[20]

The president's decision to conclude the Camp David peace agreement was ruled an act of sovereignty by the court.[21] The president's decision to invite electors to a referendum on decisions taken pursuant to Article 74 of the constitution was considered a political decision because its aim was the people's participation in and evaluation of the decisions of the president.[22] Therefore, it was an act of sovereignty.[23]

The court also decided that the decision to freeze the assets of the Arab League's Organization for Development and Agriculture was an act of sovereignty because the state took this decision within the scope of its political responsibility, under conditions of necessity, and to secure the country's economy. This decision was taken within the framework of the government's political relations with the Arab League as an international organization.[24]

The court also decided that the decision of the president to dissolve the People's Assembly and to invite electors to elect new parliamentary members was issued by the president in his capacity as the ruling authority. It was deemed an act of sovereignty not subject to judicial control.

The Supreme Administrative Court considered the declaration of the state of emergency an act of sovereignty exercised by the government in its capacity as the ruling authority and not an administrative authority. It was deemed one of the most important procedural measures taken in defense of security, public order, and the existence of the state. However, the measures taken by the authority in charge of the martial law regime, in execution of that regime, whether they are measures affecting individuals or organizations, should not be excluded from judicial control, as they are administrative decisions and thus subject to the jurisdiction of the State Council.[25]

The Supreme Administrative Court declared that the procedures followed to promulgate or amend the constitution are issues that go beyond the jurisdiction of the administrative judiciary. Accordingly, the court decided that the State Council is not competent to examine the decision of proclamation of the results of a constitutional referendum, as this is the final procedure of the amendment process.[26]

The president's decision to call for elections is an act of sovereignty that is not subject to judicial control because this decision is related to the empowerment of the sovereign people to choose its representatives and deals with relations between the People's Assembly and the government.[27]

On the other side, the president's decisions to transfer some journalists and a number of teachers, cancel the presidential decision that appointed Pope Shenouda,[28] dissolve some associations, hold a number of people in custody, cancel the licenses of certain newspapers and printed items, and hold the property of certain authorities, organizations, and groups in custody were deemed administrative decisions, even though the president adopted them on the basis of Article 74 of the constitution and even though they were politically motivated.[29]

One may wonder whether the provision that excludes claims related to acts of sovereignty from the competence of the State Council can be justified constitutionally. One may wonder the same about the declaration that immunity of acts of sovereignty is constitutional in accordance with the provisions of the Egyptian constitution, in particular Article 68, according to which "the right to litigation is inalienable for all, and every citizen has the right to refer to his competent judge. The State shall guarantee the accessibility of the judicial organs to litigants and a rapid hearing of cases." This article also says that any provision in the law stipulating the immunity of any act or administrative decision from the control of the judiciary shall be prohibited.

The constitutional prohibition against the immunization of any act or decision from judicial control would seem to put an end to anti-litigation laws. Article 12 of the State Council law allows the legislature, however, to impute the characteristics of an act of sovereignty to certain administrative measures. In this case, reference could be made to Article 68 of the constitution in order to put an end to this unconstitutional legislative provision, which immunized administrative decisions. Accordingly, Article 12 of the State Council law should be repealed. The constitutional provision is explicit as regards the impermissibility of immunizing acts of sovereignty against the control of the judiciary.

Moreover, how can the decision to dissolve the People's Assembly be considered an act of sovereignty, when such a decision has caused damage to the members of the dissolved parliament? How could it be imagined that the president's decision to appoint a minister who lacks credentials is an act of sovereignty? Public officers need to fulfill specific conditions, and an administrative court should verify the satisfaction of these conditions. Even when it comes to international relations, the judiciary could be involved in case gross damage is caused by acts of the executive authority in its handling of foreign relations.

## The Constitutional Court and Acts of Sovereignty

The 1969 Supreme Court of Egypt excluded acts of sovereignty and political acts from its field of competence. The 1979 Supreme Constitutional Court adopted the same approach before redirecting its decisions toward an implicit abandonment of this concept.

### The Supreme Court

Supreme Court Law 81/1969 did not contain any provision excluding acts of sovereignty from the scope of its control, as was the case with Law 46/1972 on the judicial authority and Law 47/1972 on the State Council.

The Supreme Court decided very early, however, to apply a theory of acts of sovereignty to exclude some acts from its jurisdiction. The court attempted to find a legal basis to support this position. Having examined administrative law jurisprudence, the court found a theory of acts of sovereignty already developed and decided to apply it to specify the scope of constitutional judicial control. According to the Supreme Court, this had become an established rule in the judicial systems of civilized countries and an established judicial principle. The court declared that it should abide by the theory and that the acts specified in the theory should be excluded from the Supreme Court's jurisdiction without the need for a further provision.[30]

In its first constitutional case, heard on 6 November 1971, the court ruled that final administrative decisions issued by the executive authority are normally subject to the control of the judiciary, following the principles of legitimacy and rule of law. Decisions relating to the internal and external sovereignty of the state, however, constitute an exception to this principle, as, by nature, such decisions could not be the subject of a judicial claim. Therefore, such cases fall outside the competence of the judiciary. The court's theory of acts of sovereignty is based on the principle that the executive authority performs two jobs in its capacity as the ruling authority and an administrative authority. The acts performed by the executive authority as the ruling authority *(sultat al-hukm)* are viewed as acts of sovereignty, whereas acts it performs as an administrative authority are administrative in nature. The criterion adopted for specifying the legal nature of any act performed by the executive authority, to determine whether such an act is an act of sovereignty or an administrative act, is the nature of the act itself. Therefore, when controlling the constitutionality of legislation, the court is not bound to abide by the description given by the legislature of the government's acts, whenever such acts are by nature contrary to such description.[31]

In another ruling, the Supreme Court viewed political acts as one form of the acts of sovereignty. The court also asserted that excluding political acts from the scope of constitutional control was based on the considerations that had excluded acts of sovereignty from the jurisdiction of both the ordinary and the administrative judiciary. This was explicitly expressed by the court as follows:

> The theory of acts of sovereignty has been established in our judicial system, as it is provided for by the successive laws regulating both the ordinary and the administrative judiciary, the latest of which is the Judicial Authority Law 46/1972 and the State Council Law 47/1972. Article 17 of the judicial authority law has excluded acts of sovereignty from the jurisdiction of the courts. Article 11 of the State Council Law has also excluded the same acts from the jurisdiction of the Council. This is attributed to the fact that acts of sovereignty are related to the internal and external sovereignty of the state and could not, by nature, constitute a subject for a judicial claim. Accordingly, such acts fall outside of court jurisdiction. The considerations requiring that judicial control over such acts be diminished have widely resonated in the constitutional judiciary in states that have adopted the system of control over the constitutionality of laws, as political issues (al-masa'il al-siyasiya) have been totally excluded from the scope of control, which is one form of act of sovereignty not subject to the control of the judiciary in the Egyptian system.[32]

The "states that have adopted the system of control over the constitutionality of laws" most probably means the United States. In fact, the abstention by the Supreme Court from controlling political acts is not based on legal concepts but rather on the court's aspiration to emulate the U.S. Supreme Court and adopt that court's policy of self-restriction.

How can a theory elaborated for the control of administrative acts be applied to the control of the constitutionality of laws and regulations, if such control, by nature, only deals with the verification of the compliance by laws and regulations with constitutional provisions? I do not agree with the Egyptian Supreme Court's approach to the exclusion of political acts from the scope of its control or its dependence on the theory of acts of sovereignty, as there is an essential difference between the constitutional control exercised by the constitutional judiciary and the control of legitimacy exercised by the administrative courts. The constitutional control aims at verifying how far the law complies with the constitution. The law, whose constitutionality is controlled by the court, is a political act by nature, laid down by a political body, as well as an expression of a number of political concepts. Therefore, the control of constitutionality inevitably will lead the constitutional judge to transcend the limits of judicial work strictly speaking and become involved in the political field. By contrast, the control of legitimacy in the Administrative Court is where the competence of the administrative official is limited to assessing the reality of the situation, in the light of which legal acts are determined.

Certainly, the control of constitutionality has an undeniable legal dimension, which means that the original duty of the judge is to verify the constitutionality of the law required to be applied to the dispute filed before him. If the judge discovers that the decision contradicts the constitution, his natural duty is to apply the constitutional provision, the higher law, and to ignore the legislative provision.

This legal aspect of the control of constitutionality, notwithstanding what is said about it, does not obscure the political aspect. The control of constitutionality could not be a purely legal control. It is, rather, legal and political control together and for a simple reason, namely that the material being controlled is itself political by nature because it has to do with the actions of politicians who regulate state affairs, acting in the role of legislators. If constitutional control of legislation is considered a political act, this could render constitutional control meaningless and valueless, as no legislative act would then be subject to judicial control.

I suggest that the political nature of legislation does not require, by way of logical necessity, the exclusion of political matters from the scope of judicial control. It rather requires that constitutional adjudication cover all legislative acts, notwithstanding their nature. It is the control by a constitutional judiciary that is always political in nature.

## Approach Adopted by the Supreme Constitutional Court

The 1979 Law on the Supreme Constitutional Court does not contain any provision excluding acts of sovereignty or political acts from the scope of its control. The court has followed, in a number of its rulings, the decisions of the Supreme Court regarding the exclusion of political acts from the scope of its control. The court has decided that it is the body competent to determine whether the issues regulated by the appealed provisions are political and thus fall outside its jurisdiction. It soon abandoned the application of this concept in practice, however.

In the first couple of years after its establishment, the court was keen to abide by the policy of the Supreme Court to view political acts as a form of act of sovereignty, excluded from the jurisdiction of the Constitutional Court, based on the same considerations on which such acts were excluded from the jurisdiction of both the administrative and the ordinary courts.[33]

For instance, the court stated in 1984 that judicial review of the constitutionality of laws is based on the principle of legality and on the rule of law as laid down by the constitution. However, this principle is limited by the rule established in jurisprudence to exclude acts of sovereignty from the field of judicial control, as the nature of such acts could not constitute a subject of a judicial case. The court added that, in France, the theory of acts of sovereignty was originally judicial and arose before the administrative court. In Egypt, however, the basis for the theory was legislative and goes back to the beginning of the modern judicial system, which explicitly established it in the text of successive legislative acts regulating the judiciary and the State Council. The most recent of these acts are the 1972 Law on Judicial Authority and the State Council Law 47/1972, which exclude acts of sovereignty from the jurisdiction of the ordinary and the administrative judiciary. According to the Supreme Constitutional Court, the exclusion of acts of sovereignty from court jurisdiction is due to political considerations that require this exclusion because of the nature of the acts and their close relationship to the political system of the state and its internal and external sovereignty.

Ultimately, this theory aims to preserve the state's internal stability, defend its sovereignty abroad, and protect its interests. In its 1984 rulings, the court noted that these considerations have resonated before constitutional courts in states that have adopted systems of control over the constitutionality of laws, especially when it comes to political issues that fall within the vital and natural field of the theory of acts of sovereignty and their exclusion from the scope of such control.[34]

The court made a distinction between acts of sovereignty and other acts subject to its control, stating that whether acts are acts of sovereignty depends on the nature of the acts, namely that they emanate from the high policy of the state, with its higher authority, and internal and external sovereignty. This high policy shall target the interests of the political group in its entirety, while respecting the rights guaranteed by the constitution, regulating the group's foreign relations, securing its integrity within and outside the state, and defending the state's territories against external aggression. The qualification depends exclusively on the discretionary authority of the judiciary.

The Supreme Constitutional Court did not maintain this approach for long, redirecting itself implicitly toward abandoning the concept of acts of sovereignty. The court's approach was surrounded by a great deal of caution, as the court found itself facing a theory that had become established in the Egyptian judicial system before both the ordinary and the administrative courts. Accordingly, it did not abandon so established a theory all at once.

The Supreme Constitutional Court started by excluding from the concept of acts of sovereignty legal provisions the content of which contradicted the restrictions and regulations laid down by the constitution. The court thus seemed to specify the framework of the concept of acts of sovereignty by way of exclusion. In other words, it specified acts that are not acts of sovereignty. The court did not deal with acts that do fall within the scope of the concept and that are considered among its contents and elements.[35] Consequently, the court had the upper hand regarding the determination of acts of sovereignty precluded from its jurisdiction. It depended on the criterion of 'nature of the act' in order to have as much flexibility as it required.

The Supreme Constitutional Court managed to reach a compromise with the established theory of acts of sovereignty in the Egyptian judicial system by maintaining it theoretically but consistently not applying it in its decisions. The court dismissed challenges to its jurisdiction that were based on arguments of acts of sovereignty. The court did not explicitly dismiss the concept, but it divested it of all practical value by making it dependent on the nature of the act itself rather than on conformity with the overarching definition hitherto used.

An Algerian soldier accidentally killed an Egyptian in Cairo while driving a car owned by the Algerian forces based on Egyptian territory during the 1973 October War. These forces were in Egypt in accordance with a joint defense convention among Arab states. The heirs of the deceased filed a claim for damages before the South Cairo Court against the minister of defense, requesting LE20,000 for the material and moral damages they suffered, based on the presumption that the Algerian soldier was affiliated to the Egyptian ministry of defense. The South Cairo Court found that according to Article 5 of the Arab Armies Organization Convention, members of the allied forces are subject to the absolute jurisdiction of their national courts regarding crimes committed by them on the territory of the host country, and that they are not subject to the jurisdiction of the ordinary judiciary or any other procedures in the host country. The convention also provided that disputes arising between them and others concerning contractual obligations or damages sustained by persons or property in general would be considered by a panel to be constituted by the secretary-general of the Arab League.

The court decided that the convention prevented the Egyptian judiciary from considering all disputes between the allied forces and Egyptian citizens, and thus deprived the family of litigation in Egypt and of the right to resort to their natural judge, as provided by Article 68 of the constitution. The case was referred to the Supreme Constitutional Court so that it could decide on the constitutionality of the convention, as this was deemed necessary for a ruling on the case.[36] The court decided its lack of competence to consider the case, as the challenged convention had been concluded within the framework of the Arab League to regulate the joint defense process among its members after the establishment of a unified Arab leadership for their military forces. Egypt had ratified the convention with the aim of preserving the state's stability and in response to the requirements of maintaining its integrity and its external security. The court said that the case was an issue related to the state's international relations and addressed by the high policy of the state. The court stated that the convention therefore came under acts of sovereignty doctrine, and should not be subject to judicial control.[37]

In 1990, the Constitutional Court declared it was not competent to consider a challenge to presidential Decree Law 404/1990, which called for a referendum on the dissolution of the People's Assembly, on the grounds that the appealed decree was a political act not subject to the court's control.[38]

According to the court, the exclusion of acts of sovereignty from the jurisdiction of the judiciary is due to political considerations that require their exclusion from judicial control. The purpose of the exclusion is to preserve the state's internal stability, defend its sovereignty abroad, and preserve its interests. The exclusion of acts of sovereignty and political acts from the jurisdiction of the courts is a form of implementation of the principle of separation of powers, which requires striking a balance between the legislative, executive, and judicial authorities so that each assumes the powers vested to it by the constitution, within stipulated limits, without infringing on the powers of the other.

Pursuant to established court rulings, the criterion for determining the legal qualification of any act performed by the executive authority as an act of sovereignty is the nature of the act itself rather than the description attributed thereto, whenever its nature contradicts such description. The court stated that because Decree Law 404/1990 was issued by the president of the republic to call for a referendum to dissolve the People's Assembly by conducting a poll among the electors, the matter was related to the most crucial issues connected with relations between the executive and legislative authorities. The court concluded that the decree was one of the most prominent matters related to the exercise of the ruling authority and thus an act of sovereignty whose political responsibility is borne totally by the executive authority, without any comment on the part of judiciary.[39]

Except for this 1990 ruling, which by itself did not prove that the court had changed its established opinion, the Supreme Constitutional Court quickly returned to the track it followed in the 1980s, refusing to consider acts challenged as political acts.

On 25 June 1983, the court ruled that it had jurisdiction to consider an appeal filed against the constitutionality of Decree Law 104/1964, which stipulated the devolution of the ownership of agricultural land to the state, without compensation, pursuant to the provisions of Decree Law 178/1952 on agricultural reform and their amendment by Decree

Law 127/1961. The court stated that the decree did not address a political act or an act of sovereignty that would exempt it from the scope of constitutional control. The 1964 legislation addressed the question of private property, which was a right duly cared for by the constitution, which provided for its protection and specified the cases in which its expropriation may be compulsory. The constitution also laid down the restrictions and regulations necessary for protecting private property, which the legislative authority should abide by. Otherwise, the legislature would be operating in contravention of the provisions of the constitution. Therefore, the decree law did not address political issues falling outside constitutional control. Ultimately, the argument presented on the court's incompetence to consider the case was ruled to have no basis and was rejected.[40]

The court continued in this vein in other cases. For instance, in 1986, it dismissed the argument of lack of jurisdiction to consider an appeal filed against the constitutionality of Article 4 of Law 33/1978 on the Protection of the Internal Front and Social Peace. The defense contended that the law had been promulgated on the basis of a referendum conducted in conformity with Article 152 of the constitution[41] with the aim of securing the integrity of the state and peaceful conditions for its political regime and of realizing the state's political interest in "the protection of the internal front and social peace." For this reason, the defense argued, the law had to be considered political in nature and thus did not fall within the scope of constitutional control over laws and regulations.

The Supreme Constitutional Court did not agree with the defense and dismissed the argument. According to the court, Article 152 of the constitution allows the president of the republic to submit matters he deems important and relevant to the national interest to the people so that the executive can know their opinion. The court said that such a referendum should not be taken as a pretext to contravene the provisions of the constitution. Furthermore, the public's agreement on specific principles proposed for referendum does not raise such principles to the level of constitutional provisions that may not be amended except by virtue of special procedures provided for in Article 189 of the constitution. Popular agreements do not rectify the defect of unconstitutionality that legal provisions thus enacted may suffer. Such provisions will, on the contrary, maintain their nature as legislative acts that do not reach the level of the constitution, and thus should be consistent with its provisions. The appealed legislative provision had been issued in relation to the right of a category of citizens to exercise its political rights as guaranteed by the constitution. Such rights should be maintained by the legislative authority; otherwise, it would be violating the constitution. Consequently, the court concluded that the provision had not addressed political issues not subject to constitutional control and that the argument that the court lacked competence to hear the case was groundless.[42]

This ruling was a turning point in the history of the Egyptian Constitutional Court. It also was an indication of the court's having abandoned its self-restriction policy. The ruling shows the court's expansion of the scope of its control to cover laws promulgated by way of referendum, even though they could have been considered political by nature and thus escaped constitutional control. In France, for instance, the Constitutional Council has considered laws adopted by referendum acts of government and thus precluded from its competence.

The Supreme Constitutional Court maintained its positive policy of extending its control to cover political acts in a number of cases. In a ruling in 1987, the court dismissed the argument of non-jurisdiction to consider a challenge to the constitutionality of Law 138/1972 on the People's Assembly, as amended by Law 114/1983. Likewise, it ruled that paragraph 5 of Article 24 of Law 73/1956 on the Exercise of Political Rights, as amended by Law 46/1984, which converted the individual election system into a list system, was justiciable as a constitutional issue.

The court refused to consider the amendments included in these laws political issues that do not fall under its control. The appealed legislation had been issued in relation to a citizen's right to be a candidate in parliamentary elections, which is a right provided in the constitution. The legislative authority may not impair this right: to do so would be a breach of the constitution. The court concluded that the law did not address political matters, as claimed by the government, and that the claim of the court's lack of competence in the matter was groundless.[43]

The positive policy adopted by the Supreme Constitutional Court becomes even clearer on the issue of division of electoral districts. The US Supreme Court has refrained from extending its control to electoral districts, claiming that the issue of division is political by nature and thus not subject to judicial control. The Egyptian Supreme Constitutional Court embraced the perspective of the French Constitutional Council, which placed legislation on the division of electoral circuits under its control.

In a 1990 ruling, the Supreme Constitutional Court dismissed the argument of non-jurisdiction to consider a case related to this issue. The legislative provisions challenged were Article 3, section 1, and Article 5 (bis) of Law 38/1972 on the People's Assembly, as amended by Law 188/1986. They concern, *inter alia*, the division of electoral constituencies, their number and scope, and the number of deputies to be elected from each. The constitution does not specify the electoral constituencies into which the state is divided, nor does it stipulate restrictions or limits on the determination of the number of constituencies or the number of representatives in each constituency.

According to the government, the absence of these provisions in the constitution means that the matter was left to the legislative authority to determine according to its discretionary powers. Therefore, it argued, the Supreme Constitutional Court is not entitled to comment on the matter, as all such issues are political and excluded from the jurisdiction of the court. The court may not compel the legislature to specify the number of electoral constituencies or to divide them in a specific way.

The court did not adopt the government's view and dismissed the argument on the basis that Law 188/1986 was promulgated in relation to the right to nomination for parliamentary membership, which is a political right secured by the constitution. The court stated that the legislative authority may not impair this right, as it would violate the constitution. Accordingly, the two challenged articles did not address political issues that fall outside the scope of constitutional control, as claimed by the government. The government's argument was deemed groundless and dismissed.[44]

In a 1993 case, the court decided to dismiss the argument of lack of competence when it was asked to consider a challenge to an international convention. International conventions generally are viewed as a perfect field for applying the theory of acts of sovereignty or political acts, as they fall within the scope of international relations and concern surrounding political considerations that have to do with the state's sovereignty and national interests.[45]

This 1993 ruling is the latest one in which the court has dealt with acts of sovereignty. Thus, it can safely be said that the court has excluded from its judicial policy the concept of political acts as a basis for self-restriction of jurisdiction.

The theory of political acts in the rulings of the Supreme Constitutional Court has often been confused with the theory of acts of sovereignty, to the extent that the two theories are mixed and the second is considered the origin of the first. The Supreme Constitutional Court appears to have refrained from applying either theory. Except in a few exceptional cases at the beginning of its history and one case in 1990, the court has reinstated the true assessment of the theory of political acts, separating the theory of acts of sovereignty, which originally was applied to legislative acts, from the theory of political acts as legislative enactments, which are considered the natural field of application of the legislative authority.

The theory of political acts, when used to restrict the jurisdiction of the Supreme Constitutional Court, is applied in the field of international relations and conventions more than in the internal field because the former is related to the state's political considerations, sovereignty, and supreme interests. It is absolutely untrue, however, that all international conventions, whatever their subject, are acts of sovereignty.

## Conclusion

The theories of acts of sovereignty and of political acts both exclude these acts from the jurisdiction of the judiciary. While the Supreme Constitutional Court lacks legal grounds to exclude political acts from its judicial review, this is not the case with the ordinary and administrative courts, where the notion of acts of sovereignty is legislatively grounded.

The relationship between certain acts and the public interest alone should not suffice for them to be considered political acts. The concept should be restricted within narrow limits. The theories should not allow abuse in the use of authority, nor any overstepping of the limits laid down by the constitution for its exercise. The theory of political acts also should not be mixed up with the theory of exceptional circumstances faced by the state, which vests the state with the power to take measures of a special nature.

The notions of acts of sovereignty and of political acts are unacceptable in the modern legislative realm if they are used to contradict the basic constitutional rules that prevent immunization of administrative decisions or other actions against judicial control. This usage was the norm during the pre-1971 constitution period in Egypt. When the constitution was promulgated, however, the legislature began working toward repealing provisions prohibiting judicial recourse in various laws and codes.

# 12

# The Government's Non-execution of Judicial Decisions

*Negad Mohamed El-Borai*

Judicial rulings are the final outcome of legal proceedings and express the decision taken by a court on the litigation referred to it. Therefore, they should be respected and executed with full transparency and impartiality. Judgments also should be final and binding on all governmental bodies. They are made to be respected and put into practice by individuals and governmental bodies alike. Since individuals are obliged by their government to enforce these judgments, the government also should be bound by all judgments, even those adopted against it. It thus not only sets an example for its citizens but also acts as an honest litigant concerned with imparting justice and conferring rights on those who deserve them. The government should not take a judicial judgment as against it personally but rather as delivered by an independent and fair judiciary acting in accordance with the principle of legality. If judicial rulings were respected by all, they would help create a safer and more secure society.

Egypt, however, has seen an increase in the phenomenon of non-execution of judicial decisions, particularly since the 1980s. The origin of this phenomenon was the creation of the State Council in 1946. The council was granted the legal capacity to void administrative decisions that violated legislative provisions or had been adopted following an abuse of power. Prior to that time, the executive authority had been accustomed to adopting decisions that could not be nullified by the judiciary.

Non-execution of judicial rulings is a sign of diminished respect for the judiciary by the executive authority. Egyptian citizens have come to believe that respect for their rights requires gaining the consent of the executive authority and that it is useless to try through legal means to compel that authority to enforce judicial decisions. Therefore, the society is swarming with corruption and bribery.

Governmental bodies can be held liable for non-execution of judicial rulings because they hold the instruments of execution. In criminal cases, only the state is vested with the power of executing judgments. In civil and administrative cases, the state is a party to the litigation and should execute the decision, even if it is against one of its bodies. Execution of such decisions by the state is the ultimate test of the extent to which the government is law abiding and responsible.

The state might refrain from executing judicial rulings, whether for the personal motives of its officials or for political motives, claiming that it thereby ensures the nation's safety or preserves public order and the public interest. The state has delayed executing or refused to execute many criminal, administrative, and even civil judgments, whether directly or surreptitiously. The various pretexts it uses for doing so may not have any justification in fact or in law, or it may not actually violate the principle of *res judicata*. The reasons announced by the administration also may not be its true motives.

I will present different forms of non-execution of judicial decisions before giving some examples and considering the legal effects of the practice.

## Different Forms of Non-execution
Non-execution of judicial decisions takes different forms according to the effects of that practice and the reasons, declared or undeclared, behind it.

### The Different Effects of Non-execution of Judicial Decisions
Recourse by the administration to different means of abstention from execution of judicial rulings varies according to the effects execution would have on the administration. If the effects would be serious, abstention is blatant; otherwise, it may take the form of negligence in the execution or of incomplete execution.

### Negligence in Execution
The administration uses the tool of negligence, for instance, when the amount of damages set by the judiciary exceeds what it is ready to pay. In that case, the litigant, who already has waited a long time for a judicial

ruling, will be compelled to accept the administration's offer, even though his or her rights are not fully realized, for fear of receiving no indemnity at all or waiting endlessly for his or her rights to be acknowledged. Hence, the executive authority relies on the claimant's frustration. Although this tool may seem a lesser act of abstention than blatant refusal, the harm incurred is by no means less important for the claimant.

### Bad or Incomplete Execution

The administration also resorts to bad or incomplete execution of judicial rulings. For instance, if the State Council invalidates a decision of the president of a university not to accept or to transfer some students, the university may implement that decision only starting the following year. Another example involves recission by the State Council of a governor's decision to authorize a citizen to exploit a piece of agricultural land; the administration circumvents the decision by appropriating the land in the interest of the same citizen. It also may arrest a foreigner and then deport him after the judiciary has nullified the arrest order. That way, the administration manages to have its original decision implemented in its original form or in a different way.

The administration also resorts to this tool in cases dealing with public servants. In this regard, however, the Supreme Administrative Court has stated:

> If a final binding ruling overturns an appealed decision, the appealed decision should be repealed and all its effects erased from the date of the decision on appeal and for the duration established by the ruling. If the overturned decision was a dismissal, then the claimant should be reintegrated in his previous job with the same salary and level, as if no dismissal decision had ever been made .... Reintegrating the dismissed person in a lower post with a lower salary is not a fully lawful execution of the decision, but an incomplete one.

The court added that it should be considered "a concealed disciplinary punishment."[1]

### Blatant Refusal

Blatant refusal of execution occurs more when rulings overturn decisions than in cases or rulings that allocate compensation. For instance, the Court of Administrative Litigation[2] decided to stop the execution of an administrative decision to prohibit individuals from commemorating Mustafa al-Nahas' death.[3] After the rejection of all requests for a stay of execution *(ishkal)* (see page 207 for the meaning of this procedure) raised by the government before competent and non-competent courts, a bailiff went on 27 November 1980, to Cairo's Chief of Security to execute the decision. The latter abstained from execution, claiming that the commemoration should have taken place on 23 August 1980. The bailiff clarified that a decision had been issued that made the ruling enforceable on 27 November or in the following days. Nevertheless, the chief persisted in abstaining, claiming that he had received instructions in that regard, and so ended the meeting.

The Court of Administrative Litigation held that:

> The administration's refusal to execute a final judicial decision
> enjoying the force of res judicata is a blatant legal violation
> for which the government is liable to pay compensation. No
> government in a civilized country would abstain from executing
> final judicial rulings illegally. Such a blatant violation would lead to
> the breakout of chaos and lack of trust in the sovereignty of law.[4]

## Pretexts Used by the Administration

The administration maneuvers to abstain from executing judicial judgments by resorting to pretexts such as the public interest, national security, public order, and even material and legal difficulties that emerge during the execution of a ruling.

### The Public Interest

This claim by the government is false in any situation because the public interest requires respect for law and enforcement of legal decisions. No other interest shall ever supersede that of enforcing judicial judgments, including judgments nullifying wrongful administrative conduct.

Since its early years, the Court of Administrative Litigation has stated:

> The insistence of the minister not to execute a judicial decision
> violates the principle of res judicata and is a legal violation
> of a basic principle and one of the fundamentals of law. . . .
> Consequently, the minister's violation shall be deemed a

personal mistake that makes him liable to provide the required compensation. Neither the fact that he has no personal interest nor the claim that he is protecting the public interest shall redeem him from providing a remedy. No public interest, indeed, is ever achieved by committing unlawful acts.[5]

The government's use of the public interest as an excuse for not executing judicial rulings is an unjustifiable act that should not be tolerated.

## National Security and Public Order

Justifications based on public order and national security interests have been rejected by the judiciary out of respect for the principle of *res judicata*, which is one of the basic legal elements of public tranquility and of the consolidation of rights and social ties.[6] Certain circumstances sometimes might force the state to place its security above all other considerations, so that all measures necessary to protect this security would be considered legitimate (for example, in cases of war, social turbulence, and political crises).[7]

If the execution of a ruling may expose public order to real disruption, the executive authority may delay it. If this delay turns out to be procrastination, however, the administrative judge may determine whether the plaintiff has incurred any special damage and may hold the executive authority liable on the basis of administrative liability for violating the principle of equality in the execution of a public responsibility. Suitable redress would then be set according to this same principle.

The Supreme Administrative Court has held that:

> An administrative decision may not obstruct the execution of a
> final judicial ruling; otherwise, it shall be considered unlawful,
> unless the immediate execution of that ruling would seriously
> damage the public interest in favor of a private one. However, this
> may only take place in exceptional circumstances. If the decision
> is made only to deny liability for paying a high amount previously
> accepted by the administration at the time of signing the contract,
> the decision shall be considered void.[8]

## Material Difficulties

Another excuse that the administration has used without any real or legal justification is 'material difficulties.'[9] For example, the government might justify non-execution by pointing to its inability to return a large number of dismissed employees to their former posts because it would mean that many others would be removed.[10] The administration itself might have created this difficulty, however, when it blindly appointed or promoted other employees to positions to which the dismissed ones should be returned.[11]

The administration often tries to avoid its financial obligations on the pretext of lack of funds, which is an excuse that should not deprive the plaintiff of his or her rights. Sometimes non-execution, especially with regard to invalidated decisions, is due to the real impossibility of restoring the situation to what it was before the illegal decision was made. However, this "impossibility" may be engineered by the administration because of the long time most litigation and legal proceedings take, the scarcity of decisions that stop the execution of appealed decisions, and the slowness of the administration itself in the execution of court rulings. Delay in the enforcement of judicial decisions is often due to the negative behavior of the administration.

### Legal Difficulties

The government might claim that a certain administrative ruling is vague and needs to be interpreted further. In such cases, the administration could be found guilty of adopting a negative decision, for which it might have to provide compensation. According to the Court of Administrative Litigation, "This shall be regarded as an illegal negative administrative decision that necessitates the provision of redress to the party involved."[12] The court also pointed out:

> Stating, as in the commissioner's report, that a slight mistake in the
> interpretation of the law does not require redress has no ground,
> since the understanding of the law and the law prescribe the
> mandatory enforcement of court decisions, and that rule implies no
> vagueness in its implementation.[13]

This should not, however, prevent the administration from going to court for the clarification of vague judgments, as long as the administration is acting in good will.

### Real Reasons for Non-execution

The administration often refers to the public interest or order or to a difficulty of execution to refrain from the execution of judicial rulings, but it usually has hidden motives. Civil servants may refuse to execute administrative rulings or may obstruct their execution if the rulings affect the party they are affiliated to or the political system in which they participate. These political motives usually come to light in lawsuits that settle administrative disputes and at the same time involve political issues.

The administration is so used to not having its decisions subject to review or invalidation that it often considers a ruling of abrogation by an administrative judge an offense. This has given rise to the undeniable abhorrence of abstention by the executive authority in carrying out judicial decisions. To boost its prestige, the administration may try to limit judicial supervision of its performance by refraining from executing judicial decisions, believing that enforcing them is only mandatory when they do not undermine its prestige or status.

In many cases, personal motives are the reason behind the obstruction of enforcement of judgments, especially if execution is assigned to a public servant who is actually litigating against the prevailing party. He or she will obstruct execution with legal and financial obstacles, such as appointing or promoting another employee to the post that a successful plaintiff should reoccupy by virtue of the ruling. The administrative judiciary has condemned such conduct.[14]

## Example: The Electoral Process
Most examples cited in this section deal with the electoral process, although abstention from executing judicial rulings occurs in other fields, as well.

## Considering Court Decisions Consultative: Article 93 of the Constitution
The administration may interfere in the execution of court decisions by considering them consultative instead of mandatory. In this way, their execution is not an obligation. Such was the case, for instance, with the decisions of the Court of Cassation about legitimacy of membership in the People's Assembly.

The Egyptian constitution has been drawn up in a way that protects members of the People's Assembly from judicial interference in determining the legitimacy of their membership. According to constitutional Article 93:

> The People's Assembly shall be the only authority competent to
> decide upon the validity of its members. The Court of Cassation
> shall be competent to investigate the validity of contestations
> presented to the Assembly, on being referred to it by the President
> of the Assembly. The contestation shall be referred to the Court of
> Cassation within fifteen days from the date on which the Assembly
> was informed of it, while the investigation shall be completed
> within ninety days from the date on which the contestation is
> referred to the Court of Cassation. The result of the investigation
> and the decision reached by the Court shall be submitted to
> the Assembly to decide upon the validity of the contestation
> within sixty days from the date of submission of the result of the
> investigation to the Assembly. Membership will not be deemed
> invalid except by a decision taken by a majority of two-thirds of the
> Assembly members.

The text prescribes that the People's Assembly, presently dominated by the ruling National Democratic Party, is the only authority that may decide the legitimacy of the mandate of its members, after an investigation conducted by the Court of Cassation. With such a provision, the assembly becomes the judge in its own case. The text clearly implies a desire to protect members of the ruling party, as the provision is used by the People's Assembly whenever the legitimacy of the membership of one of the ruling party members is contested. It actually tells a lot about the way the executive and legislative authorities consider judicial decisions. While constantly paying lip service to court decisions, these authorities actually execute only a few of the rulings, mainly those that are consistent with their interests.

This provision also deprives the administrative court of competence to decide on administrative disputes in accordance with Article 172 of the constitution. The State Council is only competent to decide disputes pertaining to measures taken prior to the process of elections, technically speaking.[15] The distinction between measures taken before and after vote counting should be invalid, as it prevents the administrative judiciary from determining the legitimacy of membership after the ballot.

The assembly has decided that the Court of Cassation, in this regard, conducts investigations and delivers consultative opinions, not binding judgments.[16] The Court of Cassation on many occasions has declared the election of candidates void in constituencies where ministers and government supporters were declared the victors. Its decisions were not carried out by the People's Assembly, however, which refused to abide by them and turned a blind eye to the voters' will and to the judicial rulings.

## Stay of Execution

The executive authority has found ways to obstruct the execution of judgments through the procedure of *ishkal*, or stay of execution, which suspends temporarily the execution of enforceable rulings. Requests for a stay of execution are not intended to be appeals against enforceable judgments; rather, they concern disputes about conditions that the law deems necessary for the enforcement of the judgment. They may be initiated by any of the litigants or by other parties. If the challenge is rejected, the executive action regains its force with regard to pursuing the execution of the judgment. If the challenge is accepted, the judgment remains suspended and cannot be executed unless the verdict ordering a stay of execution is revoked or another verdict is issued to settle the dispute that suspended the executive action.

This legal fiction is used as a tool by the executive authority to stop the execution of State Council decisions. Challenges to council decisions are presented before ordinary courts, and the execution of the decisions is suspended right away, pending the decision of the court. This tool is used particularly on the occasion of elections to challenge decisions of the State Council that deny the right of certain candidates to stand for election. The State Litigation Authority or the candidate appeals the decision before ordinary courts. This appeal stops the execution of the challenged decision, and the candidate therefore is able to run for election. Once the candidate is elected, it is up to the People's Assembly, according to Article 93 of the constitution, to decide on the validity of the election results.[17] Legal scholars are unanimous in condemning this practice. Civil courts obviously lack competence to rule on administrative decisions and ultimately declare their incompetence.[18] In the meantime, however, the ruling of the State Council is suspended until the decision of incompetence is adopted by the ordinary court.

For instance, the administration refused to carry out judicial decisions issued by the State Council concerning the parliamentary elections in 2000 and 2005. The government encouraged ruling party candidates for the People's Assembly to present challenges against the execution of judicial decisions preventing them from running in the elections. In 2005, over fifty judgments were issued throughout Egypt against the election results, including in some key constituencies like Sayyida Zaynab in Cairo, to which the speaker of the parliament belongs. Only a few of these rulings were executed, however. The government seized the opportunity to halt the election of several persons in constituencies where there were strong opponents and anti-government movements. In all other constituencies, the rulings were not executed.

## Judicial Supervision of Elections

Even judges have suffered the consequences of the government's abstention from executing judicial rulings that do not serve its interests. An instance of members of the judiciary being affected is when the State Council ruled to suspend a decision that disqualified some counselors of the council from supervising the presidential elections.[19] Although the Presidential Elections Commission was informed of the State Council's ruling, the head of the commission did not implement it and presented a request for a stay of execution on the day of the elections (7 September 2005).

## Other Examples

The ministry of the interior has refrained from executing judicial decisions concerning appeals filed by detainees against detention orders issued by the ministry under the emergency law.[20] Although the court ordered their release, the ministry transferred the detainees to the nearest police station or detention center and rearrested them under new detention orders. In doing this, the ministry violated clear judicial rulings and misused the emergency law.

In another instance, the government did not abide by the ruling that suspended the execution of the administration's order to forbid the celebration of the anniversary of Mustafa al-Nahas' death (see above). Likewise, the government did not execute the decision that suspended the detention of the father of one of the persons accused in the case of President Anwar Sadat's assassination, or the decision that suspended the confiscation of the Islamic magazine *al-Da'wa al-islamiya* and the Christian newspaper *al-Watan*.

## The State's Abstention from Executing Judicial Rulings

Legally speaking, execution of judgments falls within the competence of the executive authority, but few resources are available to force that authority to implement them.

## The Separation of Powers and the Execution of Judicial Decisions

Any refusal to execute judicial rulings violates several articles of the constitution. Article 64 stipulates that sovereignty of the law is the basis of rule in the state. Article 65 says that the state shall be subject to the law, and that the independence and immunity of the judiciary are two basic guarantees that safeguard rights and liberties. Article 68 prohibits any provision in the law that stipulates the immunity of any act or administrative decision from the control of the judiciary. The executive authority seems to ignore these articles, as well as Article 72, which states that rulings shall be passed and executed in the name of the people and that refraining from executing judicial decisions or obstructing them is a crime punishable by law. According to the same provision, those with a ruling in their favor have the right to file a direct criminal lawsuit before a competent court.

What makes matters worse is that the official capacity to execute rulings lies in the hands of the administration. It is not up to the judge, on the basis of the principle of separation of powers. If an administrative judge can declare an administrative decision void, he does not have the right to compel the administration to carry out the ruling. The administrative judiciary cannot replace the administration in interpreting the effects of a ruling in order to insure the execution of that which has been adjudged. The Supreme Administrative Court has stated its concern, saying, "The administrative judge's capacity is limited to declaring void an illegal administrative decision. The execution of this adjudged nullification belongs to the administrative body."[21] Most of the time, positive measures need to be taken by the executive authority to execute a ruling of nullification. For example, a ruling nullifying a dismissal decision cannot reinstate the dismissed person. It takes an administrative decision from the executive authority to reinstate a public servant.

On the basis of the principle of separation of powers, the State Council never has allowed itself to give orders to the administration or to replace it. It has limited itself to declaring a decision void and left it to the administration to correct the situation on the basis of its judgment.[22] For instance, the Court of Administrative Litigation voided a decision to pension off a civil servant. It stated:

This Court is not a working administrative body and is, therefore, not entitled to issue administrative orders and, in particular, to replace the administration in taking particular measures. Accordingly, the second part of the plaintiff's request regarding his return to work in the General Department of Borders until he reaches the age of retirement should not be considered, even though this demand is the logical outcome of the abrogation of the pensioning off decision, which should be respected and put into practice by the administration.[23]

Rulings on compensation claims against the administration work in a similar manner. The administration is vested with the power to use all legal means, including physical coercion, against its debtors. By contrast, the administration cannot be coerced in any way because of the lack of any means to compel execution. The administration cannot be forced to pay what it has been judged to owe. The administration can only agree to pay adjudged amounts of its own free will and following the rules stipulated in the laws on public finance and accounting.

## Remedies

A refusal to execute judicial decisions is an offence under Article 123, paragraph 2, of the penal code. Any civil servant who uses his or her authority to prevent a court ruling from being implemented eight days after the civil servant receives a warning in this regard is punishable with detention or dismissal.

Since, according to Article 87, paragraph 2, of the civil code, public property may not be disposed of, the non-execution of court orders should at least be considered an excess of power and a violation for which the responsible body should be held accountable. Delay in the execution of a judgment should require that the party pay interest on the amount overdue, in addition to the compensation. Judicial decisions are not mere recommendations but rulings that have the force of *res judicata* and must be enforced.[24]

In view of the administration's continuous disregard for rulings, the question remains, what are the effective means and tools available to the prevailing party to overcome this disregard and help execute judicial rulings? In fact, the most pressing question regarding administrative law is how to force the administration to comply with State Council rulings. In order to overcome this inadequacy in the administration, which arises on the pretext of its independence from the judiciary, the French legislature has conferred on the administrative judge the right to issue execution orders, coupled with daily fines for delay. That legislature also has conferred on administrative courts and administrative courts of appeal, in the case of non-execution of a final ruling issued by them, the right to order the necessary procedures to implement their decisions. If the procedures of execution are not defined in a decision, the competent court can specify the procedures and the period of execution, as well as order a daily fine for delay to guarantee the execution of the verdict.[25]

It would be worthwhile to entrust the Egyptian administrative judge with the ability to monitor the execution of rulings. This does not mean that the judge would replace the administration or give it orders, but the judge's intervention in most cases would urge the administration to execute judicial decisions.

## Conclusion

The principle of the submission of the state to the law entails its subjection to the judiciary, as well as the potential of it being sued and even sentenced. There is no rule of law without a truly effective judiciary and legal supervision of the performance of the executive authority. In democratic countries, the authority of the administration is limited by law and by rulings. If the administration refrains from executing rulings, it is punishable by law. The principle of legality is useless if it is not coupled with the principle of upholding and enforcing judicial rulings. Full judicial supervision can be attained only through the enforcement of judgments.

My main recommendation would be to form an administration affiliated with the judicial apparatus that would be entrusted with the execution of judicial rulings and direct and prompt punishment of transgressors. A judicial police unit could be established for the execution of court decisions. It would be affiliated with the court that issues the decisions, rather than the ministry of the interior.

# 13

# Egyptian Parties and Syndicates vis-à-vis Judicial Decisions

*Ahmed Abd El-Hafeez*

Any observer of Egyptian politics can easily track the growth of the judicial phenomenon in Egyptian political life over the past three decades. The Egyptian judiciary has become the most prominent, effective element during that period.[1] Members of the Egyptian elite, individually and collectively, have been using the judiciary in ways that are, in certain respects, both remarkable and unprecedented in Egyptian history.

Recourse to the courts by political parties is not new. It started with the 1919 Revolution and has increased in the last few years. With a few concrete examples, I will illustrate the different ways parties and syndicates resort to the judiciary.

## The Judiciary in Egyptian History

Many leaders of the 1919 Revolution were lawyers who became influential figures in political parties, especially the Wafd Party, the popular majority party that emanated from and led the revolution. No doubt because of their profession, lawyers are inclined to place legal provisions on a high pedestal. Their continued preference for resorting to courts for dispute settlement also may be due to their profession. Yet the Egyptian judiciary back then was still emerging, and as it had not yet secured itself a prominent role in public life, it was not ready to be involved in political conflicts.

Direct political mechanisms were available at the time for all conflicting parties in the political arena, as they were able to form parties and political associations, issue journals, organize demonstrations, and use various means of peaceful protest. Little reason existed in those days for the judiciary to become involved in major partisan, political, and intellectual issues. The judiciary was nonetheless the authority turned to for legal equity and to which every accused person was referred, including for charges that were politically motivated. Therefore, no urgent need emerged for expanding the scope of resort to the judiciary at that stage.

Despite the judiciary's incomplete development, the need to resort to it generated quite a controversial judicial heritage concerning the protection of public rights and freedoms. When the July Revolution overthrew the old regime, the Wafd Party resorted to the judiciary, namely the State Council, to challenge the procedures used by the revolution's leaders. The council at the time was dominated by two of the most prominent experts in Egyptian law, who were political opponents of the Wafd Party. This means that the party's attempt to use the State Council as a weapon backfired. It only increased the legitimacy of the revolution, as the use of judicial procedures gave legal tools to the leaders of the revolution to undermine the legitimacy of the regime they had overthrown.

When the revolution seized control, its leaders adopted various political, cultural, and social mechanisms to insure the regime's legitimacy. The role of the judiciary remained confined to its scope during the preceding period. It became even more limited, because the revolution decreased the competence of the judiciary through provisions that immunized certain decisions and procedures against judicial appeals and because special courts were established.

From the 1970s onward, calls for a return to constitutional legitimacy and termination of the legitimacy established by the revolution became prevalent. New laws and decisions were promulgated, and the immunization of any administrative decision against judicial review was prohibited by Article 68 of the 1971 constitution. Nevertheless, this transformation was accompanied by an unprecedented increase in the quantity of laws and exceptional courts. This created much confusion regarding the concept of legitimacy and what it required. Eventually, lawyers restored themselves to prominence and to their central position in litigation. The Bar Association became more active. When multiple political parties again emerged in the 1976 parliamentary elections, lawyers were prominent and confusion about the legitimacy of the reinvented political forms reigned, which led to a new role for the judiciary.

Lawyers came forward again, assuming leadership positions in most existing and new parties and reasserting the electoral legitimacy of previously banned parties and politicians with the assistance of the judiciary. This reemergence of lawyers and the judiciary ultimately linked concepts of political action with litigation, and the judiciary became an arena available for political and intellectual contests over legitimacy.

Events since the restoration of parties have resulted in transference to the judicial arena of conflicts of political legitimacy between ruling elites and between the ruling elite and its opponents as represented in political parties. More recently, the conflict has spread into the opposition parties themselves and negatively affected their internal relations.

The conflict levels over acquiring legitimacy have diversified. Most legislation promulgated after the 1970s was characterized by legal and procedural complications, as well as constitutional infringements, which resulted in their referral to the judiciary to compensate for legislative deficiencies. Thus, conflicts emerged over, *inter alia*, the legitimacy of establishing parties, the repeal or enforcement of certain laws and decisions, and deficiencies in the basis of legitimacy during the transitional period. Because the law provides a comprehensive set of procedures for a citizen to avail himself of rights, when the relevant procedures are blocked, the judiciary is the natural resort for completing the procedures.

## Different Forms of Resort to the Judiciary

The Egyptian judicial system is an open system that secures for everyone the right of litigation for all types of claims and actions, without limits or restrictions. Therefore, the phenomenon of judicial involvement in the life of Egyptian parties and syndicates has developed naturally. All ordinary, administrative, and constitutional judicial bodies have profoundly affected political events in Egypt. Thus, the forms for resorting to the judiciary have multiplied and diversified.

For instance, the establishment of a party is conditional on the approval of the Committee for Parties,[2] and its decisions can be challenged before the Court of Parties of the State Council.[3] The Committee for Parties can decide to freeze the newspaper of a party, and this decision also can be challenged before the Court of Parties.

The decisions of the general assemblies of syndicates, especially those pertaining to the results of elections in the syndicates, can be appealed before the State Council and the Court of Cassation or courts of appeal. The electoral rights stipulated in the different laws on trade unions or professional unions are implemented through several administrative bodies, and court appeals are possible.

As for political elites, the political imbalance in favor of the state and these elites' failure to confront the state have caused them to try to restore some balance through the judiciary, which ultimately has that authority. Courts recognized certain rights for individuals or groups of elites that they could not achieve by using their personal position as members of an elite. Parties and syndicates resort to the judiciary either to ensure the legitimacy of their existence or to defend the campaigns their newspapers launch against certain officials. The courts also serve as an arena for disagreements between members of the same party or political current or between conflicting factions within the same syndicate, especially in regard to syndicate election results or the way a syndicate is managed. Winners of court verdicts, of course, hail the court and applaud their victory, while losers condemn the verdicts.

The above-mentioned circumstances indicate some of the interrelated factors that have pushed various parties, political groups, and syndicates to take their controversies to the judiciary and submit to court rulings. They also suggest something of the context in which and process by which court decisions are used to confirm the legitimacy of actions of members of such bodies or of the bodies themselves.

## Examples of Groups Resorting to the Judiciary

The Wafd Party and the Nasserite Party, together with the Bar Association, are the most prominent examples of groups using court rulings to stress legal and constitutional legitimacy. Other parties and syndicates also have resorted to the courts in recent years. The Tagammu' Party, for instance, filed a lawsuit in 2005 in an attempt to block the referendum on amendment of Article 76 of the constitution. The Labor Party also brought a case before the courts on the press-related battles that its newspaper had gone through before it was shut down and the party frozen.

Only cases of litigation initiated by a syndicate or a party as a legal body will be presented here. The various lawsuits filed by individuals in relation to individual cases are not within the scope of this paper. Similarly, cases related to contests between syndicates or factions within the same party over authority to represent the group or to specify the scope of membership rights will not be included.

## Sequestration of the Bar Association

The 1992 Bar Association elections resulted in the Muslim Brotherhood's takeover of the association's board,[4] except for the president of the syndicate and four members. In light of this situation, a number of former boardmembers cooperated with the state to file a lawsuit requesting that the association be placed under sequestration. They obtained the ruling they sought and sequestration was imposed on the Bar Association. A group of three lawyers was appointed by the court to manage the syndicate's affairs.

This situation was challenged by attorneys individually and in groups, who used many procedures, including filing lawsuits demanding that the sequestration imposed on the Bar Association be lifted. A lawsuit filed by a female lawyer, either of her own volition or on encouragement from the Muslim Brotherhood, was deliberated in 2000 and the sequestration was canceled. Elections were held again in February 2001, resulting in a new board, again controlled by the Muslim Brotherhood, except for the position of president and a few members. This caused the board to become involved in sharp disputes that led to its inability to function. This situation accelerated after the 2005 Bar Association elections, after which the situation was so aggravated that boardmembers initiated litigation to resolve the question of whether the president of the association had competence to act without a board decision. These disputes are ongoing, although the boardmembers won two cases. These lawsuits cannot be attributed to the Bar Association as such, however. They are lawsuits brought by a group of individual members, notwithstanding how influential they are in the operation of the Bar Association.[5]

## Litigation Related to the Legitimacy of Existence

I will study here the question of the initial legitimacy of the existence of a party or a syndicate and of its reinstatement in the case of a challenge to the legitimacy of its legal representative bodies. The most prominent examples of this are the reinstatement of the legitimacy of the Bar Association, the resumption of the Wafd Party's activities, and the establishment of the Nasserite Democratic Arab Party.[6]

### Reinstatement of Legitimacy to the Bar Association

The Bar Association was transformed in the late 1970s and early 1980s into a fortress for opposing President Sadat's peace initiative with Israel.

It also resisted the arsenal of laws promulgated at the time, which were commonly called the "infamous laws" because they severely curtailed the constitutional freedoms of citizens.[7] After a while, the president of the republic and his government decided to confront the syndicate board and get rid of it. On the occasion of the general assembly of the Bar Association on 26 May 1981, the government plotted to overrun the meeting with a number of non-attorneys led by some pro-government attorneys. However, the board and its supporters avoided the government's tactics by convening the meeting at an earlier hour. The meeting concluded with the endorsement of the balance sheet and the final account and the assertion of the confidence placed in the board. The pro-government lawyers and the individuals whom they accompanied to attack the Bar Association could do nothing but convene their own meeting in the presence of the official media. They concluded by alleging that their meeting was a valid general assembly during which a decision to withdraw trust from the board had been taken and an alternative committee formed for managing the Bar Association. The attorneys and the public were astounded when all governmental mass media published accounts of the alternative committee as the legitimate meeting and of the alleged legitimacy of its decisions.

That same day, the lawyers decided to stage a sit-in at the Bar Association and to issue statements condemning the state's actions. When the matter was disclosed, President Sadat hurried to direct the People's Assembly to form a fact-finding committee to inspect the situation in the Bar Association. The committee was instructed to carry out investigations with the president of the association and the board, who refused to appear before the committee .Ultimately, the People's Assembly promulgated Law 125/1981, which provided for the dissolution of the existing board and the formation of a provisional committee to manage the Bar Association. The formation of this committee was assigned to the minister of justice, who passed his decision on the day following the promulgation of the law.

With great difficulty, the president of the Bar Association, Ahmad al-Khawaga, managed to appeal the law before the Administrative Court on the last day of the appeal period. He later argued the unconstitutionality of the law before the same court. The court accepted the defense and granted the appellant a grace period to file a constitutional lawsuit. Again with great difficulty, al-Khawaga filed the challenge before the Supreme Constitutional Court. After the assassination of President

Sadat, the new government sought to change the situation and promulgated Law 17/1983 on the Regulation of the Legal Profession. It also amended Law 125/1981 to provide for the appointment of a committee to organize new elections for the Bar Association.

The Supreme Constitutional Court declared Law 125/1981 unconstitutional, deeming it a violation of the authority of the Bar Association's general assembly and an infringement of the constitutional principle of syndicates' freedom. The election process was thus suspended and the aforementioned committee appointed to supervise it was dissolved. The legitimate board was then reinstated in full to complete its mandate until 1985.

All lawyers, headed by the board, believed this decision championed legitimacy and crowned their unceasing struggle against the government's interference in the Bar Association's affairs, as well as their rejection of the management of the association by appointed committees. The battle was resolved to a great extent in favor of unity among all categories of lawyers. The president of the syndicate and the board-members were supported by all their previous adversaries. The great lawyer, Muhammad 'Asfur, who shouldered the main burden of the legal defense of the Bar Association, became a star and was widely honored.

### The Establishment of the New Wafd Party

In early 1978, laws pertaining to political life and political parties were promulgated that provided for the political isolation of certain leaders, including the chairman and some leaders of the Wafd Party. In response to these laws, the party's general assembly decided to dissolve the party and instructed its higher council to complete the dissolution procedures. The party chairman notified the official bodies of the decision.

Nevertheless, the higher council did not complete the dissolution procedures in full. In the aftermath of the 1983 changes in political climate, the party decided to resume its activities, considering they had only been frozen. The higher council of the party met and decided to convoke the general assembly to cancel the freezing decision. On the occasion of the door being opened for nominations on party lists for municipal elections in that year, the Wafd Party submitted a list of candidates in one constituency. The administrative body in charge of organizing the elections, on the basis of a letter from the Committee for Parties, dismissed the list under the pretext that the Wafd Party had dissolved itself. The party resorted to the Administrative Court to stress its right to resume its activities. The court granted the party the right to return to political life on 29 October 1983.

## The Establishment of the Nasserite Party

As soon as a political detente started with President Hosni Mubarak's rule, Nasserites thought about establishing a Nasserite political party. The majority of them decided to be realistic and wait before applying for a license from the Committee for Parties. Nevertheless, a small group of Nasserites hastily submitted party documents that were dismissed by the Committee, whose decision was confirmed by the Court of Parties upon appeal.

A few years later, out of fear that another group would hastily file documents for a new party, the leaders of the movement decided to submit the documents necessary to found the Nasserite Democratic Arab Party. They elected Dia' al-Din Dawud to be the founders' representative. After the Committee for Parties rejected the party, the founders turned to the Court of Parties, where the matter was deliberated for about two years, although the law obligates the court to issue a decision within four months. The court finally accepted the appeal in 1992, which meant that the party was granted the right to begin operations.

The Nasserite Party in the process of establishment had taken preemptive action immediately upon issuance of the report of the State Council commissioners' body duly supporting the establishment of the party.[8] Because the court is not bound to adopt the commissioners' advisory opinion and because the court had dismissed the first party even though the commissioners had supported its establishment, the Nasserites printed a large number of reports and distributed them widely in a pamphlet entitled, "The Nasserites' Legitimate Right to Establish Their Party."

## Comments on These Two Cases

Both parties strongly asserted that their legitimacy as parties had been decided by the courts, not granted by the state, as represented by the Committee for Parties. The Wafd Party used this track openly in its 1984 parliamentary election battle, which it undertook through the newly legislated "party list system." This track also was manifest in the articles and titles of the Wafd newspaper, which was widely distributed at the time. The Nasserite Party did not have a vocal newspaper at the time, but all statements issued by its then provisional secretary-general,

Dia' al-Din Dawud, and the remaining party leaders stressed this track. The general public understood the difference between court rulings and administrative decisions, as well as the fact that the latter express the wishes and will of the state while court rulings may be contrary to the state's wishes.

This means that, in the public mind, a party created through the consent of the Committee for Parties is a tamed party that does not offer true opposition, unlike parties established by virtue of court rulings issued against the state's wishes. This idea is misguided, because the judiciary can never be separated from the political mainstream of the state. Still, a 'public body' is not the state. When public bodies reject the establishment of a certain party or political entity, its establishment will never be approved by the regular judicial hierarchy of Egyptian courts. The Court of Parties is a special court, and the opposition views such courts as not natural and thus not qualified to be the 'natural judge' of any Egyptian citizen.

### Litigation Related to Internal Conflict within Parties and Syndicates: The Syndicate of Merchants

Conflict between groups within the same party or syndicate has been a distinctive feature of Egyptian political life over the past two decades. No party, except for the Tagammu' Party, has managed to escape such conflict, especially not the multiple key professional syndicates caught up in the same trap. Nevertheless, the case pertaining to the conflict over the Syndicate of Merchants, which lasted from 1983 to 1988, is a good example of the method through which professional syndicates and parties deal with such conflicts and of relevant court rulings. This conflict had special characteristics, which other conflicts involving syndicates and parties lacked. Previous conflicts had been triggered from within the leadership and through dissension among members of the syndicate or party. In the case of the Syndicate of Merchants, however, the syndicate board was not a direct party to the conflict, which erupted among candidates for the position of president of the syndicate, none of whom was a boardmember.

The conflict started when the syndicate board decided to exclude the votes of certain electors on the pretext of fraud and to suspend announcement of the winner. The candidate concerned immediately filed an appeal before the Administrative Court against the decision of the board and obtained a ruling staying execution of the decision, which he claimed to mean acceptance of his victory. The board, which favored the other candidate, insisted that the ruling only stayed the execution of their decision not to announce the result. In response to this stance, the candidate in whose favor the ruling had been issued, accompanied by a group of proponents, went to the syndicate building and started to perform his job as president of the syndicate.

The syndicate board reported the incident to the general prosecutor and asked him to investigate the thuggery performed by said candidate. Thus, the matter was deliberated not only before the Administrative Court but also by the Office of Public Prosecution. The syndicate became an arena for violent conflict between the proponents of each candidate, which occurred at the same time as mutual appeals before courts and attempts at reconciliation and mediation.

These events were reported by the Egyptian press with an air of irony, under the satirical title, "The Commercials Serial," in which opinion journalists and caricaturists took part. The press reported all follow-ups, press investigations, and interviews with the parties to the dispute, who competed to assert the soundness of the rulings issued in their favor and to undermine the rulings issued in favor of their opponents. Neither of the two candidates managed to occupy the position of president of the syndicate, despite all the rulings and counterrulings issued by the courts and the decisions and counterdecisions issued by the syndicate board.

After a drawn-out conflict, which the late writer Ahmad Bahi al-Din likened to the civil war in Lebanon, the dispute was resolved when a court in 1988 that the statutory mandate of the board had terminated. None of the previously conflicting candidates presented himself as a candidate, and a new president and a new board were elected.

This example reveals the elite's inability to develop any common concept of legal legitimacy or behavioral limits, either legally or practically, pertaining to understanding the meaning of court rulings and their operative effects.

## Liability of the Party Chairman and Editor in Chief

Certain newspapers have launched campaigns against some senior officials in recent decades. For example, the Wafd newspaper had campaigns against the late Dr. Rif'at al-Mahjub, who was the spokesperson of the People's Assembly between 1984 and 1990, and against General Zaki Badr, the minister of the interior, during his tenure. The latter campaign was joined by *al-Sha'b* newspaper, the mouthpiece of the Socialist Labor Party, which also had campaigns against the former minister of agriculture, Yusif Wali, and the former minister of petroleum, 'Abd al-Hadi Qandil. These two officials brought cases against the Socialst Labor Party and *al-Sha'b* newspaper.

The criminal provision pertaining to publication cases used to hold that the party chairman and editor in chief were responsible for all that was published in a newspaper, which means that they were charged together with the journalist. Party chairmen and editors in chief rushed to appeal the constitutionality of this provision. The Supreme Constitutional Court ruled the provision unconstitutional because it was based on the assumption of responsibility and not on *de facto* liability. This ruling is definitely a sound one, as, although it does not immunize party chairmen and editors in chief, it grants them the right to avoid liability by proving that the material was published without their knowledge.

The fundamentals of the journalist's profession hold, however, that publishing responsibility is ultimately borne by the editor in chief, as no material should ever be published in a newspaper without his or her approval. Besides, the evasion of liability by party chairmen and editors in chief places the responsibility fully on the shoulders of the journalist who published the news and who might be a junior journalist. Every person should bear his or her share of responsibility and not pass it on to others, especially to vulnerable people who cannot protect themselves. The worst effect is that such delinking of responsibility strips the partisan newspaper campaigns of their partisan and political meaning and confines them to a narrow perspective of exclusive professional practice. It is unthinkable that political life and public liberties would ever benefit from such attitudes. Besides, the unconstitutionality ruling held that any person injured by the published material could sue the poor journalist whose name appears on the published material, rather than the editor in chief.

If such conflicts are brought before the courts, newspapers follow them in detail through headlines, pictures, and articles. While publishing the testimonies of their witnesses, they overlook the defense given by the opponents and any reference to the names of their lawyers, except when criticizing them and refuting their defenses and arguments. If the court acquits the defendant, most newspapers hail and applaud it, and even assign their main titles and editorials to the ruling, including its full grounds. If the ruling is against the newspaper, it neither refers to the ruling nor to its grounds, but rather hastily criticizes it, even blaming the court that passed it. Some of them may hastily apologize, announce their respect and appreciation for the individual under fire, and take the initiative to reach a settlement with the injured party, especially if the journalist is sentenced to prison or to pay a considerable fine. Such efforts to reconcile with the party injured do nothing to counteract the underlying harm done to press freedom and the credibility of the press, especially the political press, given the serious implications of absolving an editor in chief of a party paper of responsibility.

## Litigation in the Name of the Public: The Case of Tagammu' Against the Referendum on Article 76

Political parties may file cases in order to achieve specific goals or may support a party to a litigation in their newspapers. Political and intellectual reasons may provoke parties to become involved in such cases. For instance, the Labor, Nasserite, and Tagammu' Parties jointly filed a lawsuit before the Administrative Court to stay Cabinet decisions related to selling the public sector. The lawsuit was a failure, as the Supreme Constitutional Court ruled the sale of the public sector constitutional. The parties' chairmen attended the court hearings and eminent senior attorneys pleaded their case. In the Abu Zayd case, the Tagammu' Party and *al-Ahali* newspaper supported Dr. and Mrs. Nasr Abu Zayd against the action filed to divorce them on the pretext of apostasy.[9] The newspaper followed the case, published the defense memoranda submitted in favor of Abu Zayd, and issued special editions of the newspaper on his books, which constituted the subject of the claim of apostasy. Nonetheless, Abu Zayd was ordered by the Court of Appeal and the Court of Cassation to be divorced from his wife on the grounds of apostasy. In another case, Nasserite lawyers, induced by the party, filed a case against holding the 1992 municipal elections by the list system. That lawsuit was successful, as the Supreme Constitutional Court decided the law regulating elections was unconstitutional.

The case filed by the Tagammu' Party on the referendum on the amendment of Article 76 of the constitution deserves more clarification.[10] The case started when the party filed a lawsuit before the Administrative Court against the decision issued by the ministry of the interior regarding the referendum. The initial pleading was based on a single legal ground, namely that the referendum card did not include the text of the amended article, which was deemed an attempt to obscure the subject of the referendum. In the opening hearing, a ministry of the interior representative announced the ministry's consent to amending the referendum card by adding the text of the article to be amended. This case confirms that political parties adopt the way usually taken in all political and public cases in Egypt, that is, giving legal and technical considerations priority when preparing their pleadings or defense memoranda. The memoranda of the plaintiff in this case did not include any political meaning related to the amendment itself, its wording, or phrasing. Despite the comprehensive political nature of the case, neither the party filing the case nor any other party was interested in transforming it into a public political and constitutional case on the amendment. In the meantime, the initial pleading of the plaintiff was not used in any way to mobilize citizens against the referendum or to provoke them to boycott it, although the Tagammu' Party in particular had announced its intention to undertake street protests against the referendum.

## Conclusion

This paper demonstrates that political parties and syndicates in Egypt tend, through their newspapers and discourse, to deal with the judiciary in a deficient and selective manner, only accepting favorable rulings and overlooking opponents' viewpoints. Partisan newspapers and discourses mix news with analysis and opinion. They adopt direct and blunt propagandist manners and contradict the citizen's right to freedom of media and accurate information, in accordance with international conventions regulating such rights.

When all conflicts, opinions, and thoughts are reliant on the judiciary, the requirements for a healthy political life are undermined and the natural limits of the role of the judiciary are overextended. The question is whether the judiciary is the right place for settling political and intellectual conflicts.

# 14

# The Judicial Authority and Civil Society

## *Mustapha Kamel al-Sayyed*

The several confrontations that have occurred between the Judges'
Club and the Judges' Club of the State Council on the one hand,[1] and
the Supreme Judicial Council and the minister of justice on the other,
suggest two important features of the role of judges in Egyptian politics. These clubs are civil society organizations and they share the
aspirations of many such organizations for more freedom of association and strict respect of civil and political rights. The Supreme Judicial
Council is an arm of the state and is careful to defend the existing order
by all means, even at the risk of sanctioning violations of legal rules that
judges are supposed to uphold. The relevant rules in this respect are the
constitutional provisions that ensure the independence of the judiciary,
in addition to laws that ensure fair and free elections in the country and
punish those who tamper with them.

Any researcher of the relationship between the judicial authority
and civil society must keep these two features in mind. The position of
the judiciary on the civil and political rights of citizens is governed by
the type of political system within which the judicial authority operates,
as well as the political and ideological inclinations of individual judges,
notwithstanding the constitutional requirement of their neutrality.
Judges as individuals or even as a professional organization are free to
take whatever stand their majority prefers at any particular moment.

With this understanding of the two faces of judges in Egypt, I will
examine their relationship with civil society in four parts. In the first
part, I will demonstrate how judges, acting as an arm of the state, curb
the freedom of civil society institutions. In the second part, I will discuss the judges' involvement as a professional association through their

clubs in the fight by civil society organizations for more autonomy. In the third part, I will show how certain judicial institutions strive to move civil and political liberties forward in order to expand the range of freedoms available to civil society organizations. In the fourth part, I will survey some of the ways civil society organizations have tried to win the judiciary to their side and get them to support their struggle for more respect for the civil and political rights of citizens. These multiple faces of the judiciary should not occasion any surprise. The judicial power, like other state apparatuses, is characterized by ideological and political pluralism and is far from a homogeneous body. The period covered by this study is the duration of the Mubarak presidency, or twenty-six years at the time of writing, encompassing four presidential terms and two years of his fifth term. A few examples will be drawn from earlier periods, particularly from the post-July 1952 period.

## The Judicial Authority as an Arm of the State

Under normal conditions, perhaps excepting, for example, revolutionary times, the judicial authority would always act as an arm of the state. This position is not necessarily due to the conservative bent sometimes attributed to judges. No matter how functionally independent judges are, they are duty-bound to uphold the laws made and adopted by the other two state branches, the executive authority and the legislature. Some judicial bodies may try to interpret the law in ways not foreseen by those who drafted them, but such bodies cannot stray from the explicit provisions of the law. No court in Egypt could either legalize the Muslim Brotherhood as an association, since the group was banned by a sovereign decision of the Revolutionary Command Council in 1954, or allow it to be established as a political party against the explicit provisions of the Law of Political Parties of 1977, which prohibits the establishment of political parties based on religious discrimination. In these instances, the judges' hands are tied by the laws of an authoritarian state, no matter what they think of the two issues. In other cases, however, judges have demonstrated an activism not in the service of a nascent civil society but in curbing or even closing down organs of civil society. Two examples are sufficient to demonstrate this point.

One example is that opposition and independent newspapers occasionally run into hard times with the courts. The editors of *al-Ahali*, the newspaper of the Patriotic Progressive Unionist Rally, Tajammu', found their journal seized and banned from circulation during the last two years of the Sadat presidency on the basis of court orders, which usually came from a first instance court in Cairo. The presiding judge in this court, the late Anwar Abu Sihli, later became minister of justice.[2] Several rulings to imprison journalists on shaky libel claims have been made in recent years, the latest in the spring of 2005, which affected journalists of independent newspapers such as *al-Fajr* and *al-Dustur*. In one particular case, a journalist was condemned to one year in prison for allegedly insulting a judge in an article she wrote for an independent newspaper.

The second example is that several courts, ranging from a first instance court to the prestigious Court of Cassation, which upheld a lower court decision that ordered Cairo University professor Nasr Hamid Abu Zayd to divorce his wife. The case alleged that he had deviated in his writings from the teachings of Islam. In the judges' eyes, he was an apostate and, as such, his marriage to a Muslim woman was invalid. As Abu Zayd did not find these rulings, based on the notion of *hisba,* to be fair, and as his wife shared his view, they fled the country.[3] In a more recent case, the country's renowned poet, Ahmed 'Abd al-Muti' Higazi, was threatened in August 2007 with the forced sale of his furniture in order to pay a fine for authorizing the publication of a poem that insulted a Muslim religious leader.[4]

In these two cases, courts moved to intimidate journalists, university professors, and poets, telling them that their freedoms of expression, research, and belief had limits. Such limits are usually not known in democratic societies. The rulings cast heavy shadows on two of the most important institutions of civil society: universities and the press.

Although these rulings came from ordinary civil courts, the state in Egypt does not always trust such courts to judge civil society activists and political opponents. Egyptian judges have exhibited certain liberal leanings that they inherited from the semi-liberal past of pre-revolution Egypt and learned through their predominantly liberal education in faculties of law. Previous governments established 'special courts' to try their opponents. The Revolutionary Command Council started this practice by setting up the Court of the Revolution, the Court of Treason, and later the state security courts, as well as sequestration tribunals, anti-feudalist tribunals, and trials of civilians before military tribunals. President Anwar Sadat added the political tribunal, which tried his opponents in the Arab Socialist Union (ASU) in 1971, and the courts of values in 1980. Under the state of emergency, ongoing since

1981, state security courts authorized under the emergency law have been established and the transfer of civilians for trial in military tribunals has become common practice. At one time, the number of special tribunals acting outside the ordinary organization of the judiciary was eleven, with some staffed by judges acting under special laws and others by people with no legal qualifications or acting beyond their original jurisdiction, as in the case of military tribunals.[5]

## Judges as a Professional Body or as Organs of Civil Society

The other face of judges in Egypt is manifested in their activities as a professional organization independent from and even posing a challenge to the authority of the executive branch and the legislature. The recent history of judges as an autonomous collective actor offers three instances of the judges challenging one or both of these authorities. In this respect, they set an example for civil society organizations and act as a catalyst for establishing more favorable conditions in which to expand and empower civil society.

The first instance was the confrontation in 1968 and 1969 between the Judges' Club and the ASU, which at the time was the single mass organization in the country. The judges were concerned that certain proposals by the late Ali Sabry, secretary-general of the ASU from 1965 to 1967, would further undermine their independence and subordinate them to the organization. These proposals included integrating judges into the ASU, nominating militants of the ASU to become judges without the usual procedures that ensure proper qualifications in judges, and introducing a jury system in Egyptian courts. In March 1968, the general assembly of the Judges' Club adopted a number of resolutions that rejected all of these proposals. The assembly's stand was perceived by the executive authority, particularly the minister of justice and President Gamal 'Abd al-Nasser, as a serious challenge. The response came a year later with the suspension of the judicial authority law, the dismissal of a large number of senior judges, including elected members of the club, and the transferal of other judges to less important posts. These drastic measures are known in Egyptian history as the Massacre of the Judiciary. Many of the judges affected by these measures were reinstated on 15 December 1971, in the wake of the removal of opponents of the late President Sadat in the ASU that previous May and their trial in what was labeled by Sadat as the 'corrective revolution.'[6]

The second instance was the Judges' Club's first Justice Conference in 1986, which adopted a number of resolutions that would, if implemented, ensure the autonomy of the judiciary by limiting appointment to the Supreme Judicial Council to elected judges, allowing judges to have an independent budget, abolishing several laws that restricted citizens' civil and political rights, known in Egypt as the 'ill-reputed laws,' and guaranteeing complete judicial supervision of national elections. The resolutions also called for strict adherence to Islamic law, or *shari'a*, in the country's legislation. Few of these demands were met by the executive authority, except judicial supervision of voting in legislative elections between 2000 and 2005. The most important demands have either been ignored by the executive and legislative authorities or are still said by some spokespersons to be under consideration.[7]

Finally, the government's continuing disregard of judges' demands led the Judges' Club to threaten to boycott supervision of the presidential elections of September 2005. With this threat, the club renewed its demands concerning a law guaranteeing judicial independence, namely through the election of members of the Supreme Judicial Council, an independent budget for the judiciary, and the end of the executive authority's disciplinary powers over judges, as implemented by officials of the ministry of justice. In May 2006, the Judges' Club threatened to hold a silent protest and to picket in front of the High Judiciary Building if its demands were not met. The silent protest took place even though the president of the Supreme Judicial Council ordered disciplinary action against two of the judges, who allegedly revealed to newspapers irregularities in the first competitive presidential elections and the parliamentary elections in 2005. The government later introduced a law that met some of the demands of the club, particularly for an independent budget for the judiciary, but it continued to ignore its other demands. The tension between judges and the government continued with the appointment of Counselor Mamduh Mar'i as minister of justice, who expressed hostility toward both the Judges' Club and the Judges' Club of the State Council. The constitutional amendments of 2007 ended direct supervision of elections by judges. The government also raised the retirement age of judges to seventy—a change vehemently opposed by most judges.

In all these instances, the Judges' Club acted in the same way that many civil society organizations do, calling for autonomy in relation to the executive and legislative authorities and for strict respect for civil and political rights. No wonder its stand was welcomed immediately by established civil society organizations and by the Egyptian public in general, although spokespersons for the Cairo and Alexandria clubs continue to disclaim that they are part of civil society and insist that they are members of an authority of the state.

## Civil Society Organizations' Resort to the Courts

A number of civil society organizations of all sorts have resorted to the courts to complain of serious violations of various categories of human rights. They have asked the courts to order an end to such violations and have urged the executive authority to adhere to the constitutional and legal provisions for such rights. It is difficult to offer a complete survey of all the cases that have been filed by civil society organizations. A study of some suggests the major trends in this relationship between civil society organizations and the judiciary.

Most of the civil society organizations that have resorted to courts are advocacy organizations, particularly human rights groups. Chambers of commerce and other professional associations also have found their way to courts to challenge acts of the government they considered unlawful. Chambers of commerce complained to the courts in 1972 against a decision by the minister of supply that limited the profit margin on imported goods. The Bar Association protested the suspension of its internal elections to the State Council in 1999 and received a favorable ruling that allowed it to end the suspension and organize elections in 2000. Since then, elections in the Bar Association have been won by a coalition of lawyers in nationalist and Islamist factions, with the latter constituting the majority in national and provincial councils of the association.

This reliance on the courts reflects one feature of the political system under President Mubarak, who has left the task of settling intractable political disputes to the judiciary and who has shown himself willing to abide by court rulings, although more during the early years of his presidency than in later years. That it is mostly human rights organizations that avail themselves of the opportunity to go to court is perhaps due to their character as advocacy organizations. They adopt litigation as one of their methods of addressing the grievances of citizens. These organizations are led mostly by lawyers or depend largely on lawyers in the performance of their functions, and it is normal that lawyers would use the professional method of action that they know best. In addition, other methods of action, such as the organization of public protests and use of the mass media, are either difficult to use because of restrictions imposed by the security authorities on the freedom of assembly or are unlikely to produce tangible results. Egyptian courts in general and the State Council and the Supreme Constitutional Court in particular have stood by civil society organizations in their defense of civil and political rights. However, a few cases in which civil society organizations did not get favorable rulings are exceptions to this trend. These cases have tended to relate to the interpretation by courts of the implications of Article 2 of the constitution, which considers *sharia* the principal source of legislation, and to differences between certain courts and human rights organizations over the scope of trade union rights.

The most important issues in disputes between the government and civil society organizations have been: freedom of association, trade union rights, the fairness of elections, economic and social rights, the organizational decisions of the government, the right to equality and nondiscrimination, and unmerited decisions by local authorities.

## Freedom of Association

The Egyptian government has ratified several human rights instruments on respect for the freedom of association. Freedom of association nevertheless has been restricted in almost all its manifestations under all regimes in Egypt. The government could always claim that exercise of this right is subject to the provisions of law, but instead of facilitating the exercise of the right, the several relevant laws concerning freedom of association in Egypt have served to prevent citizens from exercising it. The exercise of the right to peaceful assembly requires a security authorization, particularly if the assembly takes the form of a march or demonstration. Such authorization is seldom given. Political parties can be established only upon approval by a committee dominated by the government or through legal battles in courts that can take several years. Elections have been suspended in no fewer than twelve professional associations since the mid-1990s in the context of a confrontation between the government and those members of the educated middle class who tend to support the Islamist movement. Trade unions are tightly controlled by the ministry of manpower, and although the Law of Associations of 2002 dropped some of the most restrictive provisions of Law 32/1964, the government still finds ways to make life difficult for associations that are not to its liking.[8] Human rights organizations, which gained legal status only recently thanks to the more liberal provisions of this law, fully realize the serious implications of restrictions on the freedom of association. It is only through the act of association that citizens can gain a voice in the government of their country and promote their own legitimate, collective interests. It is no wonder then that this freedom has been a major focus of the legal actions of human rights groups.

Egyptian lawyers resorted to the State Council to protest government procrastination in holding elections in their association. Following mass mobilization among the rank and file of the Bar Association, lawyers finally obtained a court ruling in their favor. The Bar Association thereby became the only professional syndicate since the mid-1990s to hold elections for its leading organs. It has held two rounds of elections since 2000, which were won by a coalition of opposition groups. The syndicates of engineers and of medical doctors, which found themselves in the same situation, were not as successful.

Another famous case of freedom of association centered on the right of the Egyptian Organization for Human Rights (EOHR) to legal recognition, which it failed to achieve for almost fifteen years. EOHR finally won a favorable ruling from the Court of Administrative Litigation of the State Council on 1 July 2001. That ruling called for the suspension of implementation and the annulment of the decision of the ministry of social affairs not to allow the EOHR to be counted as an association. The ruling signaled the successful end of the legal battle launched by the EOHR to achieve legal recognition by the government and the ability to conduct its activities under a semblance of normality.[9]

The Land Center also resorted to the courts to defend its freedom of association, protesting the decision of the ministry of social affairs not to give legal status to the Awlad al-Ard (Sons of the Land) Human Rights Foundation. The decision of the ministry was based on Egyptian security agencies' reluctance to allow the foundation to function. The Land Center raised its objection before the Administrative Court, which accepted the objection on 8 February 2004. The Foundation was able to start its activities soon after.[10]

## Trade Union Rights

Restrictions on trade union rights take many forms in Egypt.[11] Workers cannot choose which trade union to join as there is only one trade union for each industry and a single Federation of Trade Unions in the country. Elections in trade unions are tightly controlled by the ministry of manpower, which is empowered to issue the documents necessary for any worker to become eligible as a candidate and run for an elective office in a trade union. The right to collective bargaining is rarely used and the right to strike is limited to industrial trade unions, which rarely grant this right to shopfloor workers or to any similar group of workers. Some human rights organizations are particularly concerned with workers' rights, including Hisham Mubarak Law Center, the Land Center, and the House of Trade Union Services. The first of these has defended trade union rights on several occasions, but perhaps its most important legal fight was over obtaining an annulment of the trade union elections in 2001 on the basis of serious violations. The violations included that the elections were administered without direct judicial supervision and that the General Federation of Trade Unions chose its own candidates to serve on the committees responsible for conducting the elections. Trade unions also failed to provide candidates standing for election with the necessary membership documents. For these reasons, the chambers of the State Council in Cairo and Qalyubiya Governorates annulled the decision of the minister of manpower, who had declared the final count of the 2001 trade union elections.

On 7 February 1997, the Hisham Mubarak Law Center obtained a ruling from the Supreme Constitutional Court on the unconstitutionality of one paragraph (Article 36c) of Law 35/1976 on workers' syndicates, which the court found incompatible with articles of the constitution. Workers supported by the center argued that seventeen other articles of the law were unconstitutional, but the Supreme Constitutional Court supported their position on only one subparagraph of one article. The same court, on 2 June 2001, rejected another claim by workers supported by the Hisham Mubarak Law Center that other articles of the Law of Trade Unions are unconstitutional.[12]

## Fairness of Elections

There is no doubt that free and fair general or professional elections are a wild dream in Egypt. A major demand of most opposition political parties, civil society organizations, and enlightened public figures is for the government to allow citizens to exercise this lawful right freely and to allow the counting of votes to be carried out honestly and in a transparent manner. This has not yet happened. It was therefore a major victory when several human rights organizations succeeded in getting court rulings to allow the presence of civil society organizations inside voting stations in order to monitor the People's Assembly elections in 2005 effectively. Another favorable ruling was that television cameras be installed in voting stations to ensure transparency. The two rulings were made by the first chamber of the Court of Administrative Litigation of the State Council.

The first ruling was made in response to a case filed by the EOHR, the Group for Democratic Development, the Arab Organization for Penal Reform, the Arab Center for the Independence of the Judiciary and the Legal Profession, the Center for the Development of Democratic Dialogue on Human Rights, and the Association for Legal Aid. The ruling was made on 6 November 2005, against the objections of the minister of justice, who was the head of the Supreme Commission for Parliamentary Elections. The Arab Center for the Independence of the Judiciary and the Legal Profession, the EOHR, the Arab Organization for Penal Reform, and others obtained the second ruling on 3 December 2005. Both rulings were obtained against strong opposition from the electoral commission. A similar ruling was obtained before the presidential election of September 2005 that supported the right of civil society organizations to monitor elections inside voting stations. Unfortunately, the decision was overturned on appeal by the Supreme Administrative Court (see Chapter 15 in this volume, by Nathalie Bernard-Maugiron).

Human rights organizations have been careful to help ensure the fairness of elections in professional and business associations. The Land Center, for example, noted that elections at the regional chamber of commerce in Giza Governorate were marred by irregularities. In this case, it appealed to the minister of trade to annul the election, which had taken place on 28 May 2006, basing its objection on 1938 and 1946 rulings of administrative tribunals that considered soundness of elections the cornerstone of the democratic process.[13]

## Economic and Social Rights

Economic and social rights have been threatened by the government's gradual adoption of neoliberal economic policies since the mid-1970s. This began with the declaration of the so-called Open Door Policy and increased after Egypt signed agreements with the International Monetary Fund and the World Bank in 1991 known as the Economic Reform and Structural Adjustment Program. In 1986, the government

abandoned its policy of guaranteed employment for university graduates, leaving it largely to market forces to determine the price of basic
commodities and services and allowing the private sector to play a
larger role in the country's economy. Human rights organizations have
since sought to alleviate the suffering of the poor under these policies.
Since its establishment in 1997, the Land Center has been involved in
defending the rights of peasants, workers, women, and children against
landowners, employers, and the government administration. It has ventured to defend the civil rights of these citizens against torture and
has expanded its activities to include protection of the environment.
It publicizes various types of violations, communicates complaints to
competent authorities, including the general prosecutor, and files cases
on behalf of victims. The following table gives an idea of the scope of
the legal actions undertaken by the Land Center.

**Number of legal cases filed by the Land Center, 1997–2004**

| Year | Number of cases filed |
|------|----------------------|
| 1997 | 563 |
| 1998 | 1,021 |
| 1999 | 604 |
| 2000 | 320 |
| 2001 | 789 |
| 2002 | 597 |
| 2003 | 843 |
| 2004 | 623 |

The number of cases increased sharply in 1998 because of the disputes occasioned by the implementation of Law 96/1992, which came
into force in 1997, governing relations between owners and tenants of
agricultural land. The number of cases dropped a year later and reached
its lowest level in 2000. It rose again in the following years, although
it never reached the level of 1998. The cases filed by the center have
included claims of unconstitutionality of certain laws, which were considered by the Supreme Constitutional Court. Other cases related to
peasants', workers', women's, and children's rights or the protection of
the environment and were filed in administrative courts or civil courts.

The center was able to win cases ranging from half of the total cases it filed in 2004 to almost 90 percent in 2000.

The Land Center has not been satisfied with defending workers' and peasants' specific rights but has also moved to challenge the legal framework around the exercise of these rights. It has contested the labor code twice, for its discrimination against women and for entrusting industrial disputes to administrative rather than judicial authorities. The first occasion was a complaint by a woman agricultural worker who was arbitrarily fired from her job and denied payment of her wage following thirty-five years of service. She first complained to the local labor office, which rejected her complaint, arguing that Labor Law 137 of 1981 did not apply to female agricultural work. The Land Center filed a suit with the Giza First Instance Court. During deliberation of the case, the Land Center asked the court to refer the relevant Article (159 of Law 137/1981) to the Supreme Constitutional Court. The center held that the article was unconstitutional because it discriminated against women, in violation of provisions of the constitution that ban such discrimination.

On another occasion, a worker was fired and complained to the competent labor office. The complaint was referred to the five-member committee in charge of settling labor disputes, which was provided for in Article 71 of Unified Labor Code No. 12 of 2003. The committee is made up of two judges, the director of the local labor office, a member of the General Federation of Trade Unions of Egypt, and a member of the concerned business association. The Land Center argued that the Court of South Cairo's decision to establish such a committee was unconstitutional because it substituted an administrative organ for the judiciary in matters related to dispute settlement. Dispute settlement is an inalienable right of the judicial authority. This decision was therefore a violation of the constitution, which upholds the principles of independence of the judiciary and separation of powers. On 22 April 2004, the court of the State Council before which this case was filed agreed to refer Articles 70–71 of the Unified Labor Code to the Supreme Constitutional Court.[14]

The Hisham Mubarak Law Center has been no less active in defending workers' rights. In fact, whereas the Land Center broadened its mandate to include peasants, workers, and even middle class people, the Hisham Mubarak Law Center has focused its attention on workers' rights. The list of its engagement in the legal defense of workers' rights is a long one.

## The Organizational Decisions of the Government

Some of the issues taken up by human rights groups relate to the government's organizational decisions. In one such case, the Land Center objected to the government's decision to change the legal status of a government authority to make it a holding company. The center's main argument was that the decision was incompatible with several articles of the constitution before it was amended in 2007. These articles stressed the socialist character of the economic system of the country and declared that the state guarantees provision of cultural, social, and health services to citizens and particularly to village inhabitants. The center argued that the transformation of the Water and Sewage Authority into a holding company was only one step toward its sale to or management by the private sector, which is guided by the profit motive. It argued that this would make it difficult for villagers and poor citizens in general to obtain the basic services the authority provided.[15] I should note that this case had not been decided at the time of writing and that water became a scarce commodity in several parts of the country in the summer of 2007. Citizens in the Daqhliya and Gharbiya Governorates and even in some districts of Cairo demonstrated against the shortage of water, both for drinking and for irrigation, in rural areas. The Constitution of the Arab Republic of Egypt was amended in March 2007 to drop all those articles that ascribed a socialist character to the state or the economy.

## Right to Equality and Nondiscrimination

Although Egyptian laws generally do not discriminate among citizens on the basis of their religious beliefs, Copts in Egypt have long complained of instances of discrimination against them, whether in the text of the law or in the practices of the government at the national and local levels. Human rights organizations in general condemn such discrimination, but one organization in particular, namely the Kalima Center for Human Rights, led by Mamduh Nakhla, a Coptic lawyer, took it upon itself to fight instances of discrimination through the courts. A website favorable to the Kalima Center indicated that the center had filed twelve cases pending at the time of writing. The center has filed cases against most senior officials of the government, including the president, the prime minister, the minister of the interior, the minister of justice, and the minister of information. In one case, in 1998, it called on the president to rescind his decision to delegate his powers concerning maintenance work on churches to governors and to entrust these powers to district architects. In 1996, it filed a case against the president demanding that the first day of the Coptic calendar be declared a national holiday in the same way that the first day of the Islamic *(hijri)* calendar is a national holiday. In 1999, the center demanded that the prime minister allocate LE300 million for the Coptic Church so that it could be on equal terms with *al-Azhar*, which receives an annual grant in this amount from the government. Three years later, it demanded that churches, like mosques, be exempt from payment of water and electricity bills.

The center also asked the minister of the interior to drop the Ottoman sultan's decree specifying ten conditions for the building of churches (1996), to delete reference to religion on national identity cards (1997), and to order the removal of all religious stickers that Egyptian drivers, both Muslims and Copts, used to put on their cars (1998). In 1995, it demanded that the minister of education organize school exams on a day other than 7 January, which is Christmas Day for Copts and for other Orthodox Churches. That same year, it asked the minister of culture to cancel fees paid by foreign tourists when they enter old Coptic churches. In 1997, the minister of information was asked to show Sunday mass on television for one hour every Sunday. Finally, in 1996, the center demanded that the minister of justice rescind the bylaw on the personal status of Orthodox Copts because Copts consider it incompatible with their religious beliefs. The government responded favorably to some of these demands, either on its own, as such demands were widely supported by Copts, or in response to court rulings. The minister of information ordered that Coptic mass be broadcast live for one hour every Sunday on the Egyptian satellite television channel. Since January 1996, 7 January has been a national holiday. Since August 1996 fees paid by foreign tourists visiting old Coptic churches have been juridicially canceled.

## Contesting the Decisions of Local Authorities
The Land Center's and the Hisham Mubarak Law Center's cases have not been limited to the defense of workers' and peasants' rights or to contesting acts of the central executive authority. The Land Center also lent a hand to citizens complaining about unconstitutional acts by local authorities. An example is the cleanliness fee that was imposed by the governor of Cairo and added to the electricity bills of all inhabitants

of Cairo Governorate. The Land Center argued that the fee constituted a tax, and, because the constitution of the Republic of Egypt does
not empower local authorities to impose taxes, which are entrusted
exclusively to the People's Assembly, it pointed out that the fee was
unconstitutional. The center argued, moreover, that the fee was incompatible with previous court rulings, as the Court of Administrative
Litigation had rejected such a fee in an earlier case.[16]

In a related complaint, the Land Center objected to the seizure by
Giza Governorate of the movable properties of citizens who did not
pay the cleanliness fees and argued that the governorate, in fact, had
not cleaned streets. The matter finally was referred to the Supreme
Constitutional Court, which accepted the Land Center's argument that
the jailing of citizens or the seizure of their properties is an administrative act that violates the right of citizens to resort to courts to settle
their disputes with organs of the government. The court noted that
state authorities are subject to the law and the constitution and are
required to respect the constitution.[17]

## Conclusion

This article has demonstrated that Egyptian civil society organizations
have been capable of registering important victories in the legal battles
they have waged against violations of human rights, irrespective of the
source of these violations, which mostly has been the executive authority. Judges often have been sympathetic to the cause of human rights
as defended by these organizations. Nevertheless, a few negative trends
have emerged in recent decades.

1)  Litigation took many years in several cases because of the opposi-
    tion of the executive authority. The case of the registration of the
    EOHR is a flagrant example of slow justice. It took the organiza-
    tion close to fifteen years to obtain a ruling in its favor, which is not
    unusual.

2)  If it is unhappy with court rulings, the government simply objects to
    the implementation of certain binding court rulings, as it did with
    the ruling obtained by the Hisham Mubarak Law Center on the
    annulment of the 2001 trade union elections. The leadership of the
    general Federation of Trade Unions, which is supported by the min-
    istry of labor, simply ignored that ruling.

3)  In a number of cases, courts have handed down decisions that were
    not to the liking of some civil society organizations. The Supreme

Constitutional Court rejected the arguments of Hisham Mubarak Law Center lawyers in favor of a declaration of unconstitutionality of several provisions of the Law on Trade Unions. It is interesting that the government now is being called upon by the International Labour Organization to adopt a new trade union law that is more in line with international labor conventions.

4) A legal opinion from the State Council a few years ago gave *al-Azhar* competence to judge what it considers religious matters in literary and artistic works, an opinion highly criticized by writers and human rights organizations.

One could argue, therefore, that whereas civil society organizations are capable of getting court rulings that support their demands to lift restrictions on the exercise of human rights in the country, they have faced difficulties on specific issues that clash with the overly liberal position of Egyptian judges in social matters and with a secular stand on matters of freedom of belief and of expression.

# 15

# The Relationship between Judges and Human Rights Organizations during the 2005 Elections and the Referendum

*Nathalie Bernard-Maugiron*

The year 2005 was a particularly loaded one for voters in Egypt. The Egyptian people were asked to agree on the amendment of Article 76 of the constitution through a national referendum in anticipation of electing the president of the republic and members of the People's Assembly.[1] Many actors were mobilized to guarantee the utmost transparency of elections. Two of the actors managed to follow all or part of the electoral procedures inside the polling stations: judges and civil society organizations. Little by little, a close alliance was formed between them. The rapprochement that started with the referendum was reinforced during the presidential and legislative elections. It was manifested at various levels, as each actor extended support to the other in order to improve supervision as much as possible. The two were united against the executive authority and against the two electoral commissions established to supervise the presidential and parliamentary elections.

The judiciary already had come to the rescue of non-governmental organizations (NGOs) in the past. For instance, the Supreme Constitutional Court (SCC) handed down a judgment in 2000 declaring the unconstitutionality of Law 153/1999, the Law of Associations,[2] which NGOs had strongly criticized. In order to invalidate it on grounds of procedural error, the court characterized the text as a "law complementary to the Constitution."[3] This qualification is only applicable to laws considered fundamental, however. In order to prove that the law should be considered fundamental, the constitutional judge insisted on the importance of the freedom of association and of NGOs, stating that NGOs are a "link between individuals and the state" and a "guarantor for individual liberty." Their primary role, according to the constitutional judge, is "awakening people's conscience, extending general knowledge and culture, educating the citizen on the culture of democracy to reach a higher level of social and economic development."

The SCC also stated that the right to establish private associations was closely related to freedom of assembly, individual liberty, and freedom of expression, all of which are guaranteed by the constitution. An association aims to create a forum where individuals can debate their common concerns and express their positions and expectations peacefully. Infringement of the right of association by the executive authority is an attack on democratic values and the popular will. The SCC concluded that the Law of Associations, which touched on essential constitutional guarantees, had to be considered a fundamental law and thus complementary to the constitution. As such, it should have been submitted to the Consultative Council for its opinion in conformity with Article 195 of the Constitution before being submitted to the People's Assembly. Since the Consultative Council had not been consulted, the SCC declared Law 153/1999 unconstitutional on grounds of procedural error.[4]

Other recent examples of courts favoring NGOs and the freedom of association can be found in State Council jurisprudence, particularly after the adoption of Law 84/2002, which replaced Law 153/1999. After the Ministry for Social Affairs' refusal to register them, several NGOs filed an appeal in administrative courts, which on several occasions ruled against the ministry's decisions and required it to grant registration permits to NGOs. The New Women Foundation (Mu'assasat al-Mar'a al-Jadida), which defends women's rights, is an example. A registration permit for this foundation was turned down in June 2003 "for security reasons," probably because its board of directors included many women with a history of political activism. Through the support of another NGO, the Hisham Mubarak Law Center, the foundation filed an appeal before the Court of Administrative Litigation. On 26 October 2003, the court struck down the ministry's rejection decision on grounds of procedural error, as the administrative authority had not provided grounds for turning down the application, in violation of Article 6 of the new Law of Associations.

NGOs have extended their support to judges, as well. For instance, the Egyptian Organization for Human Rights (EOHR) awarded Yahya al-Rifaʻi, then president of the Judges' Club, its 1990 Fathi Radwan Prize for Human Rights in recognition of the role he played in the struggle for independence of the judiciary. In 1997, the Arab Center for the Independence of the Judiciary and the Legal Profession (ACIJLP) was established to defend judges and lawyers in the Arab world, which furthered the rapprochement between NGOs and magistrates.

While Egyptian judges and NGOs had interacted on several occasions in the past, the events of 2005 occasioned new manifestations and forms of support between them. Judges and NGOs supported one another in attempting to ensure the transparency of the ballot. Judges fought for the right of NGOs to enter polling stations while civil society organizations maintained their total support for judges, siding with them repeatedly through press releases, public statements, and conferences. Beyond such reciprocal support, NGOs and judges both supervised and observed the referendum and elections, and both reported the abuses and fraud that marred the elections. Their recommendations centered on the same issues, and they went beyond requests for changes to electoral procedures to demands for reforms in the legal and political environment itself.

## Judges' Support for Civil Society
Judges supported NGOs' requests to observe the elections through rulings and in a number of their individual and collective positions.

### NGO Supervision of the Presidential Elections
The decision of the Court of Administrative Litigation, handed down on 3 September 2005, was in clear support of NGO requests.

Several human rights NGOs submitted a request to the secretariat of the Presidential Elections Commission to be authorized to observe the elections inside the polling stations. They did not receive any official reply, but they came to know through the independent daily newspaper *al-Misri al-yawm* that the head of the Electoral Commission had declared,[5] during a meeting at the National Center for Judicial Studies, that local observers would never be authorized to enter polling stations because he did not want the judiciary to be subjected to any supervision, certainly not by human rights NGOs. The NGOs considered that they had not received an official reply, and challenged this implicit rejection before the administrative judiciary,[6] the State Council.

The defense of the commission was based mainly on its claim that the administrative judge was incompetent to examine such a challenge. According to newly amended Article 76 of the constitution, Presidential Elections Commission decisions cannot be challenged by any means or before any authority whatsoever. Only the commission itself can examine appeals against its own decisions—a provision that was widely criticized by opposition parties, NGOs, judges, and law professors during the constitutional amendments drafting process. Since the provision is now part of the constitution, it enjoys superiority over all other norms, and the Presidential Elections Commission has claimed jurisdictional immunity for all its decisions, including those concerning NGOs.

Everyone was astonished when the State Council declared itself competent to examine the challenge filed by the NGOs. To justify its decision, the Court of Administrative Litigation maintained that Article 76 definitely extended immunity to the decisions of the commission taken within the framework of its attributions. The court suggested, however, that Article 76 and the Law on Presidential Elections had given an exhaustive list of the competences exercised by the commission and that its decision to prevent NGOs from accessing polling stations fell outside its mandate. The commission's decision had to be considered an ordinary administrative decision and thus one that did not escape the control of the administrative judge.

On the merits, the court held that civil society organizations, including human rights NGOs, aim at reviving (*ihya'*) the idea of democracy among the various strata and categories of the people and ensuring the transparency of elections. It argued that they had to be authorized to observe the electoral process as long as they did not hinder the work of the heads of the polling stations.

NGOs praised the State Council's "historic" decision and were quite relieved that, for the first time, they would be authorized to enter polling stations. The Presidential Elections Commission held an emergency meeting and maintained that it would disregard the ruling (*'adam i'tidad*), insisting that only judges and candidates' representatives would be authorized to enter the stations. The commission also stated that the right to give authorization fell within its competence and that the judgment of the State Council had been issued by a court lacking competence and had no legal effect.[7]

The commission proceeded along legal channels and filed an appeal against the ruling issued by the Court of Administrative Litigation. NGOs remained optimistic, especially as the report submitted by the State Council's commissioners was in their favor.[8] The commissioners' report advised rejection of the appeal on the basis that the decision to authorize the NGOs was not part of the competence of the commission.[9] The report noted that observation by civil society organizations would not interfere with the work of the committees or the electoral process. On the contrary, it had to be considered laudable cooperation (*musharaka hamida*) in the democratic process, especially considering that the elections were going to be held in a single day. Supervision by judges would not be completely integral because the head of every polling station would be responsible for many ballot boxes. NGOs' participation could help judges ensure that the elections were transparent and impartial.

The 6 September decision of the Supreme Administrative Court put an end to the NGOs' hopes. On the eve of the elections, the court revoked the ruling issued by the Court of Administrative Litigation. It held that the administrative judge was effectively incompetent to examine this challenge because of the judicial immunity granted to the decisions of the Presidential Elections Commission. In an unexpected *obiter dictum*, however, the court vigorously criticized new Article 76, which it deemed in contradiction to Articles 68 and 172 of the constitution.[10] The court urged the legislature to reexamine this provision in order to bring it into conformity with the established principles pertaining to the prohibition of depriving an administrative decision from the control of the administrative judge.

This decision meant that NGOs could not observe the elections directly, but the next morning saw a reversal of sorts just a few hours after the opening of the polling stations. The Presidential Elections Commission announced that independent observers would be authorized to access the polling stations indoors, provided they obtained an authorization from the commission and did not to interfere (*'adam tadakhkhul*) in the activities of the election committees.

The commission maintained that this decision was justified by its intention to prove that there was transparency in voting, explaining that its initial refusal had been due to its desire to organize the work inside the polling stations and not due to its fear of supervision.[11] The time chosen to announce this decision raised eyebrows, however. Many people wondered whether the commission had tried to underpin the credibility of the elections without assuring any real observation of the electoral process by civil society organizations.[12] Practically speaking, the commission's last minute change of mind had little effect. Almost none of the judges heading the polling stations was officially informed,[13] and so most of them held to their earlier instructions.[14] The few judges who extended a welcome to the observers often did so in response to the recommendations issued by the Judges' Club, which had encouraged them not to respect the instructions of the commission on this issue. Their decision was not based on the commission's announcement, about which they knew virtually nothing. Moreover, NGOs had to obtain prior authorization from the Presidential Elections Commission, which was impossible for the observers stationed outside Cairo. Even those on election premises could not obtain this authorization because the commission employees seemed not to have been informed of this decision.[15]

## NGO Supervision of the Legislative Elections

The Supreme Electoral Commission, which is in charge of organizing legislative elections, also did not respond officially to requests by NGOs but announced in a press release on 24 October 2005, that NGOs and the National Council for Human Rights would be authorized to observe the elections on the condition that they coordinate their actions.[16] The participation of civil society observers also was conditioned on their being neutral, with no political affiliation, and on their members not being participants in the elections. These conditions were subject to many criticisms from NGOs and judges. How, for instance, can the neutrality of an NGO be assessed?[17] How can the prohibition of political affiliation be applied?[18]

Many NGOs that were still waiting for an official reply from the commission and refusing to collaborate with the National Council for Human Rights decided to turn to the Court of Administrative Litigation.[19] They demanded truly transparent elections and grounded their appeal on various legal texts, among which was Article 3 of the constitution on the people's sovereignty, Article 14 on citizens' right to participate in public affairs, and international legal instruments such as the Universal Declaration on Human Rights and the Declaration on the Right and Responsibility of Individuals, Groups, and Organs of Society to Promote and Protect Universally Recognized Human Rights and Fundamental Freedoms.

On 6 November, the court responded favorably to the NGOs' request and struck down the commission's tacit rejection, maintaining that civil society organizations should be granted authorization without having to coordinate with the National Council for Human Rights. The court also asserted that the supervision of the elections by judges should not prevent observation by civil society organizations. The court added that the role of civil society organizations, within the framework of the party system and of the political transformations taking place in the country, is to allow the peaceful expression of opinions and participation for the political, social, and economic edification of society. The court insisted that NGOs be present during the counting of the ballots.

In this case, the competence of the administrative judge was not raised as a legal issue, as had occurred in the case of the Presidential Election Commission, since the decisions of the Commission supervising legislative elections had not been granted the same jurisdictional immunity as that enjoyed by the Presidential Elections Commission. In practice, NGOs managed to have access to the primary polling stations where the voting process was taking place, but very few of them were authorized to attend the counting of the votes.

## Cameras in Polling Stations

Another decision of the Court of Administrative Litigation that could have equally positive effects for the transparency of the electoral process and the role of NGOs was issued on 3 December 2005. In a case brought by ACIJLP, the court decided that observers of the electoral process had to be authorized to use closed-circuit television cameras to observe the counting of ballots during the parliamentary elections. The cameras were to be installed in every general polling station and linked to television sets outside the polling stations in order to allow follow-up on the counting of ballots without the operations being disturbed. The court maintained that civil society organizations' right to observe elections at all stages was incontestable and that they should be able to use all means and instruments to facilitate the exercise of this right, including cameras and closed-circuit television. This decision, adopted after the legislative elections were over, is slated to be applied in the next elections.

## The Judges' Club

The Judges' Club has expressed repeatedly its support for civil society organizations observing the elections, and has often referred to reports published by NGOs after elections. The club has stated many times that it is a representative of civil society, even if it refuses to be registered as an NGO.[20] During the two 2005 elections, the Judges' Club maintained that NGOs should be authorized to enter polling stations and that, contrary to the allegations of the executive authority, the intervention of NGOs was not contradictory to the supervision judges exercised. On the contrary, the club argued, the two types of supervision were complementary.

By mid-August 2005, the Judges' Club started criticizing the negative stance taken by the Presidential Elections Commission vis-à-vis NGOs and requested that representatives of civil society organizations be authorized to access polling stations.[21] On 2 September, during its extraordinary general assembly, the Judges' Club made clear, after announcing that it would supervise the forthcoming elections, that its members would refuse to endorse the results for Egyptian and foreign public opinion unless four conditions were fulfilled. One of these conditions was the presence of observers from civil society organizations inside polling stations.[22]

On 23 November, during the second phase of the legislative elections, shocked by the attitude of the police and security forces, the Judges' Club called for the intervention of the armed forces to protect judges. They also requested that the presidents of primary polling stations ensure that candidates and their delegates could attend the counting of the ballots. As the previous phases of the elections had shown, the most flagrant fraud actually took place during the counting process.

For each of the two elections as well as for the referendum, the Judges' Club decided to nominate a committee from within its membership to be in charge of writing a detailed report on election processes. The first report, concerning the referendum, was almost solely based on judges' testimony, but the other two reports referred to sources in civil society organizations. The report on the presidential elections indicated that in a meeting on 13 September, the report committee decided to take into consideration reports and testimony delivered by civil society organizations. The club's report stated that the committee had received reports from a dozen organizations that observed the elections, which it listed. It specified that the presence of observers was particularly important in countries and societies where human rights violations take place and where electoral fraud occurs. Supervision of elections by civil society organizations restores to the people confidence in the elections and in their results.

The report recalled the conflict with the Presidential Elections Commission over civil society supervision and the fact that the commission's rejection at times had been justified with a statement that since judges were supervising the elections and enjoyed full credibility, NGO observers were not necessary. The report presented a counterargument, namely that judicial supervision did not preclude observation by civil society organizations. The basis of the confidence vested in judges lies in the transparency *(al-shafafiya)* with which they perform their responsibilities, whether through the publicity of their sessions, the motivations for their decisions, or the possibility of appeal. Judges thus are used to working openly. Finally, the report recommended that NGOs be authorized to observe elections.

During the preparation of its report on the legislative elections, the Judges' Club declared its readiness to receive complaints or denunciations from NGOs that had supervised the elections, as well as from candidates or their representatives and from ordinary citizens.[23] On an individual basis, many judges expressed in newspapers or on television their support for NGO observation of the presidential elections. This support was shown again during the legislative elections, even if open support was not extended by all the (properly speaking) "judicial bodies." For example, the club of the Office of Administrative Prosecution, overwhelmed by the doubts raised by NGOs regarding its judicial nature and, consequently, its competence to supervise elections, launched a fierce attack on NGOs in a press release on 16 November. This club added that a decision of the SCC had clearly stated the judicial nature of the Office of Administrative Prosecution.[24]

Judges have expressed their genuine and comprehensive support in favor of the role of civil society organizations, and on many occasions NGOs have mobilized their support for the judges.

## NGO Support for Judges

NGOs have never hesitated to extend their support to the positions taken by judges, whether through press releases or at conferences. Two days after the extraordinary general assembly of the Judges' Club on 13 May 2005, six NGOs published a joint statement in which they lauded the stand taken by the judges. They said that judges could not be held responsible for the falsification of the people's will that had taken place in recent decades.[25] NGOs expressed their solidarity with judges in their demands for the amendment of the Law on Judicial Authority and the Law on the Exercise of Political Rights, as well as the recommendations adopted by the club. A few days later, ACIJLP expressed in a press release its deep concern regarding the press release published by the Supreme Judicial Council on 16 May, in which the council announced its rejection of the recommendations adopted by the Judges' Club, claiming that they represented only a minority opinion.[26]

On 4 September 2005, when the list of judges called to participate in electoral supervision was published with more than 1,500 sitting magistrates excluded, ACIJLP organized a press conference on its premises during which participants announced their support for the excluded judges.[27] Two months later, the Supreme Judicial Council announced that it had filed a complaint with the general prosecutor requesting him to carry out investigations regarding ten judges who had expressed opinions on political matters on satellite channels, which it claimed marred judges' image. The council contended that they had offended all judges and that the offending judges ought to have used legal channels. Eighteen NGOs responded with a joint press release, saying that the position of the Supreme Judicial Council was in contradiction to the freedom of opinion and expression by judges. To the signatories, the issue of the independence of the judiciary does not concern only judges but was a general concern of citizens.[28] They expressed anxiety at the threatening tone of the council's statements and warned against a new Massacre of the Judiciary. The EOHR declared its solidarity with the judges.[29]

In February 2006, the immunity of three of the most dynamic judges in the confrontation with the executive authority was lifted by the Supreme Judicial Council in order to allow the State Security Prosecution to investigate them.[30] The judges were charged with accusing some colleagues of having shared in electoral fraud. NGOs immediately expressed their solidarity with the three judges and issued a new press release denouncing the suspension of the government's financial assistance to the Judges' Club.[31] They announced their support for the judges in their rejection of the draft amendment of the 1972 Law on Judicial Authority as presented by the Supreme Judicial Council. The EOHR also issued a press release to express its support of the three judges.[32]

NGOs' solidarity with the judges was equally manifest in their organizing conferences and debates. ACIJLP organized a conference on the reform of the 1972 Law on Judicial Authority on 2 April 2005, in which many judges participated.[33] A second conference was organized by the same NGO on 20 July on the judicial supervision of elections in light of the Law on the Exercise of Political Rights. The participants recommended that judges be in charge of updating electoral lists, that judicial supervision be conducted inside and outside polling stations, and that only sitting judges be in charge of supervision.[34] Another conference was convened by ACIJLP on 29 September to discuss the role of the judiciary, the media, and civil society organizations in the process of observation and supervision of elections. Among the final recommendations of this conference were a call directed to the legislators that they respond to the judges' requests regarding the amendment of the Law on Judicial Authority; a demand for integrated supervision of elections by the judiciary, including the announcement of results; a demand that the selection of judges called to supervise elections be done by the general assemblies of the courts; and a call for a committee of the Judges' Club to be in charge of updating lists of voters.[35] The Cairo Institute for Human Rights Studies (CIHRS) organized a conference on 13 June entitled, "Independence of the Judiciary and Transparency of Elections," in which several senior judges participated and explained the problems judges face in attempting to ensure the transparency of elections, particularly because of different forms of intervention by the executive authority.[36]

As noted above, the support given by NGOs to the Judges' Club also included communicating information when the club prepared reports on the presidential and legislative elections. Members of human rights NGOs expressed their support for the judges' struggle on a personal basis in many interviews.

Other actors spoke out in favor of the judges' demands, such as professional syndicates,[37] particularly the press syndicate. Judges did not receive the same support from opposition parties, however, namely the Wafd Party, the Tagammu' Party, and the Nasserite Party. Yahya al-Rifa'i, honorary president of the Judges' Club, criticized the leaders of these parties for not lending enough support to the judges' demands.[38] The low profile they kept is a strategy shared by all the Egyptian opposition parties, whatever the debate. In contrast, Kifaya, an opposition movement, spoke out for the judges' movement. "With secular parties weakened and street protests waning, judges like El-Bastawissy [are] the best hope for reform," stated Kifaya spokesman, 'Abd al-Halim Qandil.[39]

The 2005 referendum and elections led to an increase in the influence and cooperation of two actors that, despite the difference in their legal status, share the responsibility of supervising electoral operations and express demands that often are quite similar. Both published reports denouncing abuses in electoral operations.

## Supervision of the Elections by Judges

The principle of judicial supervision of legislative elections was laid down in 2000. Its application in 2005 faced many practical difficulties.

### The Principle of Judicial Supervision

Judges are mandated to be involved in the supervision *(ishraf)* of elections, which means they are in charge of the conduct and management of the electoral process. They complain, however, that the competence vested in them does not allow them to accomplish their designated functions properly. They have consistently demanded an expanded role in the conduct of the electoral process, one that would enable them to supervise the whole process, from the preparation of voter lists to the announcement of results.

The SCC decision of 2000 is the origin of the increased role of judges in electoral supervision.[40] Opposition parties, NGOs, and judges long had asked that the judiciary fully supervise the electoral process.[41] This was, for instance, one of the recommendations adopted by the Conference on Justice in 1986. In June 1990, the Judges' Club organized a conference on the guarantees of the integrity of elections and put out a press release calling for the judiciary's supervision of the whole electoral process.[42] The opposition also had submitted a draft law on the same issue to the president of the republic in June 1990, proposing the extension of the electoral process over several days to overcome the problem of the insufficient number of judges.[43] The government's unwillingness to pursue this proposal led to the boycott by most political parties of the 1990 elections. The modalities of supervision finally were modified by a 2000 judicial ruling.

That case originated in a challenge filed in November 1990 by an unfortunate candidate standing for the parliamentary elections who appealed to the Supreme Constitutional Court. In 2000, the court ruled that Article 24 of Law 73/1956 on the Exercise of Political Rights was unconstitutional because it made a distinction between two kinds of polling station. Until then, only general polling stations *(lajna 'amma)*, where the counting of ballots was performed, were under judicial supervision, while primary polling stations *(lajna far'iya)*, where the voting was carried out, were supervised by public servants. The SCC maintained that, according to Article 88 of the constitution,[44] the entire election process had to be performed under the supervision of "members of judicial bodies" *(hay'a qada'iya)*. The court stated in its decision that judicial supervision had to be real, not merely formal, so that electors could choose their representatives in a serene climate. It also said that the supervision must cover the voting operation itself in order to guarantee its credibility and accuracy. The SCC stated that the judicial authority is best suited to supervise elections because of the impartiality and conscientiousness of judges. It stressed that the problem of the number of members of judicial bodies must be surmounted because constitutional principles must be honored regardless of practical considerations. The court pointed out that elections do not need to take place on the same day all over the country.

Since Article 24 of Law 73/1956 had not required judicial supervision over the totality of the electoral process, it violated Article 88 of the constitution. Ten years after they had taken place, the 1990 elections were invalidated, as well as those of 1995, which took place under the same conditions of supervision.[45] The 1956 Law on the Exercise of Political Rights was amended in 2000 by the People's Assembly to require that both general and primary polling stations be overseen by members of judicial bodies.

The term 'members of judicial bodies' was itself a subject of great controversy. For judges, only sitting magistrates should be considered members of judicial bodies in the strict sense of the term. Such members amount to around 6,000 judges of ordinary courts and 2,000 judges at the State Council. The state, meanwhile, also considers the Office of Public Prosecution, the Office of Administrative Prosecution (al-Niyaba al-Idariya),[46] and the State Litigation Authority (Hay'at Qadaya al-Dawla) judicial bodies.[47] Judges refuse to confer the status of judicial bodies particularly on the last two organs, as the proper function of a judge is to deliver judgments, which these two bodies do not do. In the judges' view, they are administrative bodies under the authority of the executive branch. Beyond the dimension of strict legal terminology, the polemic has a strongly political dimension because of its consequences for the supervision of electoral processes.

The question had already been raised on the occasion of the 2000 legislative elections. The Court of Cassation delivered a decision on 12 May 2003, invalidating the elections held in a Cairo constituency

(Zaytun), which were won by a candidate of the National Democratic Party (NDP). Its decision was made on the grounds that the elections had been performed under the supervision of members of the State Litigation Authority and the Office of Administrative Prosecution. The controversy raised by this decision led the minister of justice, on request of the prime minister, to refer the case to the SCC on 29 January 2004, for an interpretation of Article 24, paragraph 2, of Law 73/1956 on the Exercise of Political Rights.[48] In its decision,[49] the SCC declared that the term 'judicial bodies' in Article 24 had to be interpreted in the light of the way the same term is used in Article 88 of the constitution. The *travaux préparatoires* of the 1971 constitution show that the intention of the constitution was to consider as judicial bodies not only the ordinary judiciary but also members of the Office of Public Prosecution, the State Council, the State Litigation Authority, and the Office of Administrative Prosecution. The court also found that Law 10/1986 amending Law 75/1963, relative to the State

Litigation Authority referred to that authority in Article 1 as an "independent judicial body." The same interpretation applies to Law 12/1989, amending Law 117/1958, on the Office of Administrative Prosecution.

Even if these two organs are not in charge of delivering judgments, the court stated, the legislature qualified them as judicial bodies because they take part in the judicial process. In conformity with the constitution (Article 167),[50] it is up to the legislature to define the organs that should be considered judicial bodies. Therefore, both should be considered judicial bodies within the meaning of Article 24, as they perform a function that contributes to the good administration of justice and as the law conferred that status on them. This decision failed to convince all the actors and did not prevent the polemic from springing up again on the occasion of the 2005 presidential elections, when more than half the primary polling stations and almost all the of general polling stations were headed by members of these two organs or of the Office of Public Prosecution.[51]

## Judicial Supervision of the 2005 Voting Processes

Judges supervised the three electoral votes that took place in 2005, meaning the referendum and the presidential and legislative elections. The conditions and effectiveness of their intervention were different in the three cases.

## The Constitutional Referendum

Article 88 of the constitution was the object of controversy on the issue of judicial supervision of hte constitutional referendum. The question was whether it applies only to legislative elections, as it was inserted in chapter 2 of section 5 of the constitution ("The System of Government") and comes under "The Legislative Authority, the People's Assembly," or to all types of public electoral votes. The government decided that Article 88 does not apply to referenda and therefore that it was not legally bound to appoint a judge to every general and primary polling station.

The governmental newspaper, *al-Ahram*, repeatedly proclaimed that the referendum had been performed under full supervision of the judiciary. If one examines more closely the modalities of organization of the referendum, however, one sees that if the 329 general polling stations indeed were overseen by members of judicial bodies, only 5,000 out of more than 54,000 primary stations were presided over by a member of a judicial body.[52] The 49,000 remaining stations were headed by public servants.

The Judges' Club denounced this fact in its report, *Egypt's Conscience*, prepared by the Committee of Investigation on the Events that Took Place during the Referendum on the Amendment of the Constitution and published in July 2005.[53] Judges pointed out that when he proclaimed the results, the minister of the interior publicly announced that the referendum had been performed under full judicial supervision at all the stages of the voting process and during the counting of the ballots. However, the report of the Judges' Club underlines that, according to statistics published by *al-Ahram*, no more than 5 percent of the 54,350 primary polling stations in the country had been under the supervision of a member of a judicial body. Judges were astonished by the fact that polling stations supervised by a judge had registered extremely low percentages of participation. Some had not seen a single voter, while others had registered an average of participation of 3 percent. By contrast, in some polling stations supervised by state employees, participation as high as 100 percent had been registered. The judges demanded, "No one was dead, or traveling, or prevented from participating for reasons of sickness, or work responsibilities, or laziness?"

The absence of full judicial supervision during the referendum had negative consequences for the credibility of the announced official statistics of 53.64 percent participation, with 82.86 percent saying "yes" and 17.14 percent saying "no."

## The Presidential Elections

The presidential elections represented an important challenge to the legitimacy of the head of state, who had initiated the amendment to Article 76 of the constitution. The issue of judicial supervision in this case was even more crucial. Here, too, a restrictive interpretation of Article 88 excluded the elections from its range of application. The Law on Presidential Elections states in Article 39 that general polling stations must be headed by a member of a judicial body and that the Presidential Elections Commission "*may* also appoint" heads of polling stations (primary polling stations) from among members of judicial bodies (author's emphasis). It is therefore a matter of option and not obligation. In addition, according to Article 76 of the constitution balloting must be performed in one day.

Faced with many protests from opposition parties, NGOs, judges, and jurists, the Presidential Elections Commission finally decided to appoint a member of a judicial body to head every primary polling station. To implement its decision, the commission grouped four to six ballot boxes in one polling station in order to reduce the number of primary polling stations to approximately 10,000 and of general polling stations to 329. This meant that every president of a primary station would have to supervise several ballot boxes simultaneously. The commission also decided that the counting of ballots would be done by each primary station and not by general stations. General polling stations would be in charge of centralizing the results and conveying them to the Presidential Elections Commission without making them public.

The controversy surrounding the concept of a member of a judicial body reemerged on this occasion. According to the minister of justice, 13,000 members of judicial bodies were called upon to participate in supervision of the election, among whom 4,199 were counselors (on the Court of Cassation and courts of appeal) and judges; 3,480 were members of the Office of Public Prosecution; 1,500 were members of the State Council; 1,513 belonged to the Office of Administrative Prosecution; and 1,873 were from the State Litigation Authority.[54] The Presidential Elections Commission excluded more than 1,500 sitting magistrates (from ordinary courts and the State Council) without explanation. The commission gave priority assignments to members of the Office of Public Prosecution, the Office of Administrative Prosecution, and the State Litigation Authority in general polling stations. Counselors of the Court of Cassation, meanwhile, who have a higher rank, were assigned to primary polling stations, which is contrary to judicial tradition and rules of seniority.

Judges, once again, protested vigorously. They asked the commission to explain its selection criteria and demanded that judicial traditions and rules of seniority be respected. During the Judges' Club's extraordinary general assembly on 2 September, they insisted on the reintegration of the judges excluded from the supervisory process and on the exclusion of freshly recruited junior prosecutors. Their demands were not met. The State Council councilors who were excluded from electoral supervision took the matter to the Court of Administrative Litigation. The court ruled in their favor, judging that, according to Article 76 of the constitution and the Law on Presidential Elections, the selection of judges must be made by a committee of the State Council itself. It decided that the Presidential Election Commission was only competent to allocate them to different polling stations.[55] The government stayed execution of this judgment through the procedure of *ishkal*.[56]

Judicial electoral supervision, even within the limits described, probably had a positive effect on the official results. The percentage of official participation was reported to be no more than 23 percent. Hosni Mubarak received 88.5 percent of the vote, and his main rival, Ayman Nour, 7.6 percent, far more than Nu'man Gum'a, who only received 2.7 percent.

In its report on the presidential elections, made public at the beginning of November 2005, the Judges' Club denounced many types of abuses witnessed by judges. The report criticized the attitude of the Presidential Elections Commission, underlining that it had refused to collaborate with the Judges' Club and had not explained the criteria followed to select judges to supervise the elections. The report added that the commission had excluded a large number of sitting judges for no reason, a matter that had created an unhealthy climate and rumors that their exclusion was related to security reasons or sanctions for having asked for full supervision of the elections. This interpretation was confirmed by the fact that most members of the board of directors of the Judges' Club of Cairo and Alexandria had been excluded. In addition, the report underlined that the allocation of judges in primary and general polling stations had been done without taking into consideration judicial seniority and customs. The judges complained about being required to supervise many ballot boxes simultaneously, which did not allow full judicial supervision. Moreover, this system created either a long queue in front of polling stations when the head of each station allowed only one person inside at a time or chaos inside the polling stations when the head of the station authorized more than one person to enter. The report noted that many voters had been allowed to leave polling stations without dipping their fingers in phosphorescent ink and that this had not been noticed by the head of the station.

The report emphasized that electoral lists had not been given to the candidates well in advance (except to NDP candidates); that some names had disappeared from electoral lists although they were on referendum electoral lists; that many voters had to leave without casting their ballots because they could not find their names on the electoral lists; and that people could vote many times in various polling stations despite the phosphorescent ink because they had been authorized to vote with their identity card only. The report recalled that Article 33 of the Presidential Election Law authorized voters to vote in a primary polling station where they were not registered provided they could present an identity card and electoral card. The head of the polling station had to sign the back of the electoral card to avoid multiple voting. The report said that oral instructions from the Presidential Elections Commission had authorized casting of votes with identity cards only.[57] Another criticism raised by the judges was of the low quality at some polling stations of the ink, which could be washed off with soap and water. Many polling stations, moreover, did not provide voting booths or just provided symbolic ones that did not provide privacy. Many delegates could not gain access to polling stations because the heads refused to accept their authorizations.

Finally, the report criticized the secrecy that surrounded the announcement of results. The authors pointed out that the commission had forbidden heads of primary and general polling stations to announce the results. They argued that, as a result of this provision, the counting took place most of the time in the absence of the delegates of the candidates, in secret, which raised suspicions around procedure and robbed the election of the transparency necessary for it to be credible. The report concluded with the statement that abuses took place and that they influenced the results in terms of the rate of participation and the percentage of votes received by each candidate. It was impossible to assess the extent of the abuses, however, and to conclude that the abuses influenced the results of the elections.

## The Legislative Elections

In order to ensure full judicial supervision of primary polling stations by members of judicial bodies, legislative elections have been organized in three successive phases since 2000. A member of a judicial body thus can be placed in every primary and general polling station.

In 2005, the territory was divided into nearly 30,000 primary polling stations and 222 general polling stations. According to the minister of justice, each polling station was planned to accommodate a maximum of 1,200 voters, and none was established in a police station.[58] Voting took place in three successive stages.

Judges again criticized the process for selecting members of judicial bodies in charge of supervising the electoral operation, mainly accusing the minister of the interior and security services of being behind the selection. *Al-Misri al-yawm* newspaper, for instance, said "sources" indicated that "sensitive" polling stations—those where symbolic NDP candidates or ministers were in close contests with Muslim Brothers or other opposition candidates—were placed under the supervision of members of the Office of Public Prosecution, the State Litigation Authority, or the Office of Administrative Prosecution in order to influence the course of the elections, and that the number of sitting judges chosen to head such polling stations was minimal.[59] Judges added that the presence of sitting judges was not even a real guarantee of independence because many of them were actually seconded (*muntadabun*) to administrative organs.[60] Thus, for Mahmud Mekki, a vice-president of the Court of Cassation, it was not enough for the elections to be supervised by sitting judges—he demanded that the judges be totally independent from the executive authority and that those currently seconded be excluded from electoral supervision.[61]

The judges also protested against the fact that, here again, the heads of primary polling stations were prohibited from proclaiming the results in their constituencies and from giving a copy of the results to the candidates' delegates. In addition, many judges noticed that electoral lists had been modified between the first and second ballot rounds, as a large number of electors on the list in the first ballot were not listed in the second ballot round.[62] The secrecy that surrounded the counting of the ballots was the object of strong criticism. According to judges, many heads of general polling stations expelled representatives of candidates and NGOs and closed their polling stations during the count. Judges claim that this was the case in 90 percent of the general polling stations.[63] In some cases, heads of primary polling stations were pushed out of the general polling station after they handed in the minutes with the results of the vote count of their stations.[64]

## NGO Observation of the Elections

Representatives of NGOs, as neutral and impartial observers, are meant to observe the electoral scene and denounce all violations they notice. They have no responsibility in organizing the elections and should not interfere in their performance. They simply should observe the election process and bear witness to its negative and positive aspects. Even if they notice abuses, they cannot intervene to stop them.

Human rights NGOs are increasingly present on the Egyptian scene. Around thirty of them participated in the supervision of the presidential and legislative elections in 2005, most of the time in the form of coalitions. Three of these coalitions were born during the presidential elections. The National Campaign for Monitoring Elections (NCME) (al-Hamla al-Wataniya li-Muraqabat al-Intikhabat), coordinated by the Arab Organization for Penal Reform, drew together four NGOs and sent nearly five hundred observers to election premises. The Independent Committee for Monitoring Elections (al-Lajna al-Misriya al-Mustaqilla li-Muraqabat al-Intikhabat), coordinated by Saad Eddin Ibrahim, director of the Ibn Khaldun Center for Development Studies, was composed of twelve NGOs and sent 2,200 observers all over the country. Finally, the Civil Coalition for Monitoring Elections (al-I'tilaf al-Madani li-Muraqabat al-Intikhabat), coordinated by the EOHR, was composed of twenty-two NGOs and sent one thousand observers all over the country. These coalitions were also present at the legislative elections, with the Independent Committee for Monitoring Elections composed at that time of sixteen NGOs and mobilizing 5,000 observers. The NCME provided nearly 3,000 observers, while the coalition of the EOHR mobilized approximately 1,200.

Before the elections, the work of these NGOs consisted in training observers, drawing up reports on the political and legal situation in the country, and assessing the conditions under which the elections were taking place. Under Presidential Elections Law 174/2005, every candidate is to be granted the same right of access to the television media. One NGO focused mainly on assessing the attitude of the audio-visual media and newspapers in relation to the different candidates in both the presidential and the legislative elections. CIHRS analyzed the attitudes of four public television stations (channels 1, 2, and 3 and Nile News),[65] two private channels (Dream 2 and al-Mihwar), and seventeen governmental and independent newspapers. The general conclusions of this survey, which substantiate claims that the media is partial to NDP candidates, particularly the newspapers, were published in CIHRS reports.

After the elections, all of the organizations in the coalitions denounced collectively on behalf of their coalition or individually in their own names the many violations that marred the balloting. NGOs together praised the positive attitude of the security and police forces at the presidential elections. They criticized, however, the way the legislative elections were marked by violence toward certain categories of voters and even toward judges. At that time, the security and police forces prevented access to some polling stations and did not hesitate to use force.[66] The two elections were characterized by many abuses, among the most flagrant being the purchase of votes, collective voting,[67] allowing voters to vote in a polling station where they were not listed (which enabled multiple voting), the absence of voting booths in many polling stations, candidates not having electoral lists in advance (except NDP candidates), the negative attitude of the electoral commissions, lists of electors not being updated and including many errors in voters' names, the premises of the primary and general polling stations not being announced sufficiently in advance, utilization of public transportation vehicles to transport groups of voters to polling stations,[68] and candidates' representatives not being authorized to attend the counting of the ballot papers.

Publishing reports is part of the traditional means of action of NGOs, but it was the first time judges resorted to it. The main conclusions of the NGOs' and Judges' Club's reports were more or less the same. Their recommendations were also quite similar. NGOs called in particular for integrated supervision of elections by judges, including in the announcement of results.[69]

## The Possibilities for Guaranteeing Truly Transparent Elections

NGOs and judges agree that beyond procedural guarantees that ensure transparent elections, which they have already requested, the country needs modifications in its judicial and political system in general. Both also request that their own organization's law be amended in order to increase their freedom from the executive authority. NGOs criticize several provisions of Law 84/2002 on Associations, which grants the ministry of social affairs important powers to control associations. Judges have been insisting for a long time that Law 46/1972 on the Judicial Authority be amended in order to decrease the hold of the ministry of justice over the judiciary. They maintain that there cannot be real, impartial judicial supervision of elections if a minimum guarantee of independence is not secured. A draft law in this vein was prepared by the Judges' Club in 1991 but has remained in the drawers of the ministry of justice. Judges threatened to boycott supervision of elections if their draft law was not adopted by the parliament or by a presidential decree law. The law finally adopted by the People's Assembly in June 2006 was not based on the text developed by the Judges' Club but on one prepared by the NDP, which was quite different from the judges' draft. The situation reached the point where some judges declared they would have preferred to keep the status quo. After the amendment of the NGO law in 1999 and again in 2002, many NGOs similarly missed the 1964 Nasserite law, which was more flexible in its application.

At its meeting in December 2005, the general assembly of the Judges' Club asked its board of directors to send a telegram to the president of the republic requesting that the state of emergency be lifted and that all exceptional laws be abrogated so that Egypt could be transformed from a police state into a lawful state.[70] NGOs have long had this same demand. NGOs and judges both have asked for the reintroduction of the 'investigating judge,' a post that was terminated in 1952.

Some judges have directly accused the executive authority of being the source of the abuses committed during the elections. For instance, Mahmud Mekki, having noticed that modifications had been introduced in the electoral lists between the two legislative rounds in favor of NDP interests, accused the minister of the interior of interfering in the elections, particularly in the constituencies where Muslim Brotherhood candidates had obtained good returns in the first round.[71] Hesham El-Bastawissy, vice-president of the Court of Cassation, accused the government of having shown its determination to end the so-called reform experience, when the judges had believed the promises of the government and had trusted its commitment to a true democratic experience through the legislative elections.[72] He said that the minister of justice, in particular, had not protected the judges, despite his promises,[73] and that the Supreme Judicial Council was an accomplice to the election fraud.[74] At the general assembly of the Judges' Club, Mahmud al-Khudayri, president of the Judges' Club in Alexandria, proposed contacting the president of the republic to ask him who was responsible for what was happening in the country. What could be said about what happened to judges at the hands of officers and hired thugs (*baltagiya*) of the ministry of the interior and of the NDP?[75] In an interview with *al-Dustur*, in reply to the question, "Do you think that the ministry of the interior can take a decision (like attacking judges) without the president's endorsement?" al-Khudayri said, "There is no doubt that it was not about a decision from the minister of the interior and that the attacks against the judges came from a political will higher than the minister of the interior."[76]

Legally speaking, judges and NGOs do not have the right to become involved in politics. Article 11 of Law 84/2002 on Associations specifies that the exercise of political activities is reserved to political parties in conformity with the Law on Political Parties and that the activities of syndicates have to be reserved to trade unions in conformity with the Law on Trade Unions. This vague wording raised fears within civil society over whether judicial aid for victims of human rights violations, criticism of government actions, calls for constitutional reform or legislative amendments, participation in electoral supervision, and the publication of reports on human rights violations would be considered political activities through that provision. Regulations implementing the law, adopted in October 2002, reassured NGOs. Article 25 specifies that the meaning of "political activities" is propaganda activities and support for programs of political parties, participation in electoral campaigns, presentation of candidates in the name of an association for elections, and financing of political parties from the budget of an association.

In their request to the State Council for the annulment of the refusal of the Parliamentary Election Commission to authorize NGOs to observe the elections, NGO applicants were careful to underline that they were not involved in any political activities: human rights NGOs do not participate in the activities of political parties or their candidates, and they do not take part in the competition for a party or a candidate. On the contrary, NGOs said, they only observe elections and ensure respect for the constitution, laws, and international standards relative to human rights by all political parties during the electoral process.

As far as judges are concerned, Article 73 of the Law on Judicial Authority prohibits the courts from expressing political opinions and judges from being involved in political activities, being candidates in People's Assembly elections, and being participants in regional assemblies or political organizations. They cannot enroll themselves in elections or belong to any political organization. A polemic has emerged on the significance of the term politics. If the government accuses judges of engaging in politics, judges defend themselves by refusing to consider their struggle as falling within the field of politics.

Judges often refer to the explanatory note of former Law 66/1943 on the Judicial Authority, according to which judges, as citizens, could express their opinions on public affairs concerning the nation without participating in political activities, that is to say, without forming or joining political parties. Judges also refer to the trust people have in them, and which they do not want to betray by legitimating fraudulent elections. They do not want people to consider them responsible for the abuses committed during the elections, and they insist that they do not favor one or another candidate but rather seek to protect the national interest.[77] El-Bastawissy has asserted that if demanding the independence of the judiciary and the transparency of elections means being involved in political activities, then all judges are in politics.[78] He added that the right to assembly, association, and expression of opinions on general political subjects, whether inside the Judges' Club or by other means, is a right that belongs to any judge and to any citizen, in conformity with Article 47 of the constitution.[79] He emphasized that the people have the right to know how judges think because they are the ones who pay the taxes from which judges' salaries are paid.[80] El-Bastawissy also referred to international instruments to the same effect,[81] among which are the Basic Principles on the Independence of the Judiciary, as adopted by the United Nations General Assembly on 20 November 1985, stating: "In accordance with the Universal Declaration of Human Rights, members of the judiciary are like other citizens entitled to freedom of expression, belief, association and assembly; provided, however, that in exercising such rights, judges shall always conduct themselves in such a manner as to preserve the dignity of their office and the impartiality and independence of the judiciary."

When the Judges' Club general assembly convened on 16 December 2005, the judges stressed that neither they nor their club *do* politics but that it is their right as citizens to express their opinions on matters that interest the nation.[82] They argued that speaking of politics is different from engaging in politics. If they are prohibited from belonging to a political party, it is nevertheless their right and obligation, as for every citizen, to speak of politics.[83] For Zakariya 'Abd al-'Aziz, supervision of elections is one of the foremost political acts. Why constitutionally entrust judges with the supervision of elections if they are prohibited to speak about politics?[84]

In the final statement issued by the general assembly of the Judges' Club in December 2005, the judges maintained that neither the club nor judges were engaged in politics but that they are an elite that seeks justice and respect of law. They said they were doing their best to fulfill the duties entrusted to them by the nation to help maintain general confidence in the system of government, because the judiciary is one of the three state authorities.

These declarations did not prevent the Supreme Judicial Council from considering the judges' stance political and therefore extrajudicial. In March 2005, it published a statement reminding judges that they should not express their opinions publicly and that participating in political seminars and commenting on political acts are not part of their mandate. A new reminder was issued in November before measures were finally taken in February 2006, with charges brought before the Office of State Security Prosecution and the lifting of immunity of senior counselors.

Will judges and NGOs be able to achieve greater independence in relation to the executive authority and to obtain concessions that guarantee a real transparent electoral process? It will depend on the future of the political reform process.

## Request for International Observers?

Faced with their inability to stop the abuses committed during the elections, particularly the legislative ones, judges and NGOs both considered the option of having international observers. The Egyptian government has always refused to authorize international observers, invoking as reasons that Egyptian society would be against it, that it would be contrary to state sovereignty, and that it would constitute an affront to the judges, who are perfectly capable of guaranteeing the integrity of the electoral process.[85]

In mid-June 2005, the EOHR called for international observation of the elections, stating that this would bring more credibility to the electoral process and that it should not be seen as foreign interference in Egyptian political life. Moreover, it suggested that such observation would encourage political participation by assuring voters that their choices would be respected. The EOHR adopted the same recommendation for the legislative elections, issuing a statement calling for the presence of international observers and underlining that Egypt had participated in observer missions in other Arab countries, particularly Yemen.[86]

Whereas their position during the presidential elections was not always clear, most political parties, disappointed by the presidential election experience, began to speak out in favor of international observers for the legislative elections. Judges, however, seemed divided on this issue. During the extraordinary general assembly of the Judges' Club on 13 May 2005, al-Khudayri declared that the obstinacy of opposing the will of the nation was the pretext used by foreign forces to become more closely interested in Egypt.[87] Another judge intervened, adding that he feared that the situation threatened to lead to what happened in Iraq.[88] Al-Rifa'i asked the reason for not inviting international observers if the government has really decided to fight fraud. Moreover, he said that it is in the interest of Europe and the United States that the elections be transparent and the system non-dictatorial in order to avoid the appearance of another Muhammad Atta.[89] Tarik al-Bishri, former vice-president of the State Council, was opposed to observation of elections by foreigners. He asked, since we refuse any pressure to be imposed on us, whatever it is, whether favoring reform or not, how could we accept foreigners to observe the elections, which represent one of the most important internal features of a people?[90]

After the presidential elections, al-Khudayri was ready to accept the presence of international observers, provided the government agreed.[91] Ahmad Mekki, a vice-president of the Court of Cassation, was of the same opinion, indicating that he was neither against nor for international supervision, but that he felt the situation should be left to the state's evaluation. He added, however, that if the political elite wants to improve the reputation of elections in Egypt, it has to take the initiative itself by inviting foreign observers.[92] El-Bastawissy called on international observers to follow the elections as witnesses without interfering in the electoral process.[93]

After the first rounds of the legislative elections, judges threatened to call for an international inquiry. Shortly thereafter the Judges' Club issued a statement calling for the intervention of the armed forces.[94]

Faced with the many abuses committed during the legislative elections and the absence of a reply from the Office of Public Prosecution to many complaints submitted by judges, the members of the committee in charge of writing the report on the parliamentary elections also angrily threatened to call for an international inquiry if the violations went unpunished. They specified a three-month grace period for the government to take the necessary measures against the perpetrators, after which, they said, they would request an international investigation. During the general assembly of the Judges' Club on 16 December 2005, 'Abd al-'Aziz said that if the results of the investigation of the violations suffered by judges in the course of the elections were not released soon, the club would call for an international inquiry.[95] El-Bastawissy stressed that he had never had recourse to institutions of international inquiry, but that the Syrian scenario was not excluded from being reproduced in Egypt in the following months if the independence of judges was not restored.[96]

In a press release issued in March 2005, after a seventh judge had been sent before the investigating judge, ACIJLP called on the United Nations Special Rapporteur on the Independence of the Judiciary and on the International Commission of Jurists to send a fact-finding mission to Egypt.[97] The International Commission of Jurists followed up on this demand by sending a letter to President Mubarak and to the Egyptian minister of justice in which it expressed its deep concern about the lifting of the immunity of the seven counselors. The commission emphasized that judges should enjoy freedom of opinion and expression. It made clear that it was studying the possibility of sending a commission of inquiry.[98]

Al-Khudayri saw an international investigation as a last resort to which judges should have recourse only if other options, such as sit-ins, demonstrations, peaceful processions, suspensions of hearings, or a strike in the courts for a full day or a few hours, did not produce results.[99]

## Conclusion

The 2005 events show that, in their struggle for independence, Egyptian judges have seized new spaces and resorted to hitherto unheard of methods, often close to those used by NGOs for many years, such as declarations in newspapers and on satellite television channels, post-election reports, boycott threats, and sit-ins. However, judges are keen to act within legal limits.

The judges' criticisms of the government matched up at various points with criticisms from NGOs. It is undeniable, however, that the magistrates' voices carry far greater weight than those of NGOs because judges represent one of the three authorities in the country. They are greatly appreciated in the heart of Egyptian society, and they are not the object of suspicion as are human rights NGOs, which frequently are accused of serving western-financed interests. The judges' criticisms, therefore, truly challenged the credibility and legitimacy of the political regime. Judges have added their voices to those of activists calling for true political reform, but the government has only reacted when the voices of the judges were seen as a threat.

In conclusion, it is unclear what motivated the coalition between judges and civil society organizations that was born in 2005. Why did judges, in particular, extend their support and seek out the support of human rights NGOs, and not that of political parties, for instance, or professional syndicates, such as the syndicate of lawyers, which are closer to them on the professional level? Why did they not resort to the National Council for Human Rights? It may be because human rights NGOs base their struggle on the protection of human rights in general and on the right to vote in particular, on the independence of the judiciary, and on the freedom of expression of all citizens. It may be because NGOs, like judges, offer a perennial challenge to the government. It also may be because NGOs are one of the most frequent victims of the executive authority. The fact that NGOs are in regular contact with the international community and that their press releases have an impact outside Egypt probably played a role in the judges' decision. If judges were reluctant to have overt links with foreign governmental or non-governmental institutions,[100] they nonetheless were aware that foreign pressure could help them obtain some of their demands.

# 16

## The Independence of the Judiciary as a Democratic Construct

*Hesham El-Bastawissy*

In any country, the independence of the judiciary as a state institution and the autonomy of judges in their individual capacity are profoundly related to the state of democracy. Neither of them could be achieved in conformity with international standards unless democratic rules and culture prevail in the state legislation and are practiced by rulers and subjects.

If the role of the judiciary is to neutrally and fairly protect the freedoms, lives, money, and honor of peoples against any aggression or transgression, it does so by applying the legislation in force. Therefore, laws should be fair and respond to the needs of the community. This can only be achieved by having legislative councils freely and directly elected by the people. In other words, the state regime has to be built upon a democratic basis, the lack of which makes it difficult for the judiciary to assume its role. Unjust laws confiscate freedoms and rights. Nevertheless, the absence of democracy does not strip the judiciary of its responsibility to address unfair provisions in the laws in order to bring them into conformity with international standards.

In such contexts, the judiciary shall use, when appropriate, constitutional texts and international instruments and agreements as tools to curb the adverse effects of such legislation. This means that judges should not wait for the dissemination of democracy, but should press for the independence of the judiciary and judges and endeavor to apply the principles of freedom and democracy. Such judicial activism becomes the principal avenue to democratic growth when it cannot be achieved by a voluntary decision from the ruling authority. In such a situation, it is through the individual practices of judges, lawyers, the media, and intellectuals that democratic development can be pushed forward. In Egypt, judges frequently have had recourse to provisions of the Universal Declaration of Human Rights to decide cases referred to courts because of unfair legal provisions, using sometimes the provisions of the Universal Declaration of Human Rights to override national legislative provisions.

It is neither correct nor true to claim that questions of economic development and the occupation of state territories should have priority over the administration and requirements of democracy, such as the independence of the judiciary and the freedom of the media and of individuals. Human experience has proven that it is possible, in the absence of democracy, to win a battle but impossible to achieve triumph in the war. Local or foreign capital will never jeopardize itself by investing in a non-democratic state whose judiciary lacks the guarantees of autonomy set by international standards. Therefore, stable and sustainable economic development and settlement of regional disputes can never be achieved except under the umbrella of democratic values, judicial autonomy, and freedom of the media and information.

The requirements of the independence of the judiciary in accordance with international standards and the wide gap between these and the current state of the judiciary in the Arab region would require many volumes to describe. My attention here is confined to one requirement: the empowerment of judges to establish their organizations, whether in the form of bar associations, clubs, or societies. I emphasize this requirement, first, because the sole protection against further deterioration in the condition and autonomy of the judiciary, as clearly demonstrated by the Egyptian experience, is the existence of a club for judges that is fully independent from all state authorities, including the Supreme Judicial Council, and whose activity is only subject to its general assembly. I emphasize it, second, because it is not given due attention. In my opinion, judges' freedom to form organizations is the first and foremost requirement for autonomy because it reinforces the ties of fraternity and solidarity among judges and facilitates the exchange of opinions regarding cases and disputes. This leads to the accumulation of legal experience and reinforces a judicial culture based on judicial values and traditions from one generation to another. It also respects the interests of judges and allows them to defend their independence.

If judges in Egypt enjoy some extent of independence denied to many colleagues in the Arab region, it is primarily because of the existence of the Judges' Club. The club's role should be viewed from two different perspectives, namely, defending the autonomy of the judiciary as a state institution and defending the independence of each judge as an individual. This paper deals with these two issues—the Judges' Club and independence of the judiciary as a state institution, and the relationship of the Judges' Club to the independence of the judges.

## The Judges' Club and the Independence of the Judiciary as a State Institution

For over half a century, the executive authority in Egypt has managed to diminish the autonomy of the judiciary as an institution through its overwhelming hegemony over the legislative authority. It has abused its constitutional right to proclaim a state of emergency in a manner that has violated the constitution itself. A state of emergency has become the permanent norm, whereas its termination and enforcement of the law have become exceptions. The executive authority has established several bodies to carry out interrogation and prosecution and has adopted extrajudicial rulings, such as the socialist public prosecutor and courts of values. In addition, it has established the Supreme Constitutional Court to constrain the normal judiciary from judicial review of the constitutionality of legislation.

The situation reached its climax when the judiciary was stripped of some of its jurisdiction, which was assigned to military courts that lack the guarantees of autonomy and neutrality. In addition, the executive authority has designated some administrative institutions as judicial bodies. One such body, the State Litigation Authority, is composed of state lawyers and another, the Office of Administrative Prosecution, is composed of state investigators. As 'judicial bodies,' their members were granted the constitutional competence to supervise parliamentary elections next to the ordinary judiciary, which was justified on the pretext that the law grants them judicial capacity. Moreover, the election process is subordinated to the hegemony of the police and the ministry of the interior, whereas the role of judges is confined to the polling stations. The preparation of voters' lists, the review of names, checking votes to ensure single voting, access to polling boxes, announcement of final results, ensuring candidates' right to electoral propaganda, and monitoring vote counts are all, in one way or another, subject to the executive authority. By designating the government lawyers of the State Litigation Authority and the Office of Administrative Prosecution members of judicial bodies, the executive authority has imposed two administrative organs that are adjuncts to the executive authority on the supervisory competence of judges during elections. Thus, the claim that parliamentary elections in Egypt are subject to judicial supervision is absolutely incorrect.

After the 1952 Revolution, the executive authority was discontented with judicial autonomy and issued legislation that curbed it. This trend culminated in the 1969 Massacre of the Judiciary. At that time, oppressive decrees and laws were passed against judges, the impact of which we still feel. The most important of this legislation was the executive decree that repealed the election of judges by their colleagues for membership on the Supreme Judicial Council. The council came back into existence in 1984 with diminished competencies and independence. The 1969 legislation also gave many competencies to the newly created Supreme Council of Judicial Bodies. To the president of the republic, it awarded the absolute right to select the head of that council. The 1972 Law on Judicial Authority and the 1979 Law on the Constitutional Court gave the president of the republic the right to choose the general prosecutor and the chief justice of the Supreme Constitutional Court, regardless of any regulations or criteria that would ensure the appropriate minimum of technical efficiency required for such prominent judicial positions. Moreover, the state has absolute control over the salaries and pensions of judges, whose monthly income is almost 90 percent composed of incentives and rewards subject to the state's discretion. In general, judges' monthly income hardly provides them with a decent standard of living.

To confront this hegemony over the judiciary, the Judges' Club prepared a draft bill to amend unjust provisions contained in the Law on Judicial Authority, filling the lacunae created by the executive authority and adopting a system for the election instead of appointment of judges to administrative judicial posts. The new system would require that some judges be given full control over the management of justice through general assemblies of courts, which would select the best and most efficient judges for administrative posts within the judiciary. The judge selected by his fellow judges would become the deputy judge, representing judges and implementing policy instead of overpowering them as an executive appointee, intervening in their work, or compromising their autonomy. Unfortunately, these amendments have not been adopted.

## The Judges' Club and the Independence of Judges

For historical reasons related to the establishment of the modern judiciary, Egyptian judges managed to establish a Judges' Club in 1939. Through the club, they have set up their independence as the optimum, and perhaps sole, way for them to maintain and defend their professional rights and interests. The establishment of the Judges' Club contributed greatly to the establishment of judicial traditions. It also helped consolidate the concept of the independence of the judiciary as an institution and of the judge as an individual, with both able to confront the executive authority and anyone else, even colleagues in court or counselors in a superior court who are in a higher position or who have professional seniority. Confrontations are practiced only through methods of appeal as prescribed by law; therefore, phone justice or phone verdicts are not known in Egypt as they are in some Arab countries. The executive authority has never dared, in any era and no matter how diminished the democratic margin, to intervene with a judge in any case, whether explicitly or implicitly, or to directly pressure a judge to take a specific decision in any dispute. It rather resorted to diminishing the independence of the judiciary as an institution.

I would like to draw attention to the fact that the absence of exceptional courts and an exceptional judiciary in some Arab countries does not necessarily mean that the judiciary is autonomous. In many cases, it means that the state has managed to undermine the independence of judges as individuals by direct influence and thus has not needed to establish exceptional courts because judges respond to the state's wishes. The Egyptian experience highlights the important fact that without an organization for judges like the Judges' Club—which was founded on a democratic basis, is removed from state intervention, and is run by judges elected to the board of directors—judges may not be able to preserve their remaining share of autonomy. It is no coincidence that the first Law on Judicial Authority in Egypt was issued in 1943, four years after the establishment of the Judges' Club. This was the law that caused discontent in the executive authority after the 1952 Revolution. Accordingly, the executive authority introduced many amendments to the law in order to curb and control the independence of the judiciary. The existence of the Judges' Club in Egypt has always impeded such attempts, although it was not able in many cases to prevent unfair legislative amendments. I reiterate that the existence of the Judges' Club has prevented further deterioration in the condition of the judiciary.

Therefore, the first and foremost step in building any autonomous judicial system is the establishment of an organization for judges, provided it is founded on a democratic basis and its board of directors is chosen through free and direct election by the judges. The board should not be subject, by any means or to any extent, to supervision or control by any other authority, even that of the Supreme Judicial Council. The only authority that should govern it is its own general assembly. Realizing this fact, the executive authority in Egypt sought above all during the Massacre of the Judiciary to undermine the Judges' Club and its board of directors and activists, who were on the list of those dismissed in 1969. It issued a decree to dissolve the club's board of directors and appointed a number of individuals in their professional capacities for its management. The judges managed to get rid of this law and restored their club and its internal regulations. The state kept interfering in Judges' Club affairs and attempted to enforce the provisions of the Law on Associations, which stipulates that every association in Egypt should be registered and subject to the supervision of the ministry of social affairs, whether on the occasion of the election of its board of directors or in the exercise by the board and the general assembly of their competencies. The state also attempted to impose on the club, as on other entities, the compulsory approval by the socialist public prosecutor of candidates for the board of directors.

Judges have held firm against such actions and refused the enforcement of these provisions, because elections relate to judges' internal affairs and the provisions would conflict with the independence of the judiciary as guaranteed by the constitution and by international standards. In all their assemblies, judges have held fast to the principle that, like any other organization, their club is subject exclusively to its own general assembly. They have demanded that no other administrative entity exercise any power over it, even if it includes judges, like the Supreme Judicial Council.

Again, the cornerstone of empowering the judiciary in Egypt to obtain autonomy is the establishment of independent organizations for judges, founded on a democratic basis free from any interference or monitoring by any authority other than its own general assembly, which represents the first and foremost guarantee of judicial autonomy in any state. Since most Arab states either prohibit the establishment of judicial organizations or only allow them under the control and monitoring of the government, a number of judges in Arab states have agreed to call for the establishment of the Union of Arab Judges, which would enjoy guarantees of autonomy and be founded on a democratic basis. In this regard, we have moved further ahead. However, we still lack funds for holding the constituent meeting of the union. We pin much hope on this union to disseminate and consolidate the concept of the independence of the judiciary and the autonomy of judges in all the Arab states.

# Appendix:
# Draft Constituent Declaration
# of the Union of Arab Judges

On the basis of the international declarations issued by the United Nations and its institutions concerning the independence of the judiciary, stressing that all its members, individually or collectively, are entitled to freedom of expression, belief, association, and assembly and are free to form and join international associations of judges or other organizations to represent their interests, to promote their professional training, and to protect their judicial independence for the sake of developing judicial and legal institutions and creating awareness and solidarity for the protection of basic human rights and freedoms in Arab societies to reinforce social and economic development. Various experiences have proved that development objectives can never be realized unless set within a humane framework that maintains a person's dignity and rights and guarantees the utmost protection for a person's basic freedoms, which can only be achieved through a truly independent judiciary, as the cornerstone of political, economic, and social reform, which represents also the basic guarantee to safeguard human rights;

Out of the belief that the Arab region has a distinctive heritage and tenets that set it apart from others in its attempt to guarantee the independence of the judiciary and recognize the role of the judiciary in safeguarding basic human rights and freedoms, and that it has the vigor to uphold its contributions with the international society to guarantee the enjoyment of such rights in order to safeguard international peace and security;

The signatories to this Declaration have decided to establish the "Union of Arab Judges" in pursuit of the following objectives:

To foster solidarity among Arab judges in order to uphold their independence and look after their scientific, cultural, and social interests.

To pursue the dissemination among Arab judges of the principles, standards, and traditions of the independence of the judiciary stipulated in international conventions and to endeavor to incorporate them into local legislation and repeal any contradictions or hindrances.

To disseminate the culture of human rights and the means to safeguard them among Arab governments, judges, and peoples, as well as to highlight its importance as an impetus for social and economic development.

To monitor the difficulties Arab judges face when assuming their professional responsibilities and to seek to surmount such difficulties through cooperation and exchange of experience among themselves and with the relevant international organizations.

To raise judges' awareness of the importance of syndicates and encourage the establishment of unions for judges in the Arab countries where no such unions exist, provided that they are founded on a democratic basis. A council composed by secret, free, and direct elections, independent from state authorities, and subordinated to its own general assembly shall represent the members, sponsor the members' interests, seek to protect their independence, and promote their professional training.

To unify the priorities of Arab judicial work and concepts of the independence of the judiciary with a view to creating an Arab reality that reflects a unified legislation for the judiciary, aiming at unifying other legislation and legal concepts throughout the Arab countries.

To focus on training and raising the scientific competence of judges, through establishment of a regional institute for judicial studies.

To establish a multilingual database for Arab legislation and rulings, linked with similar databases of international organizations and foreign bodies.

To establish a center for legal studies concerned with providing the institutions of the Arab League and any Arab government with technical support and legal studies, as well as conducting legal studies that conform with the Union's aims and objectives.

To foster bilateral and collective relations with Arab and international legal unions and organizations, and to cooperate with human rights organizations.

# Notes

## Note to the Foreword

1 All the papers from the conference were published in Arabic by the Cairo Institute for Human Rights Studies in 2006, under the supervision of Nabil Abdel Fattah.

## Notes to the Introduction

1 Article 76 of the 1971 constitution was amended to establish, for the first time, presidential elections.

2 *Damir Misr*, published in *al-'Arabi*, 3 July 2005, and *al-Misri al-yawm*, 2 July 2005.

3 According to Zakariya 'Abd al-'Aziz, president of the Cairo Judges' Club, no financial subsidy was received from the ministry of justice after October 2005. *Al-Dustur*, 19 April 2007.

4 The Office of Administrative Prosecution is a body in charge of prosecuting civil servants.

5 Noha al-Zini, *al-Misri al-yawm*, 24 November 2005.

6 *Al-Misri al-yawm*, 1 December 2005.

7 See, *al-Misri al-yawm*, 5 April 2006.

8 See chapter 3 in this book by Mahmud al-Khudayri. See also, Nathalie Bernard-Maugiron, "Vers une plus grande indépendance du pouvoir judiciaire en Egypte?" *Revue internationale de droit comparé*, no. 1, 2007, pp. 79–105.

9 See, for instance, Hesham El-Bastawissy in *al-Misri al-yawm*, 31 January 2007.

10 Although he has visited several regional judges' clubs.

11 He even refused an invitation for an *iftar* during Ramadan 2006, stating that he never eats outside his home. *Al-Misri al-yawm*, 12 October 2006.

12 See, *Sawt al-umma*, 11 September 2006, for the decision.

13 *Al-Misri al-yawm*, 29 October 2006. See also, *Nahdat Misr*, 2–3 November 2006.

14 *Al-Misri al-yawm*, 14 November 2006.

15 *Nahdat Misr*, 20 November 2006. See also, *al-Misri al-yawm*, 21 December 2006, and *al-Fajr*, 6 November 2006.

16 *Nahdat Misr*, 31 January 2007.

17 Thirty-four articles of the 1971 constitution were amended. For an analysis of these amendments, see Bernard-Maugiron, "Vers une plus grande indépendance."

18 These women were appointed directly to courts without going through the Office of Public Prosecution, as is normally the case for male judges.

19 See, *Bulletin du CEDEJ*, no. 20, Cairo, 1986, and in particular, Muhammad Nour Chehara, "Le premier congrès de la justice en Egypte," pp. 137ff. Unless otherwise stated, "Judges' Club" means the Cairo Judges' Club for civil law judges.

20 The Egyptian State Council (Majlis al-Dawla) is based on the model of the French *Conseil d'Etat*, but with significant differences.

21 *Sawt al-umma*, 15 January and 5 February 2007. See also, *Nahdat Misr*, 8–9 February 2007.

22 *Al-Misri al-yawm*, 2 February 2007. Five members out of seven of the Supreme Judicial Council would have reached retirement age in 2007. *Al-Dustur*, 26 April 2007.

23 See, *Nahdat Misr*, 4 April 2007.

24 *Ruz al-Yusuf*, 26 April 2007.

25 *Nahdat Misr*, 18 April 2007.

26 *Al-Badil*, 10 September 2007.

27 A woman was appointed to the Supreme Constitutional Court in 2003.

28 The president of the Court of Cassation is chosen from among the vice-presidents of the court, after hearing the opinion of the Supreme Judicial Council (Art. 44, paragraph 2). The draft amendment of the Judges' Club requested he be elected by the general assembly of the court.

29 Counselors complained in August 2007, however, that a secret inspection direction for counselors, called the direction of counselors' complaints (*idarat shakawat al-mustasharin*), had been established illegally within the ministry of justice. *Al-Misri al-yawm*, 13 August 2007.

30 Ahmad Mekki, in *Ruz al-Yusuf*, 8 January 2007.

31 Hisham Muhammad Ra'uf, "al-Ishraf al-qada'i al-kamil 'ala-l-intikhabat," in Negad Mohamed El-Borai, *Islah al-nizam al-intikhabi* (Cairo: Gama'at al-Tanmiyat al-Dimuqratiya, 1998), pp. 226ff.

32 Supreme Constitutional Court, case no. 11/13, 8 July 2000, *al-Ahkam al-lati asdaratha al-mahkama al-dusturiya al-'ulya*, vol. 9, pp. 667ff.

33 Before its amendment in 2007, Article 88 read, "the ballot shall be conducted under the supervision of members of judicial bodies."

34 See, for instance, Muqbil Shakir, in *al-Dustur*, 17 January 2007.

35 *Ruz al-Yusuf*, 15 November 2006.

36 *Majallat Uktubir*, 28 January 2007. See also, *Ruz al-Yusuf*, 15 November 2006.

37 *Al-Ahram Weekly*, 25–31 January 2007.

38 Counselor Husayn 'Abd-Allah, former president of the Cairo Court of Appeal, *Ruz al-Yusuf*, 5 February 2007.

39 *Al-Misri al-yawm*, 24–25 March 2007.

## Notes to Chapter 2

1 See, generally, Michael J. Reimer, *Colonial Bridgehead: Government and Society in Alexandria: 1807–1882* (Oxford: Westview Press, 1997), pp. 107–21.

Mediterranean trade before 1850 was the logic behind the political, economic, social, and cultural transformations throughout the Ottoman Empire, especially in Egypt.

2   Delphine Gérard-Plasmans supports my hypothesis that, since 1854, the year of the concession awarded by Viceroy Sa'id to Ferdinand de Lesseps to dig the canal, French capital owners have had a deep interest in Egypt. See, Delphine Gérard-Plasmans, *La présence française en Egypte entre 1914 et 1936: de l'impérialisme à l'influence et de l'influence à la coopération* (Darnétal: éd. Darnétalaises, 2005), p. 21. At the purely legal and judicial levels, the Suez Canal is deemed the origin of the main reforms that took place in Egypt during the last quarter of the nineteenth century.

3   Under the Ottoman Empire, the reform movement that affected all sectors was called *tanzimat* (regulations). See, Robert Mantran, ed., *Histoire de l'Empire ottoman* (Paris: Fayard, 1989).

4   Under the reign of Khedive Isma'il, the vast movement of codification equally concerned Islamic law, the codes of real status and personal status (Hanafi rite), which were prepared by the minister of justice, Qadri Pasha.

5   Capitulations were a kind of treaty between the Sublime Porte and foreign countries. In the nineteenth century, they favored European countries and their subjects residing in the Ottoman Empire. Europeans and Ottoman protégés of European countries enjoyed cultural, political, religious, judicial, and legal privileges. See, Pelissié du Rausas, *Le régime des capitulations dans l'Empire ottoman* (Paris: Arthur Rousseau Editions, 1911), vols. 1 and 2.

6   To tackle increasing numbers of commercial disputes between Ottomans and foreigners, mixed commercial courts were established in 1820 at Constantinople and in 1861 in Egypt under the reign of Sa'id Pasha. These courts were staffed by Ottoman judges and European merchants. See, Salvatore Messina, "Les tribunaux mixtes et les rapports inter-juridictionnels en Egypte," The Hague Academy of International Law, *Recueil des cours*, vol. 41, 1932, part III, p. 20. The concept of judicial control of administrative and legislative activity was addressed in the regulations of the mixed courts of 1875.

7   I am not claiming that the mixed courts played a heroic role from the political and social point of view. A study of the relations between lawyers working within this judicial realm and the Egyptian national movement would be welcome, however.

8   Prior to the promulgation of the Egyptian Nationality Law in 1926, there was no difference between Egyptians and other Ottoman citizens. There was then only one nationality, namely the Ottoman nationality.

9   Maxime Pupikofer, "Liminaire," in *Les juridictions mixtes (1876–1926): Le livre d'or à l'occasion du cinquantenaire des Tribunaux de la Réforme* (Alexandria: ed. Journal des Tribunaux mixtes, 1926), p. 21.

10  Nubar Pasha's message to Mr. Russel, 24 July 1867, in the Nubar Archive, the document of Zareh Bey Nubar, file 2, sub-file F, no. 3, Paris, p. 1.

11  The Ottoman Sultan 'Abd al-'Aziz issued the decree *(firman)*, dated 8 June 1876, by which he granted his subordinate viceroy, Isma'il, the title of Khedive

of Egypt (a word derived from the Persian, meaning the master, the prince, the viceroy, or sovereign). See, Jean-Jacques Luthi, *La vie quotidienne en Egypte au temps des khédives* (Paris: L'Harmattan, 1998), p. 11. It was Nubar Pasha's interpretation that, except for the "general Ottoman principles included in the Khatt-i-Humayoun of Gulkhane of 1839" (a kind of charter that included judicial, financial, administrative, and military matters), Egypt at that time did not need Constantinople's permission to accept companies, to undertake great works, to grant loans, or to draft regulations (especially judicial) for the country. Nevertheless, Nubar Pasha's letters, kept at Nubar's library in Paris, indicate that, but for the political support of his old friend, the Ottoman grand vizier, Ali Pasha, Nubar Pasha would never have been given the sultan's permission for this judicial reform.

12   Nubar Pasha, *Mémoires* (Beirut: Mirrit Boutros Ghali Publishing House, 1983).

13   Nubar Pasha's letter to Mr. Russel, in the Nubar Archive, the document of Zareh Bey Nubar, file 2, sub-file F, no. 4, Paris.

14   See, Nubar Pasha, *Mémoires*, p. 275.

15   Ibid., p. 6. Nubar Pasha says in a letter dated 24 July 1867 that Italy imported Egyptian products and exported silk textiles to Egypt in an amount exceeding one million [currency unknown], salted food for roughly 600,000 piasters, wine and liquor for 300,000 francs, and marble and stones.

16   Pasquale Mancini was an Italian politician and lawyer who played an essential role during the discussions that took place during the international conferences held from 1867 to 1870 on the reform of the Egyptian judiciary.

17   Furthermore, most of the French in Egypt (like the other members of the "European colonies") were hostile to the reform. Only some members of the French elite, such as Ferdinand de Lesseps, showed interest in the project. The numerous controversies that set Nubar Pasha in opposition to the Universal Suez Ship Canal Company between 1854 and 1870 did not, of course, enhance the support that could have been extended by de Lesseps. This explains why France was the last European power to ratify the reform, on the eve of the opening of the mixed courts in 1875.

18   Since the Belgian revolution of 1830, which put an end to the oppressive administrative practices of the Napoleonic regime in 1831, Belgium has vested ordinary courts with the judicial defense of civil and political rights against administrative infringements by virtue of Articles 92, 93, and 107 of its constitution. Hostility to the French administrative justice system also emerged among some French legal scholars at the time. Finally, two years before the first round of talks on Egyptian judicial reform, Italy abrogated the principle of administrative jurisdiction, pursuant to the law of 20 March 1865. See V.E. Orlando, *La giustiza amnistrativa*, in Trattato Orlando (Milan: N.p., 1991), III, pp. 644–53.

19   Abdel Salam Zohny, *La responsabilité de l'Etat égyptien à raison de l'exercice de la puissance publique* (Paris-Lyon: Paul Geuthner, 1914), vols. 1, 2, and 3.

20   As soon as the foreign countries (European and American) and the Sublime Porte approved the reform, Nubar Pasha asked his friend, Jacques Maunoury,

former French advisor of the Universal Suez Ship Canal Company and a lawyer in Alexandria, to draft six codes known as the mixed codes. These codes were composed of a civil code, a commercial code, a maritime commercial code, a civil and commercial procedures code, a criminal code, and a criminal investigation code. See the French diplomatic archive of the ministry of foreign affairs at Nantes and Paris, the English archives at the British ministry of foreign affairs, and the Nubar Pasha archives in Paris. Regarding the impact of French law in Egypt, see, Isabelle Lendrevie-Tournan, "Réception et diffusion de certains principes du code civil français de 1804 en Egypte (1875–1948)," in *Cahiers aixois d'histoire des droits de l'Outre Mer français*, no. 2, Presses Universitaires d'Aix-Marseille, 2004, pp. 139–157. See also, Pierre Arminjon, "Le code civil et l'Egypte," in *Le livre du centenaire du Code Civil*, ed. Societé d'études legislatives (Paris: ed. A. Rousseau, 1904), vol. 2, p. 735ff.

21   Octave Borelli, "Règlement d'organisation judiciaire pour les procès mixtes en Egypte," in *La législation égyptienne annotée: les codes égyptiens pour les procès mixtes* (Cairo: Librairie Barbier, 1882), p. 2.

22   A copy of a private letter sent by Mr. Alfred Vacher to Mr. Emile Valot, the personnel manager at the ministry of justice in Versailles, Alexandria, 26 May 1876, in the diplomatic archives of the Ministry for Foreign Affairs (Quai d'Orsay), Affaires politiques diverses, Egypte-Réforme judiciaire (1867–1879), vol. 1., p. 4.

23   Maurice De Wee, *La compétence des juridictions mixtes d'Egypte* (Brussels: Librairie des sciences juridiques, 1926), p. 19.

24   Private letter sent by Mr. Alfred Vacher, 26 May 1876.

25   Ramzi Seif, *Les conflits de juridiction entre les tribunaux mixtes et les tribunaux indigènes (en matières civiles et commerciales)*, law thesis, Cairo University, 1938, p. 62.

26   Edouard Lafferière, *Traité de la juridiction administrative* (Paris/Nancy: Berger-Levrault and Cie, 1888); See, Christian Debbasch, *Contentieux administratif* (Paris: précis Dalloz, 1994), p. 57.

27   See *Decisions of the Courts of the Reform in Egypt*, Official collection, rulings and decisions issued by special circuits of the Mixed Court of Appeal from 1876 until 1877 on settlement of pending disputes between the government and foreign individuals, vols. I and II. These collections are kept in the Institut d'Egypte in Cairo.

28   Decision 10/4/1883, *Gazette des Tribunaux mixtes*, vol. 7, 145. Decision 4/2/1885, *Gazette des Tribunaux mixtes*, vol. 10, 4C.

29   This opinion could be found in Ottomans' PhD dissertations and works written by Egyptian professors of comparative law of the time. A group of these Egyptian scholars defended their dissertations in Europe and especially in France.

30   Zohny, *La responsabilité de L'Etat égyptien.*

31   Salvatore Messina, "Les sources du droit mixte, I-La loi," in *Egypte contemporaine*, 1924, p. 65.

32   The collection of judgments issued by the Mixed Court of Appeal is available for reading and reference at many institutions in Egypt and France, including at

the Supreme Court House (Dar al-Qada' al-'Ali), particularly in the library of the Court of Cassation, at the Institut d'Egypte (al-Majma' al-'Alami al-Misri), at the Centre d'études et de documentation économiques, juridiques, et sociales (CEDEJ) in Cairo, at the Court of Appeal in Alexandria, and at the French National Library in Paris.

33 Fabrice Desplechin, *Les Tribunaux mixtes égyptiens,* master's thesis, Laboratoire d'anthropologie juridique de University Paris I, 1987, p. 130.

34 Diplomatic archives, Archive of the French ministry of foreign affairs.

35 After the judicial reform of 1875, Khedive Isma'il contracted many foreign companies. See, Isabelle Lendrevie-Tournan, "Le service public égyptien dans la chronique judiciaire mixte à la fin du XIXe siècle et au début du XXe siècle," in G.J. Fuglielmi, ed., *Histoire et Service Public* (Paris: PUF, 2004), pp. 143–59.

36 The Cairo French Law School was founded in 1890 during the reign of Khedive Tawfik.

37 The Cairo Khedival Law School was founded in 1868 during the reign of Khedive Isma'il.

38 Decision of the Special Chamber of Alexandria, in *La jurisprudence des tribunaux de la Réforme,* Official Record (parts 1, 2, and 3), Jugements et décisions des chambres spéciales, Alexandria, 1876–1877.

39 Mixed Court of Appeal, Alexandria, 13 April 1892, *Bulletin de législation et de jurisprudence égyptiennes,* no. 18 (16 August 1892), pp. 273–74.

40 For a definition of *waqf*s (or *awqaf*), see, Kamel T. Barbar and Gilles Kepel, *Les Waqfs dans l'Egypte Contemporaine,* Dossiers du CEDEJ, 1981, p. 101.

41 This issue is tackled in Isabelle Lendrevie-Tournan, "Apports et rapports de l'anthropologie du droit à l'histoire du droit à partir d'une expérience égyptienne," in *Anthropologie et droit, intersections et confrontations, Cahiers d'anthropologie du droit* (Paris: Karthala, 2004), pp. 249–55.

42 In particular, the Ottoman law of the nineteenth century, capitulations law, Hanafite Islamic law, European laws such as French law, local customs, colonial laws, and Tunisian and Algerian Islamic laws. See, Isabelle Lendrevie-Tournan, "Réception et diffusion de certains principes du code civil français de 1804 en Égypte (1875–1948)," in *Cahiers aixois d'histoire des droits de l'Outre Mer français,* no. 2 (2004), pp. 152–53.

43 Raymond Schemeil, "L'oeuvre créatrice de la jurisprudence mixte," in *Les juridictions mixtes (1876–1926): Le livre d'or à l'occasion du cinquantenaire des Tribunaux de la Réforme* (Alexandria: ed. Journal des Tribunaux mixtes, 1926), p. 153.

44 See, Isabelle Lendrevie-Tournan, *Les services publics égyptiens dans la chronique judiciaire mixte à la fin du XIXe siècle et au début du XXe siècle,* in G.J. Fuglielmi, ed., *Histoire et Service Public* (Paris: PUF, 2004), pp. 143–59.

45 Desplechin, *Les Tribunaux mixtes égyptiens,* p. 153.

46 See, *Gazette des Tribunaux mixtes,* vol. 23, no. 265.

47 Jacques Boedels, *Les habits du pouvoir: La justice* (Paris: Édition Antébi, 1992).

48 Article 15 of the Regulations for the Organization of the Judiciary in National Courts corresponds to Article 43 of the Regulations for the Organization of the

Mixed Judiciary. See the Regulations for the Organization of the Judiciary in National Courts in the preliminaries of codes indigènes, 1883.

49  Letter of Mr. Cogordan to the minister for foreign affairs, 30 December 1896, in the diplomatic archives of the French Ministry for Foreign Affairs, Nouvelle série, Egypte, no. 41, Question juridique/Tribunaux mixtes-Réforme judiciaire (January 1896–February 1898) (Paris: Imprimerie Nationale, 1973), p. 5.

50  Ibid., p. 10.

51  Ibid., p. 25.

52  See on this case, Mark S.W. Hoyle, *Mixed Courts of Egypt* (London: Graham and Trotman, 1991), the chapter entitled, "The Khedive's Debt." On the cessation of European capital exportation to Egypt see, Samir Saul, *La France et l'Egypte de 1882 à 1914: intérêts économiques et implications politiques* (Paris: Comité pour l'histoire économique et financière de la France, 1997), p. 11.

53  Decision issued on 3 and 16 May 1876 of the Mixed Court of Appeal in Alexandria, in *La jurisprudence des tribunaux de la Réforme en Egypte, jugements et decisions rendus parle chambres spéciales*, 1876–1877, vols. 1, 2, and 3.

54  Copy of private letter sent by Mr. Alfred Sacher to Mr. Emile Valot, 26 May 1875.

55  Ibid., pp. 22–25.

56  Decision of the Court of Appeal, 2 December 1896, in *Bulletin de législation et de jurisprudence égyptiennes (1896–1897)*, Alexandria, pp. 21–32. This decision was given on appeal of a judgment given by the mixed first instance court, 8 June 1896.

57  Decision of the Alexandria Mixed Court of Appeal, "Egyptian Government v. Herbault, Nemours, and consorts, commission of State Domains, Debt Fund, and others," 2 December 1896, in *Bulletin de législation et de jurisprudence égyptiennes (1896–1897)*, 1897, p. 22.

58  Ibid., p. 23.

59  Ibid., p. 24.

60  Ibid., at 25.

61  Philippe Chevrant-Breton, "L'abolition des capitulations et la suppression des tribunaux mixtes en Egypte 1919–1949," PhD dissertation, Ecole nationale de Chartres, 2000, 3 vols., p. 112. According to the author, "When the Egyptian national movement became interested, during the interval between the two world wars, in establishing the economic base for achieving independence, it generalized the model of joint stock companies whose statutes provided that shares and actions may not be attributed to foreigners. The purpose of this was to evade the jurisdiction of the Mixed Courts. One of the prototype models of such companies is Misr Bank founded by Tal'at Harb."

62  The British started by launching an attack on the political and cultural influence that France was still exercising at that time in Egypt. They first dismissed French employees from the government and the administration in general. Then the colonial authorities completely reformed the educational system, especially the Cairo Khedival Law School. The French diplomatic records report in detail the diplomatic incident that took place between France and Britain because of the resignation of the French director of the law school

in 1907. He was Edward Lambert, the famous comparative law specialist. The British had already issued a decree on 28 November 1904 stripping the Administration of the Railway, the Telegraph, and Alexandria Port of its mixed legal personality. From that date on, this administration was an extension of the Anglo-Egyptian government. One of the British goals was to deprive the mixed courts of their competence to decide on old litigation between certain branches of the local administration (considered as mixed administrative branches) and Ottoman subjects.

63   In this case, the two contractors made a claim both to the Egyptian and the Sudanese governments, jointly, for the payment of the works executed at Port Sudan. They argued that the Sudanese provinces were an integral part of the Egyptian territory and that the Anglo-Egyptian government, therefore, was responsible for the contracting obligations undertaken by the Sudanese government. The Anglo-Egyptian government invoked the incompetence of the mixed courts in this case and said it was not responsible, arguing that the 1899 convention concluded with the British government granted Sudan an absolutely autonomous government, distinct and separate from the Anglo-Egyptian government.

## Notes to Chapter 3

1   See Art 10 .of Law 66/1943 on the Independence of the Judiciary.

2   Law 46/1972 was amended again in April 2007 to increase the age of retirement and limit secondment abroad to four years) editor's note.(

3   Article 77 bis (1) of Law 46/1972.

4   Law 46/1972 was amended again in April 2007 to increase the age of retirement.

## Notes to Chapter 4

1   As presented in the introduction to this book, in Egypt, the Public Prosecution (ministère public) *(niyaba)* is part of the judiciary and separate (or supposed to be) from the ministry of justice.

2   The office was occupied first by a Belgian, then by a Frenchman.

3   In the French and Egyptian inquisitorial system, as opposed to "adversarial" systems, the investigative judge (juge d'instruction) is usually a judicial personage of fairly high rank in the judiciary who supervises conduct of the investigation of serious crimes.

4   1923 constitution, Art. 128.

5   The capitulations were agreements that placed foreigners under the jurisdiction of their own laws as administered by their consular tribunals.

6   Law 66/1943 on the Independence of the Judiciary, Art. 78 and 79.

7   Ibid., Art. 71.

8   Ibid., Art. 72.

9   Ibid., Art. 84.

10  Ibid., Art. 85.

11  Decree Law 188/1952 on the Independence of the Judiciary, Art. 84.

12  Decree Law 188/1952 on the Independence of the Judiciary, Art. 76. The
Supreme Judicial Council is presided over by the president of the Court
of Cassation and composed of the president of the Cairo Court of Appeal,
the general prosecutor, the two most senior vice-presidents of the Court of
Cassation, and the two most senior presidents of courts of appeal other than
the Cairo Court of Appeal. Decree Law 188/1952 on the Independence of the
Judiciary, Art. 84.

13  Decree Law 188/1952 on the Independence of the Judiciary, Art. 75.

14  Ibid., Art. 83.

15  Law 56/1959 on the Judicial Authority, Art. 133.

16  Ibid., Art. 137.

17  Ibid., Art. 121.

18  See, Ahmed Fathi Surur, *al-Wasit fi qanun al-ijra'at al-jina'iya* (Cairo: Judges' Club
Edition), 1983, p. 137ff. See also, *The Public Prosecution: Egyptian National Report*,
2004, United Nations Development Programme Governance Program in Arab
Countries.

19  Statistics of the ministry of justice for judicial year 2004/2005.

20  Article 116 refers to Article 38 of Law 46/1972 on the Judicial Authority.

21  Law 46/1972 Art. 116, as amended by Law 142/2006 Art.1 .

22  See, *al-Wafd*, 16 March 2006.

23  Law 46/1972 on Judicial Authority, Art. 125.

24  Ibid., Art. 26 and 125, as amended by Law 142/2006.

25  Ibid., Art. 125, as amended by Law 142/2006.

26  Ibid., Art. 94, paragraph 4, as amended by Law 142/2006.

27  Ibid., Art. 129, as amended by Law 142/2006.

28  Ibid.

29  Art. 121, as amended by Law 142/2006.

30  The State Security Affairs Office was established under Emergency Law
162/1958. It is affiliated to the prime minister in his capacity as the deputy
general military ruler.

31  The National Council for Human Rights was established by Law 94/2003.
Article 13 stipulates that the council shall prepare an annual report on its efforts
and activities regarding the enhancement of the protection of human rights.

32  *Annual Report of the National Council for Human Rights*, 2005/2006, p. 37.

33  See, Mahmud Najib Husni, *Sharh qanun al-ijra'at al-jina'iya* (Cairo: Dar al-Nahda
al-'Arabiya, 2nd ed., 1988), p. 623.

34  Mahmud Mustafa, *Tatawwur qanun al-ijra'at al-jina'iya fi Misr wa ghayriha min
al-duwal al-'arabiya* (Cairo: Dar al-Nahda al-'Arabiya, 1969), p. 87.

35  Egyptian Organization for Human Rights, "Sujana' bila huquq," in *Difan 'an
huquq al-insan*, vol. II, May 1993–December 2004, p. 131ff.

## Notes to Chapter 5

1 See, Nabil 'Abd al-Fattah, *al-Yutubya wa al-hajim: Qadaya al-hadath wa-l-'awlama fi Misr* (Amman: Dar Azmina, 2005), pp. 107–109.

2 See, Nabil 'Abd al-Fattah, "al-Qudah wa-l-sulta al-tanfiziya al-sai'a ila al-istiqlal," in Amr Hashim Rabi', *Misr wa mustaqbal al-islah ba'd al-intikhabat* (Cairo: al-Ahram Center for Political and Strategic Studies, 2006), pp. 11–29.

3 Sayf Dayf-Allah, ed., *Nazahat al-intikhabat wa istiqlal al-qada'* (Cairo: Cairo Institute for Human Rights Studies, 2005), pp. 135–53.

4 Amr Hashim Rabi' et al., ed., *Nuzum idarat al-intikhabat fi Misr* (Cairo: al-Ahram Center for Political Research and Studies, 2006), pp. 11–46.

5 On 18 and 19 January 1977, Egyptians took to the streets to protest the decision of the government to end subsidies on flour, rice, and cooking oil.

6 This ruling can be found in Husayn 'Abd al-Raziq, *Misr fi 18–19 Yanayir* (Cairo: Dar Shuhdi, 1984), 3rd ed., pp. 232, 333–34.

7 This provision was amended again in March 2007 to read" ,The Arab Republic of Egypt is *a democratic system based on citizenship*. The Egyptian people are part of the Arab nation and work for the realization of its comprehensive unity." (author's emphasis).

8 Mustafa Abu-Zayd Fahmi, *al-Nizam al-dusturi al-misri wa riqabat dusturiyat al-qawanin* (Cairo: Munshat al-Ma'arif, 1992), p. 146.

9 This provision was amended again in March 2007 to read, "The economy of the Arab Republic of Egypt is based on freedom of economic action, social justice, safeguarding the different forms of ownership, and preserving the rights of workers."

10 The constitutional amendments of March 2007 rid the constitution of most of its socialist provisions.

11 This provision was not amended in 1980 or in 2007.

12 Article 24 was amended in March 2007 to read, "The state will protect production and will strive to achieve economic and social development."

13 Article 30 was amended in March 2007 to read, "Public ownership is the ownership of the people and is represented by state and individual ownership."

14 For an analysis of this point and cooperative and private property, see, Muhammad Rif'at 'Abd al-Wahab, *al-Qanun al-dusturi* (Cairo: Munshat al-Ma'arif, 1990), p. 221.

15 Supreme Constitutional Court, case no. 7, judicial year 16, 1 February 1997, *al-Ahkam allati asdaratha al-mahkama al-dusturiya al-'ulya*, vol. VIII, p. 344.

16 Faruk 'Abd al-Bar, *Dur Majlis al-dawla fi himayat al-huquq wa-l-hurriyat al-'amma* (Cairo: privately published, 1998), particularly the second chapter, pp. 429–98.

17 Court of Cassation, case no. 20471, judicial year 60, 14 November 1999.

18 Royal decree *(firman 'ali)* of 1856, regulating matters of non-Muslim communities, known as *al-Khat al-hamayuni*.

19 Supreme Administrative Court, case no. 6510, judicial year 5, 16 December 1952.

20 High State Security Court (emergency), case no. 4190, 16 April 1987.

21 High State Security Court, case no. 266, 1980.

22  Jamal 'Ali Zahran, "al-Dur al-siyasi li-l-qada' al-misri fi 'amaliyat san' al-qarar," in 'Ali al-Din Hilal, *al-Nizam al-siyasi al-masri: al-taghayyur wa-l-istimrar* (Cairo: al-Nahda al-Misriya Publishers, 1988), pp. 277ff.

23  Ibid., pp. 288–89.

24  *Official Gazette*, no. 28, 11 June 1985, pp. 1271–79. Also see, Jamal 'Ali Zahran, "al-Dur al-siyasi," pp. 288–89.

25  'Asam Raf'at, *al-Wafd* , 26 February 1990.

26  See, Court of Administrative Litigation, 4 February 2003, on the legality of peaceful marches. See also, Nabil Abdel Fattah, *Siyasat al-adyan: al-Sira'at wa darurat al-islah*, 3rd ed. (Cairo: Maktabat al-Usra, 2005), p. 531.

27  For an analysis of some decisions on the right to assembly, see, Hasan Muhammad Hind, *al-Nizam al-qanuni li-huriyat al-ta'bir* (Cairo: Tubagi Institution, 2003), pp. 196–206.

## Notes to Chapter 6

1  A large body of literature is available in Arabic, English, and French on the Egyptian Supreme Constitutional Court (SCC). Since it is only possible for me to sketch the broadest outlines of SCC rulings in a paper this size, I point the reader to more detailed analyses in the following studies: Hisham Fawzi Muhammad, *Riqabat dusturiyat al-qawanin: Dirasat muqarana bayn Amrika wa Misr* (Cairo: Cairo Institute for Human Rights Studies, 1999); Yahya al-Gamal, *al-Qada' al-dusturi fi Misr* (Cairo: Dar al-Nahda al-'Arabiya, 2000); Faruk 'Abd al-Bir, *The Supreme Constitutional Court and the Protection of Human Rights* (Cairo: Dar al-Nahda al-'Arabiya, 2003); Kevin Boyle and Adel Omar Sherif, eds., *Human Rights and Democracy: The Role of the Supreme Constitutional Court of Egypt* (London: Kluwer Law International, 1996); Eugene Cotran and Adel Omar Sherif, eds., *Democracy, the Rule of Law, and Islam* (London: Kluwer Law International, 1999); Nathalie Bernard-Maugiron, *Le politique à l'épreuve du judiciaire: la justice constitutionnelle en Egypte* (Brussels: Bruylant, 2003); Bruce Rutherford, "The Struggle for Constitutionalism in Egypt: Understanding the Obstacles to Democratic Transition in the Arab World," PhD dissertation, Yale University, 1999; Tamir Moustafa, "Law Versus the State: The Judicialization of Politics in Egypt," *Law and Social Inquiry* 28 (2003), pp. 883–930. For a complete list of the rulings, see, *al-Mahkama al-dusturiya al-'ulya*, vols. 1–9.

2  SCC, 26 June 1986, *al-Mahkama al-dusturiya al-'ulya* (hereafter *al-Mahkama*), vol. 3, p. 353.

3  SCC, 7 May 1988, *al-Mahkama*, vol. 4, p. 98.

4  SCC, 16 May 1987, *al-Mahkama*, vol. 4, p. 31; SCC, 19 May 1990, *al-Mahkama*, vol. 4, p. 256

5  SCC, 15 April 1989, *al-Mahkama*, vol. 4, p. 205; SCC, 15 April 1989, *al-Mahkama*, vol. 4, p. 191.

6  Prior to these rulings, the government managed the political field by granting only a handful of parties exclusive representation of the opposition

in parliament. In a classic corporatist arrangement, the parties were left to exercise *internal* control over activists who dared to challenge the government outside the bounds that were implicitly negotiated between the government and opposition parties. After the SCC introduced electoral reforms, however, opposition activists were no longer beholden to the leadership of opposition parties, which controlled party platforms, party membership, and the position of candidates on party lists. For a more detailed analysis, see, Tamir Moustafa, "Law versus the State: The Expansion of Constitutional Power in Egypt," PhD dissertation, University of Washington, 2002, pp. 98–111.

7   The SCC also issued a number of rulings protecting other important civil liberties throughout this period, but because of space constraints, I will discuss only those pertaining to press liberties. Other notable rulings overturned laws allowing the guilt of the accused to be presumed and laws empowering the executive authority to punish suspects without trial. See, SCC, 2 January 1993, *al-Mahkama*, vol. 5.2, p. 103, and SCC, 15 June 1996, *al-Mahkama*, vol. 7, p. 739. For an expanded summary of SCC activity during this period, see Tamir Moustafa, "Law Versus the State," pp. 134–256.

8   SCC, 6 February 1993, *al-Mahkama*, vol. 5.2, p. 183.

9   For a useful analysis of vicarious criminal liability in the Egyptian legal system, see, Adel Omar Sherif, "The Supreme Constitutional Court of Egypt and Vicarious Criminal Liability," in Cotran and Sherif, eds., *The Role of the Judiciary in the Protection of Human Rights* (London: Kluwer Law International, 1997).

10  SCC, 3 July 1995, *al-Mahkama*, vol. 7, p. 45. This also was one of the first cases in which the SCC explicitly invoked international human rights frameworks and treaties to lend legal and moral weight to its ruling. The SCC ruled that Law 40 contradicted Articles 10 and 11 of the Universal Declaration of Human Rights and the principles of justice "shared by all civilized nations." For more on the "internationalization" of the SCC's legal doctrine, see, Boyle and Sherif, *Human Rights and Democracy*, and Moustafa, "Law Versus the State," pp. 204–209.

11  SCC, 1 February 1997, *al-Mahkama*, vol. 8, p. 286.

12  The center initiated seventy-one cases in its first year, 142 in 1996, and 146 in 1997, in addition to providing legal advice to fourteen hundred women in its first three years of activity.

13  With Land Reform Law No. 96 of 1992 coming into full effect in October 1997, hundreds of thousands of peasants faced potential eviction in the late 1990s, and lawsuits between landlords and tenants began to enter the courts by the thousands. Between 1996 and 2000, the Land Center represented peasants in over four thousand cases and provided legal advice to thousands more. Interview with Mahmoud Gabr, director of the legal unit, Land Center for Human Rights, 18 November 2000.

14  In each of its first five years of operation, the Human Rights Center for the Assistance of Prisoners launched over two hundred court cases and gave free assistance (legal and other) to between seven and eight thousand victims per year. Correspondence with Muhammad Zar'i, director of the Human Rights Center for the Assistance of Prisoners, 24 January 2002.

15  Interview with Muhammad Gum'a, vice chairman of the Wafd Committee for Legal Aid, 17 February 2001.

16  Personal interview with 'Abd al-Raziq, 16 April 2000.

17  SCC, 1 February 1997, *al-Mahkama*, vol. 8, p. 286. The Center for Human Rights Legal Aid filed appeals with the SCC in five additional cases in which it represented journalists prosecuted under Article 195.

18  SCC, *al-Mahkama*, vol. 8, p. 1165.

19  The Center for Human Rights Legal Aid was further encouraged by activist judges in the regular judiciary who publicly encouraged groups in civil society to challenge the constitutionality of government legislation. Some activist judges went so far as to publicize their opinions of laws in opposition newspapers and to vow that if particular laws were challenged in their court, they would transfer the relevant constitutional questions to the SCC without delay.

20  Several other human rights groups, such as the Land Center for Human Rights, successfully transferred cases to the SCC for consideration.

21  The ability to circumvent difficulties of collective action is one of the most significant benefits of legal mobilization even in consolidated democracies where civil liberties are relatively secure. Frances Zemans, "Legal Mobilization: The Neglected Role of the Law in the Political System," *American Political Science Review* 77 (1983), pp. 690–703. The possibility of initiating litigation in lieu of a broad social movement is even more crucial for opposition activists in authoritarian systems where the state forcefully interferes with political organizing.

22  Emergency state security courts *(mahkamat amn al-dawla li-ltawari)* handle all trials prosecuted under the emergency law. They are staffed with judges from the regular judiciary and two military officers, if so desired by the president, but there is no appeal for the defendant. After the court renders a decision, it is sent to the president, who has the power to overturn the court's ruling or to demand a retrial. The loose wording of the emergency law gives the government wide latitude to transfer cases perceived as politically threatening out of the jurisdiction of the regular judicial system. The broad powers of the president over the emergency state security courts ensure that once cases enter this parallel legal track, the government will almost certainly win favorable rulings. For more on the structure, composition, and procedures of these courts and the military courts, see, Nathan J. Brown, *The Rule of Law in the Arab World: Courts in Egypt and the Gulf* (Cambridge: Cambridge University Press, 1997) and the Center for Human Rights Legal Aid, "*al-Qada' al-'askari fi Misr: Qada' bi-ghayr damanat . . . qada' bidun hasana mathamun bila huquq,* 1995 (Cairo: Center for Human Rights Legal Aid).

23  Article 68 reads, "The right to litigation is inalienable for all. Every citizen has the right to refer to his competent judge. The state shall guarantee the accessibility of the judicial organs to litigants, and the rapidity of rendering decisions on cases. Any provision in the law stipulating the immunity of any act or administrative decision from the control of the judiciary shall be prohibited." Article 172 reads, "The State Council shall be an independent judicial organ

competent to take decisions in administrative disputes and disciplinary cases. The law shall determine its other competences."

24   SCC, 16 June 1984, *al-Mahkama*, vol. 3, p. 80.

25   Article 171 of the constitution reads, "The law shall regulate the organization of the State Security Courts and shall prescribe their competences and the conditions to be fulfilled by those who occupy the office of judge in them."

26   See, *al-Mahkama*, vol. 3, pp. 90–95.

27   See, *al-Mahkama*, vol. 3, pp. 108–13, 152–57, 189–94.

28   For example, in 1990, an emergency court acquitted Sheikh Omar 'Abd al-Rahman and forty-eight of his followers when it was revealed in court that their confessions were extracted through torture. The government was able to overturn the verdict on "procedural grounds" and retry the defendants, but only after an uncomfortable exposition of the government's disregard for human rights. In another trial of twenty-four Islamists charged with assassinating parliamentary speaker Rif'at al-Mahgub in the early 1990s, the panel of judges dismissed the case when it found that confessions were extracted through torture. Judge Wahid Mahmoud Ibrahim did not spare any details, announcing that medical reports proved the defendants had been severely beaten, hung upside-down, and subjected to electric shocks to their genitals. Michael Farhang, "Recent Development: Terrorism and Military Trials in Egypt: Presidential Decree No. 375 and the Consequences for Judicial Authority," *Harvard International Law Journal* 35 (1994), pp. 225ff. Additional acquittals based on allegations of torture are provided in Brown, *Rule of Law*, pp. 98–99.

29   The first such case was transferred to a military court by Mubarak via Presidential Decree 375/1992. From December 1992 through April 1995 alone, a total of 483 civilians were transferred to military courts for trial. Sixty-four of them were sentenced to death. According to the Arab Center for the Independence of the Judiciary and the Legal Profession 1998 annual report, civilian transfers to military courts reached a high of 317 in 1997 alone.

30   Presidential Decree 297/1995 transferred the cases of forty-nine members of the Muslim Brotherhood from Lawsuit 8, military no. 136, 1995, in the Higher State Security Court to the military judiciary. In 1996, the government transferred twelve members of the emerging Wasat Party to a military court.

31   Brown, *Rule of Law*, p. 115.

32   Article 74 of the constitution reads, "If any danger threatens the national unity or the safety of the motherland, or obstructs the constitutional role of State institutions, the president of the republic shall take urgent measures to face this danger, direct a statement to the people, and conduct a referendum on those measures within sixty days of their adoption."

33   Article 6, paragraph 2 of Military Law 25/1966 states, "During a state of emergency, the president of the republic has the right to refer to the military judiciary any crime which is punishable under the Penal Code or under any other law."

34   Some mistakenly understood this ruling to be the SCC's confirmation of the constitutionality of the law, but interpretation of legislation is another function of the SCC that is completely independent of judicial review.

35  The constitutional challenge was raised by Salim al-'Awa, a prominent Islamist lawyer, and 'Atif al-Banna, a Wafd Party activist and Cairo University professor.

36  In an interview, former Chief Justice 'Awad al-Murr described the Egyptian political system as a "red-line system," in which there is an implicit understanding between the government and the opposition over how much political activism is tolerated. Personal interview with 'Awad al-Murr, 11 June 2000.

37  The problem of recurrent detention was aggravated by "anti-terrorism" Law 97/1992, which expanded the authority of the general prosecutor's office and weakened the oversight of the administrative courts.

38  Egyptian Organization for Human Rights, *Annual Report 1996*.

39  For examples of administrative court rulings concerned with administrative detention and recurrent detention, see Egyptian Organization for Human Rights, *Annual Report 1996*, pp. 41–45.

40  Brown makes this excellent observation: "Having successfully maintained channels of moving outside the normal judiciary, the regime has insured that the reemergence of liberal legality need not affect the most sensitive political cases. . . . The harshness of the military courts, in this sense, has made possible the independence of the rest of the judiciary." Brown, *Rule of Law*, p. 116.

41  The procedural argument for the unconstitutionality of the law was that it was unnecessary for Mubarak to circumvent the People's Assembly and issue an executive decree. The substantive arguments were based on constitutional provisions protecting property rights and access to justice. For example, see, Nu'man Gum'a, "The Legislation is Contradictory to the Constitution and an Aggression on the Function of the Court," *al-Wafd*, 12 July 1998; "Amending the Law of the SCC is an Aggression on the Rights of Citizens," *al-Ahali*, 15 July 1998; Muhammad Hilal, "Three Reasons Behind the Attack on the Supreme Constitutional Court," *al-Sha'b*, 4 August 1998; Muhammad Shukri 'Abd al-Fattah, "Remove Your Hands from the Constitutional Court," *al-Haqiqa*, 8 August 1998.

42  See the extensive report by the Arab Center for the Independence of the Judiciary and the Legal Profession printed in *al-Wafd*, 14 July 1998. Also see the extensive critique provided by the Legal Research and Resource Center for Human Rights, printed in *al-Wafd*, 17 July 1998. The Center for Human Rights Legal Aid issued its own report a few days later in *al-Wafd*, 20 July 1998.

43  See, 'Abd al-'Aziz Muhammad, "Treasonous Amendment to the Constitution and to the Law!" *al-Wafd*, 16 July 1998.

44  Seif al-Nasr, "Three Reasons behind Amending the Law of the SCC," *al-Ahram al-Masa'i*, 13 July 1988; Muhammad Mursi (chair of the Legislative Committee in the People's Assembly), "I Agree with the Law of the Government to Amend the Law of the Rulings [sic] of the Constitutional Court and Here are My Reasons!" *Akhbar al-yawm*, 18 July 1998; Muhammad Badran, "The Decree is a Step in the Right Direction," *al-Ahram*, 27 July 1997.

45  SCC, case no. 163, judicial year 21, 3 June 2000.

46  The case was raised ten years earlier by Kamal Khalid and Gamal al-Nisharti, both candidates who ran for seats in the People's Assembly elections of 1990, in coordination with opposition parties, which recognized the full importance

of constitutional litigation as an avenue for challenging the regime after the dissolution of the People's Assembly in 1987 and 1990.

47  Nagib was appointed first deputy president of the Court of Cassation one year before his appointment to the SCC. Just prior to Nagib's appointment as chief justice, Mubarak extended the mandatory retirement age of judges from sixty-four to sixty-six years of age. Although the shift in the mandatory retirement age was not explicitly designed to extend Nagib's service to the regime, it was well understood by both regime insiders and the opposition that the timing of the extension was formulated with Nagib in mind.

48  The constitutional provisions for the SCC (embodied in Articles 174–178) do not specify the number of justices who sit on the court. Law 48/1979, which governs the functions of the court, also does not prescribe a set number of justices. The explanatory memorandum of Law 48 states, "The law does not specify the number of the members of the court, to leave ample room for expansion in accordance with the work requirements that unfold as the court proceeds with its tasks." According to Article 5 of Law 49/1979 governing the SCC, new appointments to the court are made by the president from between two candidates, one chosen by the general assembly of the SCC and the other by the chief justice of the SCC. It is unclear whether or not there was resistance to Nagib's recruitment efforts from other SCC justices, because deliberations over new appointments are closed to the public.

49  Interview with Fathi Nagib, 27 March 2002.

50  *Al-Jarida al-rasmiya*, no. 10, 9/3/2004 (ruling issued 7 March 2004).

51  Ibid.

52  A minimum of sixty-five of the 250 supporters are required to be from the People's Assembly, a minimum of twenty-five supporters are required to be from the Shura Council, and a minimum of ten members are required to be from the local councils from each of at least fourteen governorates.

53  The party must have been operating for five consecutive years, and the candidate must occupy a leading position within the party for at least one year prior to nomination.

54  Moreover, the Bush Administration could claim a victory in "advancing democracy" through the Broader Middle East Initiative at a time of flagging credibility, with Iraq mired in violence.

55  Amendments to the political parties law gave the regime ample ability to sideline political parties at will.

56  The five members of the judiciary would be the chief justice of the SCC, the head of the Cairo Court of Appeal, the first deputy chief justice of the SCC, the first deputy chairman of the Court of Cassation, and the first deputy chairman of the State Council.

57  Law 48/1979, Article 29, on the procedures of the SCC.

58  *Al-Musawwar*, 15 March 1996, pp. 34–36, 82–83. Also see Hisham Fawzi's analysis in *Riqabat dusturiyat al-qawanin*, pp. 316–18.

59  *Al-Musawwar*, 22 March 1996, pp. 20–23.

60  Lecture by 'Awad al-Murr at Cairo University, 25 September 2000.

61  Mar'i was appointed minister of justice in August 2006.

62  "Mubarak is First Elected President of Egypt," *al-Ahram*, 10 September 2005, p. 1.

63  Tayyab Mahmud, "Jurisprudence of Successful Treason: Coup d'Etat and Common Law," *Cornell International Law Journal* 27 (1994); Anthony Pereira, *Political (In)Justice: Authoritarianism and the Rule of Law in Brazil, Chile, and Argentina* (Pittsburg: University of Pittsburgh Press, 2005); Paula R. Newberg, *Judging the State: Courts and Constitutional Politics in Pakistan* (Cambridge: Cambridge University Press, 1995).

64  "Former Top Judge Says US Risks Edging Near to Dictatorship," *The Guardian*, 13 March 2006.

65  Keck and Sikkink explain that "voices that are suppressed in their own societies may find that networks can project and amplify their concerns to an international arena, which in turn can echo back into their own countries. Transnational networks multiply the voices that are heard in international and domestic policies." Margaret Keck and Katheryn Sikkink, *Activists Beyond Borders: Advocacy Networks in International Politics* (Ithaca: Cornell University Press, 1998).

# Notes to Chapter 7

1  This paper is dedicated to Yahya al-Rifa'i, the symbol of the judges' struggle to defend their independence. It is also dedicated to the great counselors and judges, Ahmad Mekki, Mahmud al-Khudayri, Hesham El-Bastawissy, Mahmud Mekki, Muhammad Naji Darbala, 'Asem 'Abd al-Jabbar, Yahya Jalal, Husam al-Ghoryan, Zakarya 'Abd al-'Aziz, and Ahmad Sabir, as well as all other judges who will remain great as benchmarks in the history of the independence of the judiciary in contemporary Egypt.

2  The board of directors of the club has fifteen members: five are ranking counselors of courts of appeal and the Court of Cassation, of whom one is a retired judge; five are from the Public Prosecution (chiefs and members); and five are presidents of courts or judges.

3  The number of these regional clubs was twenty at the time of writing. All clubs are independent from one another, even though since its establishment the Cairo Judges' Club has been considered the representative of all judges in Egypt. In many cases, the government (and some 'pro-government' judges) has tried to use the regional clubs to decrease the strength of the Cairo club. The government has also tried to enhance divisions among judges by encouraging splits between regional clubs and between them and the Cairo club.

4  According to its register at April 7 2004, the club had 8,715 members. In addition, it had fifty-five associate members and two thousand retired members who were judges. These figures were given to me by a person responsible for statistics on members who had paid membership fees in 2003, although the actual membership was around ten thousand members.

5  Many judges and key people in the club reject the idea that the ministry of justice would use money to pressure the club. All those concerned realize that

the ministry of justice suspended financial support in order to put pressure on the club because of its stances.

6   *Al-'Arabi*, 1 May 2005.

7   See, 'Uthman Husayn, "The Social Guarantees for the Independence of the Judge: Judges' Right to Form their Assemblies and Express their Opinions," *al-Majalla al-jina'iya al-qawmiya* (1995), pp. 580–879.

8   Counselor Ahmad Sabir's presentation before the assembly was entitled, "Jam'iyat al-ta'kid 'ala istiqlal nadi al-qudah wa hisanat mudawalat a'da'ihi," *Qudah*, September 2003–August 2004.

9   *Qudah*, January–August 2002, p. 1.

10   Yahya al-Rifa'i, *al-Ahram*, 19 January 1984.

11   This paper was written before the Egyptian parliament enacted the new law for the judicial authority in 2006, which, despite the degree to which it empowers the Supreme Judicial Council in relation to the ministry of justice in terms of judicial affairs in Egypt, has been criticized by the Judges' Club and human rights groups for being minimal with respect to what the judges sought to ensure their independence.

12   The draft law was prepared by a committee of the club that included Counselors Yahya al-Rifa'i, Wajdi 'Abd al-Samad, Ahmad Mekki, Fathi Najib, and Sirri Siyam.

13   The law was finally amended in 2007 to increase the retirement age from sixty-eight to seventy years.

14   *Qudah*, 18 January 1991.

15   Without going into too much detail in comparing the 1991 and 2004 drafts, I point out that this general philosophy resulted in slight amendments to the new draft.

16   The central security forces staged a rebellion in 1986 when a rumor spread that their term of service would be extended from three years to four years. They set hotels and nightclubs on fire in the tourist areas of Cairo and near the pyramids at Giza. A general curfew was declared and army units restored order after the rioting had gone on for four days and had spread to other parts of Egypt.

17   *Al-Ahram*, 19 January 1991.

18   Statement of the Judges' Club, 24 March 2003, *Al-Ahram Weekly*, 3–9 April 2003.

19   *Qudah*, January–June 1990, p. 10.

20   Available at http://www.islamonline.net/iol-arabic/dowalia/qpolitic-jul-2000/qpolitic16.asp.

21   It is worth noting here that by virtue of the constitutional amendments of 2007, which include changes to Article 88 of the constitution, the debate over what is meant by 'judicial body' has become irrelevant to supervising public elections in the country. The reason for this, as indicated earlier in this paper, is the elimination of direct supervision of elections by the judicial authority.

22   Being based temporarily abroad, I relied solely on briefs from the 2005 general assemblies as published in Egyptian newspapers and a summary of the fact-finding report regarding judicial participation in the constitutional amendment referendum on 25 May 2005.

23  *Al-'Arabi*, 10 May 2005; *al-Wafd*, 14 May 2005.

24  *Al-Wafd*, 3 September 2005; *al-Ahali*, 7–14 September 2005; *al-'Arabi*, 4 Sepember 2005.

25  *Al-'Arabi*, 18 December 2005; *al-Wafd*, 18 December 2005.

26  The general assembly on 17 March 2006 started with a sit-in and condemned the referral of senior judges for investigation. It reaffirmed judges' demands for the adoption of a new law that would guarantee their independence. The assembly decided to organize another sit-in on 25 May 2006 to commemorate the referendum on the amendment of Article 76 of the constitution. The report on parliamentary elections was not released.

27  See *al-'Arabi*, 3 July 2005.

28  The Judges' Club issues two magazines entitled *Qudah* in Arabic. One is a monthly publication that presents debates and articles in addition to an overview of the club's activities; the other is seasonal and oriented toward legal research. From 1991 to 2001, the monthly magazine was almost canceled, and it focused on legal studies only (plus some editorials). Currently, because of practical considerations, the monthly magazine is not issued regularly. I believe that *Qudah* is a veritable treasure of information through which a reader can become better acquainted with the views of judges and the insights of their club concerning the judiciary and law in Egypt.

29  I cannot give a complete summary of means used by the club as above mentioned. Such means and tools as I have mentioned are drawn from the observation and analysis of some of the club's papers and activities undertaken by researchers.

30  *Al-Misri al-yawm*, 19 April 2005.

31  Yahya al-Rifa'i, "Qudah fi muwaghat al-istibdad" in *Istiqlal al-qada' wa mihnat al-intikhabat* (Cairo: al-Maktab al-Misri al-Jadid, 2000), vol. 3, p. 207.

32  *Al-'Arabi*, 1 May 2005.

33  *Qudah*, vol. 10, January–June 1990.

34  *Al-Misri al-yawm*, 18 March 2006.

35  *Al-Misri al-yawm*, 12 March 2006.

36  Ibid.

## Notes to Chapter 8

1  See, Mona al-Ghobashy, "Taming Leviathan: Constitutionalist Contention in Contemporary Egypt," PhD dissertation, Columbia University, forthcoming. Also see, James H. Rosberg, "Roads to the Rule of Law: The Emergence of an Independent Judiciary in Contemporary Egypt," PhD dissertation, Massachusetts Institute of Technology, 1995; Bruce Rutherford, "The Struggle for Constitutionalism in Egypt: Understanding the Obstacles to Democratic Transition in the Arab World," PhD dissertation, Yale University, 1999.

2  See, Linn Hammergren, "Do Judicial Councils Further Judicial Reform? Lessons from Latin America," Carnegie Endowment for International Peace, paper 28, June 2002.

3 See, Latifa Muhammad Salim, *al-Nizam al-qada'i al-misri* (Cairo: al-Ahram Political and Strategic Studies Center, 1986). See also, Nathan J. Brown, *The Rule of Law in the Arab World: Courts in Egypt and the Gulf* (Cambridge: Cambridge University Press, 1997).

## Notes to Chapter 9

1 In the Massacre of the State Council, in 1954, then chief justice of the State Council, 'Abd al-Razzaq al-Sanhuri, an eminent jurist and scholar, was physically attacked on the premises, injured, and forced into retirement.

2 See, Yahya al-Rifa'i, *Istiqlal al-qada' wa mihnat al-intikhabat*, 1st ed. (Cairo: Modern Egyptian Office, 2000), p. 281. The recommendations of the conference include: "The Conference recommends that parliamentary elections be organized under judicial supervision in all their stages to allow serious and effective control and that judges preside over all election committees, even if this would lead to holding elections in several phases, and that the judiciary would be in charge of deciding on electoral challenges."

3 Although the current, 1971, constitution does not expressly provide for the separation of powers and is not based on it, Article 166 stipulates that "judges are independent, subject to no other authority but the law. No authority may intervene in the cases or in the affairs of justice." The text is copied from Article 175 of the 1956 constitution and Article 152 of the 1964 constitution. A similar text is found in Articles 124 and 113 of the 1923 and 1930 constitutions, respectively, which demonstrates that judicial problems with the post-1952 regime are not due to the constitutional text but to the status of the constitution and legislation within the political system.

4 According to Article 88 of the 1971 constitution, "The rules of election and referendum shall be determined by law, while balloting is conducted under the supervision of members of judicial bodies."

5 Until 2000, judges supervised only general polling stations, where the vote counting took place, while auxiliary polling stations, where the balloting took place, were supervised by civil servants.

6 He was chosen as honorary president for life of the Judges' Club in appreciation of his historic role in defending the independence of the judiciary with his participation in the 1968 revolt against attempts to incorporate judges into the Arab Socialist Union, which resulted in his dismissal, as one of the victims of the famous 1969 Massacre of the Judges. See, Hamada Husni, *'Abd al-Nasir wa-l-qada': Dirasa watha'iqiya* (n.p., 2005), pp. 63–94. After onerous efforts, he succeeded in persuading President Sadat to promulgate a law in June 1973 through the People's Assembly to bring back all the judges who had been sacked. See, Husni, *'Abd al-Nasir*, pp. 104–105.

7 See *Qudah*, May 2005, pp. 12–18. It is a special issue on the convocation of the extraordinary general assembly of 13 May 2005.

8 See, Yahya al-Rifa'i *Istiqlal al-qada'*, pp. 230–42. The judgment was issued under the chairmanship of Counselor Muhammad Jalal on his last day in office.

9   Ibid., p. 240.

10  The Alexandria Judges' Club held two general assemblies, on 18 March and 15 April 2005.

11  See, general assembly, 2 September 2005.

12  This drew criticism from a number of writers and journalists. See, Husayn 'Abd al-Razik, *al-Wafd*, 21 April 2005.

13  See, extraordinary general assembly, 13 May 2005.

14  Ibid.

15  See, general assembly, 2 September 2005.

16  Ibid.

17  See, extraordinary general assembly, 16 December 2005.

18  See, Counselor Ahmad Mekki, *Qudah*, May 2005, p. 19. According to Mekki, "The people's confidence in the efficiency and integrity [of the judiciary] is the basis of its existence. It is the people's trust in the judiciary that makes them have recourse to it to settle their conflicts."

19  See, Nabil 'Abd al-Fattah, in Sayid Dayf-Allah, ed., *Nazahat al-intikhabat wa istiqlal al-qada'* (Cairo: Cairo Institute for Human Rights Studies, 2005), pp. 135–53. See also chapter in this book Ahmed Abd El-Hafeez.

20  See, extraordinary general assembly, 13 May 2005.

21  See, extraordinary general assembly, 2 September 2005.

22  I am not well informed on Coptic judges' attitude toward this type of legitimacy.

23  See, "Declaration of Free and Fair Election Standards," *Qudah*, 2005. Published in a special issue of the magazine on the invitation of judges to attend the general assembly on 2 September 2005, the "Declaration of Free and Fair Election Standards" was unanimously approved by the Inter-Parliamentary Council at its 154th session in 1994 (pp. 55–58 of *Qudah*, 2005).

24  See, extraordinary general assembly, 13 May 2005. See also, general assembly, 2 September 2005, during which al-Khudayri said, "Great people of Egypt, galvanize your force against those responsible for rigging. Despise and boycott them." He also presented his discourse as the best politics for the regime, stating that those who perform rigging strip rulers of their legitimacy, which "allows rebellion and resistance against them," confirming that "power derives its legitimacy from its submission to the law." These were expressions of hope that the regime would reverse its determination to continue election rigging.

25  Extraordinary general assembly, 16 December 2005. At the same meeting, Counselor Ashraf al-Barudi was quoted as saying, "Fair election simply needs a fair government. . . . The state demands not the culture of right but rather that of 'yes, Mr. President.'"

26  See, extraordinary general assembly, 16 December 2005.

27  See, Article 77 bis (1) of Law 46/1972 on Judicial Authority.

28  Article 2 of the statutes of the Judges' Club states, "The purpose of the club is to entrench further ties of fraternity and solidarity among the judiciary and members of the Office of Public Prosecution and to facilitate means and ways

of meeting and acquaintance, while preserving their interests and consolidating the independence of the judiciary and of its men."

29  Report of the Committee in charge of implementing the decisions adopted at the general assembly meeting of 13 May 2005.

30  This judicial immunity has been extensively slashed by the 1971 constitution, although the judiciary still gives immunity to some presidential decrees by considering them acts of sovereignty. See Chapter 11, by Mohamed Maher Abouelenen, in this volume.

31  See, Muhammad 'Afifi Isma'il, extraordinary general assembly, 13 May 2005. In this assembly, he mentioned lounges for judges, medical treatment, pay increases, transportation at the expense of the state, and other benefits. See also, *Qudah*, May 2005, p. 28, and Mahmud al-Khudayri, extraordinary general assembly, Alexandria Judges' Club, 15 April 2005.

32  See, Muhammad Mirghani Khayri, in Sayed Dayf Allah, ed., *Nazahat al-intikhabat*, pp. 29–30. Khayri is a professor of constitutional law who criticized this confusion in a series on reform issues, *Qadaya al-islah*, published by the Cairo Institute for Human Rights Studies.

33  This takes place through the appointment of heads of courts of first instance and the fact that the general assemblies of courts delegate the competence of case distribution to them. Concerning the importance of not naming in advance the judge who is to consider a certain case, see, Tariq al-Bishri, "Istiqlal al-qada' wa mihna al-intikhabat," in Yahya al-Rifa'i, ed., *Istiqlal al-qada'*, pp. 211–16.

## Notes to Chapter 10

1  Constitution of Egypt, Art. 68.

2  Decree Law 344/1952, Art. 1.

3  Orders of the Revolution Command Council of 13 September 1953 and 16 September 1953.

4  Anwar Sadat was appointed a judge in the first Court of the Revolution.

5  Pursuant to Article 7 of Law 162/1958 on the State of Emergency.

6  See also, Constitution of Egypt, Art. 183: "The law shall organize a military judiciary, prescribing their competencies in the framework of the principles in the Constitution."

7  Law No. 16 of 23 April 2007, amending some provisions of the military law.

8  If the defendant surrenders or is arrested before the end of trial or the lapse of penalty that nullifies *in absentia* status.

9  On the basis of Article 33 of the Law on the Supreme Constitutional Court.

10  SCC, case no. 1, Judicial Year 5 (interpretation), 30 January 1993.

11  Constitution of Egypt, Art. 179: "The Socialist Public Prosecutor shall be responsible for taking the procedures which secure the people's rights, the safety of society and its political system, the preservation of socialist achievements, and commitment to socialist behavior. The law shall define his other competencies. He shall be subject to the control of the People's Assembly in accordance with what is prescribed by law."

12 Amended by Law 177/2005. Previously amended by Law 30/1981 and by Decree Law 221/1994.

13 Since the amendment by Law 177/2005.

14 Art. 8, sec. 12, Law 40/1977, as amended by Law 177/2005.

## Notes to Chapter 11

1 For the development of legislation in terms of acts of sovereignty, see, for instance, the thesis of Muhammad Zuhayr Jarana, *L'ordre administratif*, Cairo University, 1935.

2 Court of Administrative Litigation, case no. 5, judicial year 1, 10 March 1947.

3 Court of Administrative Litigation, case no. 304, judicial year 1, 21 April 1948.

4 Court of Administrative Litigation, case no. 252, judicial year 1, 13 April 1948.

5 Court of Administrative Litigation, case no. 587, judicial year 5, 26 June 1951.

6 Court of Administrative Litigation, case no. 13, judicial year 7, 19 January 1956.

7 Supreme Administrative Court, case no. 807, judicial year 10, 12 December 1966.

8 Court of Administrative Litigation, case no. 13, judicial year 7, 19 January 1956.

9 Court of Administrative Litigation, case no. 587, judicial year 5, 26 June 1951.

10 Court of Administrative Litigation, case no. 4079, judicial year 7, 7 March 1956.

11 Court of Administrative Litigation, case no. 3715, judicial year 7, 25 April 1957.

12 Supreme Administrative Court, case no. 1609, judicial year 6, 29 June 1963.

13 Court of Administrative Litigation, case no. 5, judicial year 1, 10 March 1947.

14 Court of Administrative Litigation, case no. 587, judicial year 5, 26 June 1951.

15 Court of Administrative Litigation, case no. 304, judicial year 1, 21 April 1948.

16 Court of Administrative Litigation, case no. 252, judicial year 1, 13 April 1948.

17 Supreme Administrative Court, case no. 377, judicial year 20, 5 April 1975.

18 Court of Administrative Litigation, case no. 2550, judicial year 54, 19 June 2001.

19 Court of Administrative Litigation, case no. 12106, judicial year 55, 5 February 2002.

20 Court of Administrative Litigation, case no. 23668, judicial year 57, 25 May 2004.

21 Court of Administrative Litigation, case no. 287, judicial year 33, 1 May 1979.

22 Constitution of Egypt, Art. 74, as amended in 2007: "If any immediate and serious danger threatens the national unity or the safety of the motherland or obstructs state institutions from exercising their constitutional roles, the president of the republic shall take urgent measures to face this danger after taking the opinions of the prime minister, the speakers of the People's Assembly, and the Consultative Council. He shall then direct a statement to the people and conduct a referendum on these measures within sixty days of their adoption. The People's Assembly cannot be dissolved during the time of exercising these powers."

23 Court of Administrative Litigation, case no. 3123, judicial year 35, 22 December 1981.

24 Court of Administrative Litigation, case no. 1729, judicial year 36, 7 January 1986.

25 Supreme Administrative Court, case no. 830, judicial year 20, 29 December 1979; case no. 1438, judicial year 31, 6 March 1988; case no. 1439, judicial year 31,

25 June 1989. See also, Court of Administrative Litigation, case no. 667, judicial year 45, 27 November 1990.

26   Supreme Administrative Court, case no. 675, judicial year 30, 11 January 1986.

27   Supreme Administrative Court, case no. 1939, judicial year 30, 12 December 1987; case no. 2184, judicial year 30, 5 January 1991.

28   Pope Shenouda is the head of the Egyptian Coptic Orthodox Church.

29   Court of Administrative Litigation, case no. 3123, judicial year 35, 22 December 1981. These measures were taken by President Sadat in 1981.

30   Supreme Constitutional Court, case no. 22, judicial year 6, 5 February 1977; Case No. 8, judicial year 7, 7 May 1977; case no. 5, judicial year 7, 1 April 1978.

31   Supreme Constitutional Court, cases no. 6, 2, and 9, judicial year 1, 6 November 1971.

32   Supreme Constitutional Court, case no. 5, judicial year 5, 3 July 1979.

33   'Adil 'Umar Sharif, *Qada' al-dusturiya: al-Qada' al-dusturi fi Misr* (Cairo: Dar al-Sha'b, 1988), p. 167.

34   Supreme Constitutional Court, case no. 48, judicial year 4, 21 January 1984.

35   See, Sharif, *Qada' al-dusturiya*, p. 163.

36   The unconstitutionality of a legal provision can be raised by the judge or by a party to litigation during the examination of a case before the trial court.

37   Supreme Constitutional Court, case no. 48, judicial year 4, 21 January 1984.

38   Supreme Constitutional Court, case no. 4, judicial year 12, 9 October 1990.

39   Ibid.

40   Supreme Constitutional Court, case no. 3, judicial year 1, 25 June 1983.

41   Constitution of Egypt, Art. 152: "The president of the republic may call a referendum of the People on important matters related to the supreme interests of the country."

42   Supreme Constitutional Court, case no. 56, judicial year 6, 21 June 1986.

43   Supreme Constitutional Court, case no. 131, judicial year 6, 16 May 1987.

44   Supreme Constitutional Court, case no. 37, judicial year 9, 19 May 1990.

45   Supreme Constitutional Court, case no. 1, judicial year 14, 19 June 1993.

## Notes to Chapter 12

1   Supreme Administrative Court, cases no. 5, 6, 7, and 8, judicial year 1, 26 April 1960.

2   Court of Administrative Litigation, case no. 2056, judicial year 34 11 August 1980.

3   Mustafa al-Nahas was one of the founders of the Wafd Party. He headed the party after the death of Sa'd Zaghlul in 1927.

4   Court of Administrative Litigation, case no. 1181, judicial year 5, 19 June 1952.

5   Court of Administrative Litigation, case no. 88, judicial year 3, 29 June 1950.

6   Ibid.

7   See, Na'im 'Atta, "al-Idara wa-l-hurriyat fi-l-awqat ghayr al-'adiya," *Administrative Science Magazine*, December 1979, pp. 7–8.

8   Supreme Administrative Court, case no. 1309/12, 18 February 1967.

9   Husni Sa'd 'Abd al-Wahid, *Tanfiz ahkam al-qada' al-idari* (N.p.: n.p., n.d.), 1st ed., p. 432.

10  Court of Administrative Litigation, case no. 894, judicial year 51, 11 June 1962.

11  Supreme Administrative Court, cases no. 5, 6, 7, and 8, judicial year 1, 26 April 1960.

12  Court of Administrative Litigation, case no. 6255, judicial year 8, 30 June 1957.

13  Ibid.

14  Local authorities, notably small ones, abide by judicial rulings less than any other authority. This may be because their judicial disputes are sometimes an extension of personal rows or party conflicts or because the execution is done by biased civil servants. Legality and law are less observed, emotions are given full reign, and the feeling of humiliation is much more intense.

15  Such as registration in electoral lists, submission of nomination papers, and conditions for being a candidate.

16  See, Jihad 'Uda, Negad El-Borai, and Hafez Abu Seada, *A Door onto the Desert: Egyptian Legislative Elections of 2000* (Cairo: Association for Democratic Development, 2001), p. 91.

17  Ibid., p. 92.

18  Articles 40 and 50 of Law 47/1972 on the State Council stipulate that the request for a stay of execution has to be introduced before the appeal investigation circuit and does not automatically result in a stay of execution.

19  Case no. 41187, judicial year 59, 6 September 2005.

20  Law 162/1958 on the State of Emergency allows people to be held in detention almost indefinitely, without trial, at the discretion of the minister of the interior. Petitions for release can be filed by detainees at thirty-day intervals, but these applications are heard by the emergency High State Security Court, with no right of appeal.

21  Supreme Administrative Court, case no. 289, judicial year 16, 24 February 1974.

22  For more detailed information on the powers of the administrative judge in facing the executive authority, see, Hamdi 'Ali 'Umar, *Sultat al-qadi al-idari fi tawjih awamir al-idara: Dirasa muqarana* (Cairo: Dar al-Nahda al-'Arabiya, 2003); Yusri Muhammad al-'Assar, *Mabda' hadhr tawjih awamir min al-qadi al-idari li-l-idara wa hadhr hulul mahallaha wa tatawarratuh al-haditha* (Cairo: Dar al-Nahda al-'Arabiya, 2000).

23  Court of Administrative Litigation, case no. 72, judicial year 1, 28 May 1947.

24  See' Abd-al-Wahid ,*Tanfiz ahkam al-qada'*, p. 310.

25  'Umar, *Sultat al-qadi al-idari,* pp. 123ff. The prevailing party also may resort to a mediator in order to compel the administration to execute a ruling. A mediator is a parliament member who mediates between the prevailing party and the administration. His role is similar to that of the dispute settlement committees common in Egypt, but he is more effective. However, the mediator is not vested with power to abrogate or amend the administrative decision or even to impose a penalty on the administration or the public servant. He is authorized only to recommend submitting reports to the parliament to raise the question of imposing criminal or punitive measures against those officials. Hamdi 'Ali 'Umar, *Sultat al-qadi al-idari,* pp. 89ff.

## Notes to Chapter 13

1 See, for instance, 'Abd al-Mun'aym 'Abd al-'Azim Gabra, "Dur al-qadi al-madani fi wad' al-qawa'id al-qanuniya," *Quarterly Judiciary Journal* 27 (July–December 1994), pp. 56ff. See also, Latifa Muhammad Salim, *al-Nizam al-qada'i al-misri* (Cairo: al-Ahram Political and Strategic Studies Center, 1986).

2 According to Article 8 of Law No. 40 of 1977 on Political Parties, as amended by Law No. 177 of 2005, the Committee for Parties is made up of the speaker of the Consultative Council, the ministers of the interior and parliamentary affairs, three former heads or deputy heads of judicial bodies, and three independent public figures chosen by a decree of the president of the republic.

3 According to Article 8 of Law No. 40 of 1977 on Political Parties, as amended by Law No. 177 of 2005, the Court of Parties is the first circuit of the Supreme Administrative Court of the State Council, headed by the president of the State Council and consisting of five counselors of the State Council, joined by five public figures appointed by a decision of the minister of justice, with the approval of the Supreme Council of Judicial Bodies.

4 The board is made up of twenty-five members.

5 See, Mustafa 'Iwis, *al-Harb al-ahliya fi niqabat al-muhamiyin* (**[city?]**: Human Rights Legal Studies and Information Center, 1997), 1st ed. Also see, Raga' al-Mirghani, *Niqabat al-sahafiyin* (Cairo: al-Ahram Political and Strategic Studies Center, 2005).

6 See, Ahmed Abd El-Hafeez, "Dur al-qada' fi takwin al-ahzab al-siyasiya," in Amr Hashem Rabi', ed., *al-Ahzab al-saghira wa-l-nizam al-hizbi fi Misr* (Cairo: al-Ahram Political and Strategic Strategic Studies Center, 2003).

7 Ahmad Faris 'Abd al- Mun'aym, *al-Dur al-siyasi li-niqabat al-muhamiyin, 1912–1981*, photocopy of the version found in the Bar Association Public Library, Cairo.

8 The commissioners' body is in charge of preparing reports on all cases submitted to the State Council.

9 Nasr Hamid Abu Zayd, professor of literature at Cairo University, was condemned by the courts to divorce his wife on the grounds of his alleged apostasy.

10 Article 76 of the 1971 constitution was amended in May 2005 to provide for presidential elections. This amendment was adopted by referendum.

## Notes to Chapter 14

1 Administrative law judges of the State Council have established their own club, which is totally independent from the Judges' Club of the civil law judges.

2 For details, see, 'Abd al-Raziq Husayn, *al-Ahali, sahifa taht al-hisar* (Cairo: Dar al-'Alam al-Thalith, 1994), pp. 48–50.

3 On the case of Nasr Hamid Abu Zayd, see, Nadia Abou al-Magd, "When the Professor Can't Teach," *Al-Ahram Weekly*, no. 486, 15–21 June 2000.

4 Gabir 'Asfur, "Ayyuha al-muthaqqafun: Ittahidu," *al-Ahram*, 13 August 2007, p. 12.

5   On exceptional courts in Egypt, see, Ahmed Seif al-Islam, "Exceptional Law and Exceptional Courts," in Nathalie Bernard-Maugiron and Baudouin Dupret, eds., *Egypt and Its Laws* (London: Kluwer Law International, 2002), pp. 359–77.

6   See the details in, Muhammad 'Abd al-Salam, *Sanawat 'asiba: Zikrayat na'ib 'amm* (Cairo: Dar al-Shuruq, 1995), pp. 166–81.

7   Center for Political and Strategic Studies, *al-Taqrir al-istratiji al-'arabi* (Cairo: Center for Political and Strategic Studies, 1987), pp. 376–77.

8   For the details, see the reports of human rights organizations on Egypt, particularly those of the Egyptian Organization for Human Rights, Amnesty International, and Middle East Watch.

9   Documents presented by the Egyptian Organization for Human Rights.

10  Information obtained at the Land Center.

11  For more details concerning workers' rights and resort to courts, see *al-'Ummal wa-l-muwazzafin wa ahkam al-qada'* and *al-'Ummal wa-l-muqawama al-ijtima'iya* (Cairo: Hisham Mubarak Law Center, n.d.).

12  Documents presented to the author by the Hisham Mubarak Law Center.

13  Information obtained at the Land Center in May 2007.

14  Memorandum obtained by the Land Center.

15  See the challenge submitted by the Land Center to the Supreme Constitutional Court, 2004, and presented to the author by the Land Center.

16  See the Land Center's challenge of the constitutionality of the decision of the governor of Cairo to collect the cleanliness fee as part of the electricity bill, Cairo, 2006.

17  Ibid.

# Notes to Chapter 15

1   The constitutional referendum took place on 25 May 2005. It was about a provision for electing the president of the republic directly for the first time (instead of with the former indirect system of validating the parliament's choice of candidate) through public and secret ballot. The presidential election took place on 7 September 2005. Voting for the People's Assembly was set up in three phases from 8 November to 7 December 2005.

2   SCC, case no. 153, judicial year 21, 3 June 2000, *al-Ahkam al-lati asdaratha al-mahkama al-dusturiya al-'ulya*, vol. 9, pp. 582ff.

3   According to Article 195, draft laws "complementary to the Constitution" have to be submitted to the Consultative Council for its opinion, a procedure that was not followed for that law.

4   Having identified a procedural error, the SCC did not examine the merits, in conformity with its jurisprudence.

5   *Al-Misri al-yawm*, 16 August 2005.

6   The NGOs that filed the appeal were the Arab Organization for Penal Reform, the Group for Democratic Development, the Center for Democratic Dialogue, the Andalusia Center for the Study of Tolerance and Combating Violence, and the Egyptian Organization for Human Rights.

7   *Al-Ahram*, 4 September 2005.

8   The State Council's commissioners are junior magistrates assigned to investigate every case and submit a report to the court.

9   It is noteworthy that the report's authors expressed surprise that the appeal against the decision of the Court of Administrative Litigation was not introduced by the electoral commission but rather by the State Litigation Authority, which is a body assigned to defend the state's interests before the courts. The commissioners pointed out that according to the constitution, the Presidential Election Commission is an independent organ not subordinate to the state or to the executive authority. How, then, could its interests be defended before the courts by state lawyers? The report concluded that the state did not have the capacity (read, legal standing) *(sifa)* to introduce such an appeal and that it should have been presented by the head of the Presidential Elections Commission—a procedure that was finally carried out.

10   Article 68 states, "Any provision in the law stipulating the immunity of any act or administrative decision from the control of the judicature is prohibited." Article 172 states, "The State Council is an independent judicial organization competent to take decisions in administrative disputes and disciplinary cases. The law shall determine its other competencies."

11   *Al-Ahram Weekly*, 8–14 September 2005.

12   In its report on the presidential elections, the Judges' Club questioned the reasons for this change in the attitude of the commission.

13   See, for instance, the report published by the Independent Committee for Elections Monitoring, "Independent Committee for Election Monitoring Preliminary Report on Election Day Voting and Counting Process," 8 September 2005.

14   According to the report submitted by the Arab Center for the Independence of the Judiciary and the Legal Profession, this was particularly the case with members of the Office of Public Prosecution.

15   See, Ibn Khaldoun Center For Development Studies, "Egyptian Democracy Support Network Update," 8 September 2005.

16   The National Council for Human Rights was created in 2003 in response to an invitation by the United Nations Commission for Human Rights to create national institutions for the defense of human rights. The outcome of its first three years of activities is highly controversial.

17   Mahmud al-Khudayri, *al-Misri al-yawm*, 27 October 2005.

18   Hesham El-Bastawissy, *al-Misri al-yawm*, 27 October 2005.

19   The Egyptian Organization for Human Rights, the Group for Democratic Development, the Arab Organization for Penal Reform, the Arab Center for the Independence of the Judiciary and the Legal Profession, the Center for Development of Democratic Dialogue on Human Rights, and the Association for Legal Aid.

20   The refusal to be registered is based on the corporate interest of judges being contrary to Article 11 of Law 84/2002 on the Law of Associations, which prohibits associations from pursuing the same activities as syndicates.

21   *Nahdat Misr*, 17 August 2005.

22   The other three conditions were that junior prosecutors recently nominated should not supervise the elections because they do not have sufficient experience; a copy of the minutes of the counting of the ballots should be communicated to the candidates' delegates; and the judges excluded from electoral supervision should be reintegrated.

23   *Al-Misri al-yawm*, 3 January 2006.

24   *Nahdat Misr*, 17 November 2005. Reference is to the opinion of the SCC of 7 March 2004; *see infra*.

25   ACIJLP, "Human Rights Groups Express Solidarity with the Egyptian Judiciary," 15 May 2005.

26   ACIJLP, "ACIJLP Urges the Egyptian Judiciary to Resist Supreme Judicial Council Pressure," 19 May 2005.

27   *Al-Misri al-yawm*, 5 September 2005.

28   ACIJLP, "Human Rights Organizations Warn against Harming Egypt's Honest Judges," 29 November 2005.

29   EOHR, "EOHR Welcomes Judges' Guarantees, Urges Judiciary High Council to Reconsider Stance," 30 November 2005.

30   Mahmud Mekki, Hesham El-Bastawissy, and Mahmud al-Khudayri, who are vice-presidents of the Court of Cassation. The investigation was finally withdrawn from the Office of State Security Prosecution and transferred to an investigating judge. Four other reformist judges were subjected to the same measures: Ahmad Mekki, Yahya Galal, 'Asim 'Abd al-Gabbar, and Nagui Dirbala, who also are vice-presidents of the Court of Cassation.

31   ACIJLP, "Civil Society Organizations in Solidarity with Egypt's Judges," 20 February 2006.

32   EOHR, "EOHR Calls upon President Mubarak to Annul Immunity-Lifting Decree on Deputies of Court of Cassation Chair," 18 February 2006.

33   For a summary of the debates, see, *al-Misri al-yawm*, 3 and 4 April 2005.

34   ACIJLP, "Judicial Supervision of the Elections in the Light of the Law on the Exercise of Political Rights: Recommendations," 24 July 2005.

35   ACIJLP, "Recommendations of the Conference on the Role of the Judiciary, Media, and Civil Society Associations in Observation and Supervision of the Elections," 2 October 2005.

36   The participating senior judges were Mahmud Mekki, Ahmad Mekki, Hesham El-Bastawissy, Mahmud al-Khudayri, and Yahya al-Rifa'i. For a summary of the debate, see, CIHRS, "Nazahat al-intikhabat wa istiqlal al-qada'," 2005.

37   See *al-Misri al-yawm*, 3 and 12 May 2005.

38   Ibid., 4 June 2005.

39   *New York Times*, 27 February 2006.

40   SCC, case no. 11/13, 8 July 2000, *al-Ahkam al-lati asdaratha al-mahkama al-dusturiya al-'ulya*, vol. 9, pp. 667ff.

41   Muhammad Ra'uf, "al-Ishraf al-qada'i al-kamil 'ala-l-intikhabat," in Negad Mohamed El-Borai, ed., *Islah al-nizam al-intikhabi* (Cairo: Gama'at Tanmiyat al-Dimuqratiya, 1998), pp. 226ff.

42   Ibid.

43 Murad M. Hilmi, "Damanat nazahat al-intikhabat al-'amma," in Negad Mohamed El-Borai, *Islah al-nizam al-intikhabi* (Cairo: Gama'at al-Tanmiyat al-Dimuqratiya, 1998), p. 165.

44 Article 88 states, "The necessary conditions stipulated by the members of the People's Assembly shall be defined by law. The rules of election and referendum shall be determined by law, while the ballot shall be conducted under the supervision of members of a judicial body."

45 The court stressed, however, that the laws adopted by the parliament before the publication of its decision in the *Official Gazette* would not be affected by the invalidation of the elections.

46 The Office of Administrative Prosecution is organized by Law 117/1958, as amended by Law 12/1989. It is in charge of conducting prosecution in the disciplinary affairs of state employees.

47 The State Litigation Authority is organized by Law 75/1963, as amended by Law 10/1986. It is in charge of defending the interests of the state before the courts.

48 See, for instance, *al-Wafd*, 24–25 July 2003. This decision led to divisions within the Court of Cassation itself, as illustrated by the appeal filed by the president of that court before its penal chamber for procedural error. The penal chamber turned down the appeal, deciding that the president of the Court of Cassation was not competent to file such an appeal. See, *al-Wafd*, 12 February 2004. Article 175 of the constitution gives the SCC the competence to interpret laws and decree laws.

49 SCC, 7 March 2004, *Official Gazette*, no. 10 bis, 9 March 2004.

50 Constitution of Egypt, Art. 167: "The law shall determine the judicial bodies and their functions, organize the way of their formation, and prescribe the conditions and measures for the appointment and transfer for their members."

51 The polemic decreased, however, when a female member of the Office of Administrative Prosecution, in an article published on 24 November 2005 by *al-Misri al-yawm*, publicly denounced the fraud that had taken place in the electoral district that was under her supervision and which had led to the proclamation of the victory of an NDP candidate when, in almost the totality of the primary polling stations, the Muslim Brothers' candidate was in the lead. Judges praised that woman's courage and some apologized for having indirectly attacked the Office of Administrative Prosecution.

52 See also, *al-Wafd*, 18 May 2005, which refers to a press release of the ministry of justice.

53 The report was published in *al-'Arabi*, 3 July 2005. See also, *al-Misri al-yawm*, 2 July 2005.

54 *Ruz al-Yusuf*, 4 September 2005.

55 Court of Administrative Litigation, 6 September 2005.

56 A legal device that consists of introducing a request to stay the execution of an administrative ruling before the ordinary courts, in order to suspend its effect on a provisional basis, while the ordinary courts are themselves incompetent to examine that request since the judgment is issued by the administrative judiciary. See Chapter 12, by Negad Mohamed El-Borai, in this volume.

57 Because of the bad quality of the phosphorescent ink, which allowed multiple voting.

58 *Al-Ahram*, 21 November 2005.

59 *Al-Misri al-yawm*, 20 November 2005.

60 This would be the case for the controversial heads of general polling stations at Doqqi and Damanhur, where, according to various corroborating sources, rigging took place at the level of ballot counting. According to *al-Misri al-yawm* (26 November 2005), the head of the general committee at Doqqi had been seconded to the People's Assembly for three years and the head of Damanhur had been seconded as a counselor at the ministry of housing.

61 *Al-Misri al-yawm*, 26 November 2005.

62 See, Mahmud Mekki and Hesham El-Bastawissy, *Sawt al-umma*, 28 November 2005.

63 Hesham El-Bastawissy, *al-'Arabi*, 4 December 2005.

64 Ibid.

65 It also analyzed other public channels for the legislative elections.

66 Especially during the last two phases of the legislative elections.

67 In particular, public servants were transported by buses to the polling stations, where they were strongly encouraged to vote for NDP candidates.

68 This violated Article 21 of the Law on Presidential Elections.

69 See also, ACJILP, "Free, Partial, and Unfair Presidential Elections," 11 September 2005.

70 *Al-Wafd*, 18 December 2005.

71 *Sawt al-umma*, 28 November 2005.

72 Ibid.

73 Ibid. Ahmad Mekki.

74 Ibid. Hesham El-Bastawissy.

75 *Sawt al-umma*, 19 December 2005.

76 *Al-Dustur*, 29 December 2005.

77 *Nahdat Misr*, 14 December 2005.

78 *Al-Misri al-yawm*, 2 September 2005.

79 *Al-'Arabi*, 4 December 2005.

80 Ibid.

81 Ibid.

82 *Al-Wafd*, 18 December 2005.

83 Ibid.

84 *Nahdat Misr*, 18 December 2005.

85 This did not prevent Egypt from sending observers to Palestine in January 2006, and to Zimbabwe and Tanzania to observe elections.

86 EOHR, "EOHR Calls upon Parliamentary Elections Committee to Accept Local and International Elections Supervision," 27 September 2005.

87 *Al-Wafd*, 15 May 2005.

88 Ibid.

89 *Al-'Arabi*, 24 April 2005. Muhammad Atta is one of the terrorists, of Egyptian nationality, who participated in the 11 September 2001 attack on New York City.

90  Ibid.

91  *Al-Misri al-yawm*, 2 October 2005.

92  Ibid.

93  *Al-Misri al-yawm*, 19 December 2005.

94  Statement dated 23 November 2005.

95  *Al-Wafd*, 18 December 2005.

96  *Nahdat Misr*, 18 February 2006.

97  ACIJLP, "ACIJLP Calls upon the ICJ to Send a Fact-finding Mission Concerning the Crisis of Egypt's Judges," 19 March 2006.

98  *Nahdat Misr*, 8 April 2006. See also, *al-Wafd*, 6 April 2006.

99  *Al-Misri al-yawm*, 31 December 2005

100 As demonstrated by the conflict in April 2006 between supporters and opponents of the visit of the administrative council of Human Rights Watch to the Judges' Club. After governmental pressure and accusations that the club favored foreign intervention in Egypt's interior affairs, the meeting was canceled.